# Economics and World History

# Economics and World History

## Myths and Paradoxes

Paul Bairoch

**The University of Chicago Press**

The University of Chicago Press, Chicago 60637
Harvester Wheatsheaf, Hemel Hempstead, U.K.
A division of Simon & Schuster International Group

Printed in the United States of America

02 01 00 99 98 97 96 95      3 4 5

ISBN: 0-226-03462-3 (cloth)
ISBN: 0-226-03463-1 (paperback)

Library of Congress Cataloging-in-Publication data
are available from the Library of Congress

**This book is printed on acid-free paper**

# Contents

# Contents

# Statistical Tables

# General Introduction

To paraphrase Leo Tolstoy, economic history is a deaf man answering questions no economist has put to him.[1] This may be rather provocative, and the fact that I was invited to deliver the Schumpeter Lecture at the Third Congress of the European Economic Association in Bologna, August 1988 is proof that the words 'no economist' are an exaggeration. Nevertheless, Tolstoy's quotation is apt, since it appears that the longer the whole post-World War II period becomes, the more economists view it as a valid example of previous economic evolution. This is, after all, a natural bias since it is one of the most important periods in contemporary history. Although this is a reason to devote more time to the post-World War II period, it is not a sufficient one to ignore pre-World War II history.

I was impressed 30 years ago, when engaged on my PhD dissertation on the Industrial Revolution, by the wrong ideas most economists held about economic growth during the nineteenth century. Questioning my fellow economists, I found that they believed the nineteenth century to be a period of very rapid growth, much faster than we were experiencing then (between 1950 and 1960 the annual GNP per capita increase in the Western developed countries was 2.8%). Even on the incomplete data we had in 1961, the nineteenth-century rate of growth appeared much lower than that suggested by most economists. I published my second paper under the title 'The myth of the rapid economic growth in the nineteenth century',[2] where I stated 1.5% to be the average yearly increase in developed countries' GNP per capita for the 1800–1913 period (the actual figure can now be put at 1.1%). In addition to evidence on available data, I made a 'common sense' estimate showing that if growth had been higher than or even similar to that of the 1950s, it would imply either a much too high 1960 level or a much too low 1800 one. Due to numerous discussions on the slowing down of economic growth after

1973/4, this myth has almost totally disappeared. Many other myths remain and some of thos  concern the twentieth century. All this was the motivation of the subject of my Schumpeter lecture and of this book.

## The relative meaning of a myth

Since the term 'myth' is at the core of this book it is worth outlining the meaning I give it here. By 'myth' I mean incorrect knowledge of the history of the economy that is shared by many economists, social scientists and the general public. The myth is much less widespread among economic historians, even if due to the subdivision of this field, the profession resembles that of the other social sciences. Except where the origin of the myth can be traced to a specific publication, I will not list even a small number of the texts or authors that share this myth. In some instances the myth I am exposing is shared more by other social scientists than by economists (for example, belief that a depression preceded World War I).

Among the twenty myths examined and rejected in this book the two most important concern two very different and often antagonistic groups of people. The first could be described (with some exaggeration) as a conservative group that romanticizes the nineteenth century and makes free trade almost into a sacred doctrine. This group either ignores or forgets the fact that until the early 1960s the commercial history of the developed countries was almost entirely one of protectionism. Excluding England, which became liberal only a century and a half after the Industrial Revolution, European liberal policy lasted only two decades and coincided with – indeed led to – the most negative economic period of the nineteenth century. (Incidentally, the United States did not share this brief interlude of free trade and this was that country's best economic period of the nineteenth century.) All this and other aspects of the free trade myth will be exposed in greater detail in Part I of this book.

The second group, which can (also with some exaggeration) be described as leftist or radical economists, see the history of colonialization as one of whites becoming rich by oppressing the Third World. In this respect very often the fact that the Third World lost much more than it gained from the colonial or neo-colonial period is seen as a proof that the West benefited greatly. The realities are much more subtle. As a general rule, countries that had very few economic ties with the Third World fared better than the large colonial powers. If there is no doubt that the contribution of the Third World, especially through the availability of cheap raw materials and energy, was one of the factors in the rapid growth of the Western economies in the 1955–73 period, the situation was quite different in the nineteenth century and during the first half of the twentieth. During this period the developed world even exported energy to the Third World and was almost totally self-sufficient in raw materials. So, other times, other situations. The arguments can continue and still do. In Part II of this book I will present those arguments as well as other myths concerning the role of the Third World in Western development. Part III will be devoted to myths about the Third World which are shared by both groups. In any case, there are no myths that are exclusive to any specific economic group.

## The structure of this book

Since the October 1987 stock market crash is still haunting the economic and financial world, and since the recession of the early 1990s has revived the fear of a long depression, I begin with a chapter on the myths about the 1929 crash and the Great Depression. This is followed by Chapter 2 on the myth of the 'Golden Era of European free trade' and on the fallacy of the negative impact of protectionism. These three major topics and other minor ones make up Part I. Part II concerns the myths about the historical role of the Third World in the economic development of the West. Then Part III describes the myths concerning the historical roots of underdevelopment and the more recent situation in the Third World, for which myths are also numerous. Part IV deals with some less important myths and some major but often unnoticed turning points in modern economic history.

Some parts of this book have been published previously, mainly in the form of scientific journal articles, but in many instances I have carried out detailed research to complement the existing data, especially with some of the tables.

Being by training more an economist than an historian, I cannot begin this book, which presents a number of important myths that are more common to economists than to historians, without making the following comment. A book could certainly be written presenting the myths historians have about economics, and it is probable that the list of myths would be at least as long. But this is a task more suitable for an historian than an economist, and the title of such a book could, instead of *Economics and World History*, be *World History and Economics*.

## Acknowledgements

In writing a book almost any author will owe a large number of debts. In the field of economics, but even more so of history, a book has to rely on a large spectrum of previous research by many specialists. As is almost always the case, and especially here, only a very small number of these authors can be found in the references.

I would like to express my gratitude to all the librarians who helped me to gain ready access to the work I needed to carry out my research, particularly in those institutions whose resources I most regularly consulted: the International Labour Office, the Faculty of Economics and Social Sciences of the University of Geneva, the United Nations, the Graduate Institute of International Studies in Geneva, and the Bibliothèque Publique et Universitaire in Geneva.

I wish to thank Professor Edmond Malinvaud, who very kindly invited me to deliver the Schumpeter Lecture at the Third Congress of the European Economic Association, which ultimately led to this book.

Finally, I have had the good fortune to benefit from the kind interest in my work by my colleagues and friends, who read and commented on it. Herbert Glejser helped with the article which preceded this book. Nikki R. Keddie, during the last meeting of the International Economic History Congress (Leuven, 1990), took the time to improve considerably the title of this book as well as those of most of the chapters. Catherine Mayer went through the almost final version of the manuscript, pointing out many mistakes and suggesting many improvements. Bouda Etemad was very helpful in providing me with some references and Paul Krugman made useful comments from which I even 'stole' a few phrases in this Introduction. Special thanks to Donald Fillinger for his polishing of the final text. Last, and certainly not least, I wish to thank Robert Bolick for his splendid editorial performance which greatly exceeded in quality, depth, and importance the normal task of an editor and also the staff of Harvester Wheatsheaf who worked with dedication to help produce the book.

## Notes

1 For the inspiration of this paraphrase, I am grateful to Professor Jean-François Bergier's quotation of Tolstoy in the spring of 1987 at the twentieth anniversary of the first annual meeting of economic historians at the Datini Institute in Prato.
2 Bairoch, P., 'Le mythe de la croissance économique rapide au XIXe siècle', *Revue de l'Institut de Sociologie*, No. 2, Brussels, 1962, pp. 307–31.

# PART I

# *Major Myths About the Developed World*

The success story of the developed world is certainly important *per se*. But even if history seldom repeats itself, the past is often, too often, invoked to justify present policies, and this not only in the developed world but also in the strategies for the Third World's economic development. One key element in those strategies is the trade policies to be adopted, and generally there is a completely wrong assessment of the policies pursued and their effects on the economic history of the developed world, and in turn an incorrect application of this assessment to the situation in the Third World. This justifies my beginning this book with myths about the economic history of the developed world and not only with those concerning trade policies.

# 1

# *The 1929 Crash and the Great Depression*

Why begin this book with the inter-war period? To start, it was the 'mirror' to which we all turned when fears of another Great Depression were raised by the October 1987 stock market crash. Indeed if the 1987 crash was far from being as severe as in 1929, it was the worst since that year. Commercial policies had a central place in discussions concerning the measures to be taken to avoid such a depression, and the almost general view was that we should avoid protectionist measures, since it was protectionism that caused the 1929 crash and especially its following depression. Economic history shows that there are at least three myths underlying this assumption. The first concerns the timing of the commercial policies: the 1920s are generally described as being years of increasing protectionism. The second relates to the magnitude of the depression, which was much less severe and general than is thought. The last myth concerns the performance of the fascist economies during the depression, which was not as exceptional as generally thought.

## *Were the 1920s years of increasing protectionism?*

Let us first consider the decade preceding the 1929 crash. The years between 1920 and 1929 are generally described, mistakenly, as being a period of increasing protectionism in Europe. One of the reasons for this misapprehension may be connected with the 1927 International Economic Conference organized by the League of Nations, which aimed, among other things, at modifying existing trade policies, believed to incline excessively towards protectionism. In fact the assessment of the weighted average of customs duties on manufactures in Continental

3

Europe was 24.6% in 1913 and 24.9% in 1927.[1] It is true that this lack of
change in the average level conceals the diverging trends of various goods
and countries, but I shall only note in passing that, so far as average rates
are concerned, there was a fall in the level of duties in the following
countries (listed in decreasing order of fall): Poland, Austria, Sweden,
Belgium; and an increase in others (in order of increase): Italy, Germany,
Hungary, Spain, Czechoslovakia, Romania, Yugoslavia, Switzerland
and Bulgaria.

The protectionist trend, however, had been somewhat greater outside
Europe. Among other measures, anti-dumping legislation was enacted in
the early 1920s in Japan, Australia, New Zealand and the United States.
On the other hand, and this is extremely important, during 1928 and
1929, partly due to the recommendations of the International Economic
Conference of 1927, customs duties were lowered in almost all developed
countries and more liberal measures were adopted. Therefore it is
incorrect to consider that the 1929 crisis was preceded by increased tariff
levels.

As far as quantitative restrictions, and especially quotas, were
concerned, which resulted largely from World War I, except for some
cases in central and eastern Europe the situation had already reversed to
'normal' by 1923. As a result, the League of Nations noted the following:

> After the Armistice, the return to prewar methods and practices involving
> the abolition of quantitative controls was fairly rapid outside Europe and in
> Great Britain and certain of the Western and Northern European
> countries. In the case of some of these European countries, the movement
> was premature and could not be maintained. For example, France, which
> abolished its general control system in 1920, felt obliged to reimpose a
> number of quantitative restrictions in 1922 in order to protect its currency.
> Switzerland imposed import controls in 1922 as a defense against exchange
> dumping. But, by and large, within a few years of the Armistice, the
> problem was no longer of major importance outside Central and Eastern
> Europe.[2]

Furthermore, the 1927 conference led to an improvement in the few
remaining cases. As a result, from an overall point of view, the period
preceding the Great Depression can be considered to have been in
Europe a time when there was a tendency towards more open trade
policies. This does not mean that it was a period of free trade, since in
practically all countries, tariffs were as high as just before World War I, a
period, as we will see in Chapter 2, of high tariff levels.

Finally, a few words about the trend in the volume of international
trade, even if this is not a good indicator of trade policies. Despite the
withdrawal of Russia from world trade, the pre-war level was reached in

1924, and between 1924 and 1929 the volume of world exports increased by an annual rate of 6%, a rate of expansion that was unprecedented.

Why should we have the misconception that the 1920s were a period of increasing protectionism? On the eve of the 1929 crisis, the United States had begun the process of changing its tariff policy towards an increase in protectionism. In January 1929 a new tariff was under discussion, and the final vote was taken in the Senate and the House of Representatives on 13 and 14 June, 1929. The economic crisis cannot be considered to have started before the Wall Street crash in October 1929; industrial production in November 1929 was 7% higher than in November 1928 and began to decline only in January 1930.[3] Clearly, the signing of the Smoot–Hawley (tariff) Act by President Hoover, taking place on 17 June 1930, in spite of a petition by more than a thousand economists, put a slightly different complexion on events. But probably even without the crisis, the president would not have vetoed the law. Although it had passed in the Senate by a narrow margin (44 against 42), it had been approved by a wide majority in the House of Representatives (222 against 153).

Under the June 1930 tariff, protectionism in the United States reached an unprecedented height. This was especially the case for manufactured goods, for which customs duties rose often to more than 60% and were, on average, around 45–50%, which means 5 percentage points above the previous peak of 1891/4 (see Table 3.1 in Chapter 3). Before the end of 1931, as a reprisal, 25 countries had raised their duties on US products, and this led to an escalation in customs duties. Nevertheless, by then the world was involved in the depression, and those protectionist measures were a result of this depression, and not vice versa, as is too often claimed.

Finally, it should be noted that another fact has contributed to our negative misconception of commercial policies in the 1920s, i.e. differences in the actions taken after each of the two world wars. As Kindleberger noted in his introduction to his survey on commercial policies between the wars:

> A loosely concerted attempt was made after the war (World War I) to patch up the fabric of trade relationships, but with nothing like the fervor exhibited after the World War II. There was virtually no planning of post-war trade policies, despite President Wilson's third of the fourteen points that called for 'removal, as far as possible, of all economic barriers and the establishment of an equality of trade conditions among all nations consenting to the peace and associating themselves with its maintenance'.[4]

Therefore, globally, the 1920s were not years of increasing protectionism. This period was only a continuation of the major trend in nineteenth-century commercial policies and there was an even more liberal trend in the last two years of the decade. But it is also true that, if one wrongly sees the nineteenth century as a liberal period, the perception of the 1920s becomes different. The myth of a liberal nineteenth century will be dealt with in the next chapter.

## The magnitude of the 1930s depression

The magnitude of the depression? It is obvious that, for a number of countries, the 1930–39 period was a very negative one. This was especially the case in the United States. The 1939 volume of US per capita GNP was some 3–4% lower than that of 1929, and the total unemployment rate for the 1931–9 period reached an annual average of 18%, which compares to below 5% between 1920 and 1929. Also, since in the 1930s the United States was already the dominant economy (and the most studied one), it is normal to generalize from the US case. Furthermore, in a number of countries – especially Germany, the Netherlands and Norway – the situation in the early 1930s was even worse (higher levels of unemployment and a greater decrease in per capita GNP).

However, the picture must be qualified; so let us begin with a global appraisal of economic development during the depression compared to other periods. Table 1.1 presents data on the growth of the volume of GNP per capita, which is the best (or, if one prefers, the least incomplete) single indicator of economic evolution. One important shortcoming of GNP is that it also includes external negative costs of economic development. For example, increased traffic congestion in cities means an increase in GNP through higher petrol consumption and additional health care incurred by the pollution resulting from this consumption. But even if there is much research in this field, no better single indicator of economic development has yet been implemented. To be comprehensive Table 1.1 also includes data for the Third World, but, for obvious reasons (especially the dominant role of agriculture), this region will be omitted from our analysis.

Compared to the preceding five to six years, the 1930s do show a major slowing of economic growth but not declining GNP per capita. For the developed countries,[5] per capita GNP increased annually by 1.1% between 1929 and 1939 (see Table 1.1). Also, it must be stressed that, if we disregard the reconstruction period (1920–5), the 1925–9 period was not only a very good one but was the best in the history of the world's economic growth until the 1950s. However, if we take the whole 1913–29 period and even count those 16 years as a 12-year span to exclude the war, we arrive at a rate of growth of only 0.5 percentage points above that of the 1929–39 period (respectively, 1.6% and 1.1%). Finally, and this is the

**Table 1.1** Historical trends in economic growth, 1800–1990 (annual growth rates of the volume of GNP per capita; based on three-year averages for 1800–1900)

|           | Developed countries | Third World[a] | World |
|-----------|:-------------------:|:--------------:|:-----:|
| 1800–30   | 0.6  | −0.2 | 0.1  |
| 1830–70   | 1.1  | 0.0  | 0.4  |
| 1870–80   | 0.8  | 0.0  | 0.5  |
| 1880–90   | 1.1  | 0.1  | 0.8  |
| 1890–1900 | 1.7  | 0.2  | 1.2  |
| 1900–13   | 1.6  | 1.0  | 1.5  |
| 1913–20   | −1.3 | 0.2  | −0.8 |
| 1920–9    | 3.1  | 0.1  | 2.4  |
| 1929–39   | 1.1  | 0.3  | 0.8  |
| 1939–50   | 1.5  | 0.4  | 0.8  |
| 1950–60   | 3.3  | 1.6  | 2.5  |
| 1960–70   | 4.6  | 1.7  | 3.5  |
| 1970–80   | 2.5  | 1.7  | 2.0  |
| 1980–90   | 1.8  | 0.0  | 0.9  |

[a] Excluding China, and after 1950 also the other planned economies of Asia; very approximate figures until 1950.

*Note:* For the total of the developed countries, the following are the per capita growth rates for brief periods between 1913 and 1939:

    1913–20 −1.25   1929–33 −3.96
    1920–5   3.58   1933–9   4.67
    1925–9   2.51

*Sources:* Bairoch, P., 'The main trends in national economic disparities since the Industrial Revolution', in Bairoch, P. and Levy-Leboyer, M. (eds), *Disparities in Economic Development since the Industrial Revolution*, London, 1981, pp. 3–17 (with updated figures).

most important qualification, the performance in the 1930s was close to or better than those of periods of similar duration between 1830 and 1890 (not to mention the period before 1830).

However, as we shall see later in this chapter, as far as unemployment is concerned, especially industrial unemployment, the 1930s were not only worse than the 1920s but were probably the worst ever recorded. This does not, however, mean that, contrary to general opinion, the 1920s were years of full employment. It is even likely that the unemployment level was higher in the 1920s than in the 1900–13 period. But let us first return to economic growth.

As always, global figures conceal differences on national and sectoral levels, and often these differences are very important. The fact that we began this section with figures on the decrease of per capita GNP in the United States is already an indication of international differences. Table 1.2, which provides data on the performance of a selected group of developed countries, shows that the evolution was very divergent.

A few words of justification for the period chosen. I retained 1938 as the end period for the 1930s for two reasons: for some countries the data

**Table 1.2** Annual growth rates in the volume of GNP per capita, 1890–1938

|  | 1890–1913 | 1913–29 | 1925–9 | 1929–38 | 1913–38 |
|---|---|---|---|---|---|
| **Developed countries** | 1.6 | 1.2 | 2.5 | 0.8 | 1.0 |
| EUROPE | 1.4 | 0.4 | 2.6 | 1.8 | 0.9 |
| Austria | 1.4 | 0.3 | 2.4 | −1.0 | −0.2 |
| Belgium | 1.7 | 1.4 | 2.9 | −0.2 | 0.6 |
| Denmark | 2.3 | 0.6 | 2.7 | 1.2 | 0.5 |
| Finland | 1.5 | 0.8 | 2.9 | 3.3 | 2.1 |
| France | 1.1 | 1.8 | 2.0 | −0.4 | 1.0 |
| Germany | 1.7 | 0.1 | 2.4 | 4.2 | 1.3 |
| Italy | 1.4 | 1.0 | 1.8 | 0.7 | 0.6 |
| Netherlands | 1.2 | 1.1 | 2.6 | −0.5 | 0.7 |
| Norway | 1.6 | 1.2 | 4.6 | 2.1 | 1.5 |
| Sweden | 2.4 | 1.0 | 3.7 | 2.2 | 1.2 |
| Switzerland | 1.4 | 1.0 | 5.4 | −0.2 | 0.7 |
| United Kingdom | 1.0 | 0.4 | 2.0 | 1.1 | 0.5 |
| USSR | 2.1 | 0.1 | 6.0 | 4.3 | 1.8 |
| **Other developed countries** | | | | | |
| Australia | 0.5 | −0.4 | −2.8 | 1.0 | 0.0 |
| Canada | 2.0 | 0.4 | 4.4 | −1.6 | −0.2 |
| Japan | 1.1 | 1.2 | 1.1 | 5.0 | 2.2 |
| New Zealand | 1.3 | 1.1 | 1.3 | 0.1 | 0.8 |
| South Africa | 0.6 | 0.6 | 2.9 | 2.1 | 1.0 |
| United States | 1.9 | 1.1 | 2.3 | −1.3 | 0.4 |

*Sources:* See Table 1.1.

for 1939 are lacking, and since 1939 was the best year of the 1930s inclusion of this would improve the overall performance of the 1930s. It can also be argued that 1939 was a year strongly influenced by preparations for war (see Table 1.4 below). The year 1925 is the first where total GNP reached the pre-war level. The peak of the 1920s was 1929. Therefore, globally, we tend rather to underestimate than over-estimate the relative performance of the 1930s.

There are at least eight countries for which the 1930s were, in terms of economic growth, a better decade than the 1920s. Those include Britain and Germany, the two major economic powers in Europe. For Britain, which did not suffer from the effects of World War I in terms of a damaged infrastructure, we must take into consideration the pre-1925 period, which was very negative. Between 1929 and 1939 the per capita GNP increased faster than during the 1920–9 period.[6] The German case will be dealt with later. The other countries that prospered during the 1930s were Denmark, Japan, Norway, South Africa and the USSR (which was a very specific case). In terms of population, these eight represent 46% of all the developed countries.

It is interesting to note that the two small highly industrialized countries that did not participate in war had very different performances in the 1930s. While Sweden's per capita GNP increased at an annual rate of 2.2%, Swiss GNP per capita decreased by 0.2%, and this despite the fact that the 1929–31 crisis was much less severe in Switzerland. This can be largely explained by the wide range of socio-economic measures taken by the Swedish government and the lack of intervention by the Swiss federal authorities.

I have mentioned sectoral differences. I shall not detail the differences in performance of the various sectors of economic activities. The only fact worth mentioning here is that, due to increased protectionism in European countries in the 1930s, agriculture had a more positive evolution in Europe than in, for example, Argentina, Canada and the United States, who were important grain exporters to Europe. Thus, for example, according to the League of Nations calculations,[7] agricultural production in Europe (excluding the USSR) between 1925/9 and 1935/8 increased by 12% compared to a decrease of 3% in North America (Canada and United States).

This brings us to another very important sectoral development, that of international trade. In this area the 1930s saw a collapse in terms of both price and volume. Between 1929 and 1932 the value of world trade declined by some 60%; a decline of the order of 35% in volume. Even though international trade increased after 1932, in 1938 its volume was still below that of 1929.

There is no doubt that this collapse was largely due to the extreme protectionist measures that most countries adopted in the first years of the depression. Even if quantitative controls were not used for the first time, there was an increasing sophistication in both quotas and licensing, which are the principal forms of direct quantitative trade controls. Among other import-limitation measures applied during this period there were monopolies and cartels, veterinary and packaging regulations, foreign exchange controls, etc. But despite this collapse in international trade, as far as economic growth is concerned, as we have seen, the 1930s were not at the world level, and in many countries, such poor years as have been generally described.

## Were only the fascist economies able to overcome the depression?

One important misconception of this period is that only the fascist economies (i.e. Germany and Italy) were able to overcome the depression. In this respect it should be admitted that, even if the performances of all fascist economies were not significantly better than those of the democracies, Germany was, to a large extent, unusually successful. Even Winston Churchill praised Germany's success in this field. It is true that Germany had one of the best economic performances of the 1930s: its per capita GNP increased annually by 4.2% between 1929 and 1938. Furthermore, and this is also very important, unemployment decreased rapidly and reached a very low level in the final years of the 1930s (see Table 1.3). As we shall see, from 1936 onwards these positive developments were largely due to a military build-up which along with other factors tarnish this positive evolution.

While Germany's economic performance in the 1930s appeared to be good its 1929 level was very low; so if we take the whole 1913–38 period this brings the annual growth rate to 1.3% compared to 4.2% for the 1929–38 period. If we compare the 1913–38 period internationally we can find a large number of countries that performed better or, at least, not much worse (see Table 1.2). Among those with better performances than Germany were Finland and Norway and probably also Czechoslovakia and Romania (not included in Table 1.2). In the list of countries with performances not much worse we find France, New Zealand and South Africa.

As the reader may have noted, we have not mentioned the two examples of better performance than that of Germany in the 1930s: Japan and the USSR. The Japanese success was the result of early economic development and military spending in the 1937–8 period (see Table 1.4 below). The uniqueness of the case of the USSR is obvious, but in the perspective of the actual situation in that country, which was characterized by the failure of its economic system, it should be noted that the figures in Table 1.3 are not official (Stalinist) propaganda but Western (probably valid) estimates. The 1929–38 annual increase in the per capita GNP was of the order of 4–5%, so despite the fact that the economic level in 1928 was more or less the same as that of 1913, the 1913–38 performance (close to 2%) was among the best in the world. In the USSR economic planning succeeded in the creation of heavy industries and transport and utilities infrastructures, but not in the rest of the economy; and a very high human cost was paid in the largely unsuccessful programme for agricultural modernization.

On the other hand, and here the comparisons are more meaningful, in the 1930s the other fascist economies did much less well than Germany: Italy saw its per capita GNP increasing annually by a mere 0.7% and Portugal by 1.0%. This can be compared to 1.2% for Denmark, 1.1% for the United Kingdom, 2.2% for Sweden, 2.1% for Norway and South Africa, and 3.3% for Finland.

Furthermore, and this is not a minor aspect, the military build-up (and, in the case of Italy, the war in Abyssinia (now called Ethiopia)) enabled

**Table 1.3** Unemployment rates among industrial workers[a] in selected developed countries, 1900/13–1934/8 (in percentages of total industrial workers)

| | 1900/13 | 1920/29 | 1930/33 | 1934/38 | Year | Data | 1935 |
|---|---|---|---|---|---|---|---|
| | | | | | Yearly maximum in the 1930/38 period | | |
| **Europe** | | | | | | | |
| Belgium | (2.6)[b] | 2.4[f] | 12.6 | 15.1 | 1932 | 19.0 | 17.8 |
| Denmark | 8.8 | 16.0 | 23.0 | 20.9 | 1932 | 31.7 | 19.7 |
| Czechoslovakia | – | (2.4)[g] | (10.8) | (12.5) | 1934 | (17.4) | (15.9) |
| France | 4.2[c] | 3.8[f] | 9.5 | 10.8 | 1932 | 15.4 | 14.5 |
| Germany | 3.5 | 8.7 | 34.2 | 11.8 | 1932 | 43.8 | 16.2 |
| Netherlands | 3.0[d] | 8.0 | 18.7 | 28.9 | 1936 | 32.7 | 31.7 |
| Norway | 2.0 | 15.4 | 25.8 | 23.4 | 1932 | 30.8 | 25.3 |
| Poland | – | (5.8)[h] | (11.3) | (15.2) | 1935 | (16.7) | (16.7) |
| Sweden | 5.1[d] | 13.4 | 18.6 | 13.5 | 1933 | 23.3 | 15.0 |
| Switzerland | – | (2.2)[g] | (17.3) | (15.5) | 1932 | (21.3) | (17.7) |
| United Kingdom | 3.3 | 11.1 | 19.9 | 13.8 | 1931 | 21.3 | 15.5 |
| **Other developed countries** | | | | | | | |
| Australia | 5.4[e] | 7.9 | 24.3 | 12.5 | 1932 | 28.1 | 15.6 |
| Canada | – | 5.4 | 20.7 | 16.8 | 1933 | 26.6 | 19.2 |
| Japan | – | – | (6.0) | (4.1) | 1932 | (6.8) | (4.6) |
| United States | 10.0 | 7.8 | 28.4 | 27.5 | 1933 | 37.6 | 30.2 |

[a] Including mining and construction.
[b] 1903/13 less comprehensive data.
[c] 1901 and 1906.
[d] 1911/13.
[e] 1913.
[f] 1921/9.
[g] 1926/9.
[h] 1927/9.

*Notes:* For data for Italy, see text. Figures in parentheses are more approximate and less comparable to the others; see the sources below.

*Sources:* Australia, Belgium, Canada, Denmark, France, Germany, the Netherlands, Norway, Sweden and United Kingdom: Eichengreen, B. and Hatton, T. J., 'Interwar unemployment in international perspective: an overview' in Eichengreen, B. and Hatton, T. J. (eds), *Interwar Unemployment in International Perspective*, Dordrecht, 1988, pp. 1–50. Data for these countries can be considered fairly comparable.
United States: Lebergott, S., *Manpower in Economic Growth: the American Record since 1800*, New York, 1964, p. 512. Concerns non-farm employees.
Rest of the countries: ILO, 'World index number of unemployment', *International Labour Review*, **XXXIX**, No. 1, January 1939, pp. 118–29; and ILO, *Year-book of Labour Statistics*, Geneva, various issues. Czechoslovakia and Poland include salaried workers in agriculture and the tertiary sectors; Japan: foreign workers excluded; Switzerland including the tertiary sectors.

the fascist economies, especially Germany, to lower their unemployment levels considerably. Germany's unemployment level reached a peak in 1932 at 30% of its total working population and 44% of its industrial workers (see Table 1.3). As a rule, and especially for pre-war periods, the unemployment rate for industrial workers is a better (but not perfect) yardstick to compare international unemployment levels than the unemployment rate for the total working population. This is due to the three following factors:

1. In practical (and even more so in statistical) terms, there was no unemployment in agriculture, and in the 1930s the share of agriculture in the total working population varied greatly; for example, 6% for Great Britain, 46% for Italy.
2. An important part of employment in services is composed of activities that have no cyclical fluctuations (education, medical care, government, etc.).
3. There is no real unemployment among the non-salaried active population.

On 30 January 1933 Hitler became Chancellor of Germany, and the industrial unemployment rate fell from an average of 43.8% in 1933 to 36.2% in 1934. In 1935 it stood at 16.2%, in 1936 at 12.0% and in 1938 at 3.2%. From 1936 onwards the success can be attributed almost entirely to Germany's rearmament. As can be seen from Table 1.4, military expenditure, which represented 3.2% of GNP in 1933, increased rapidly to 8.9% in 1935 and 14.4% in 1937. Germany's level of expenditure for armaments for the 1935/7 period was 52% higher than that of France; 61% higher than that of the United Kingdom; and 950% higher than that of the United States.

However, even Germany's success in 1934/5 was doubly relative. The country's 1935 unemployment level was probably[8] higher than that of France, Sweden, the United Kingdom and Australia, to take only the countries for which reasonably reliable statistics exist. More important is the fact that in Germany the unemployment level was reduced artificially by taking out of the labour market a substantial number of people (principally women, bachelors, teenagers). For example, in 1935, those groups represented close to 1 million people[9] or 3% of the industrial workforce.

Last but not least, the other major fascist economy was in a much worse situation. Italy's unemployment figures are unreliable. According to the most recent attempt to measure it, the 1935 unemployment rate in the industrial sector was 11.5% if we take the lower-bound estimate and 23.2% for the upper bound.[10] If we take the average (17.4%) this means

**Table 1.4** Indicators of the importance of the military sector in selected countries, 1929/32–1938

| | Germany | Italy | France | United Kingdom | United States | USSR | Japan |
|---|---|---|---|---|---|---|---|
| **Military expenditures in % of GNP** | | | | | | | |
| 1929/32 | 0.9 | 3.7 | 3.8 | 2.0 | 0.9 | 3.4 | 2.5 |
| 1933 | 3.2 | 5.5 | 4.0 | 2.1 | 1.0 | 4.1 | 1.6 |
| 1934 | 4.4 | 6.8 | 6.3 | 3.9 | 1.2 | 18.3 | 2.4 |
| 1935 | 8.9 | 7.3 | 7.4 | 5.1 | 1.1 | 26.4 | 2.3 |
| 1936 | 11.4 | 15.7 | 8.2 | 7.1 | 1.1 | 12.8 | 2.1 |
| 1937 | 14.4 | 16.1 | 7.1 | 9.4 | 1.1 | 13.7 | 5.2 |
| 1938 | 28.2 | 9.2 | 7.2 | 12.8 | 1.3 | 19.7 | 9.8 |
| **Number of military personnel (1000s)** | | | | | | | |
| 1929/32 | 114 | 319 | 433 | 338 | 235 | 562 | 485 |
| 1933 | 118 | 330 | 422 | 325 | 228 | 562 | 555 |
| 1934 | 315 | 331 | 449 | 318 | 230 | 940 | 589 |
| 1935 | 461 | 336 | 458 | 321 | 234 | 1300 | 597 |
| 1936 | 596 | 343 | 548 | 336 | 274 | 1300 | 598 |
| 1937 | 603 | 362 | 613 | 350 | 294 | 1433 | 561 |
| 1938 | 782 | 383 | 581 | 376 | 304 | 1566 | 525 |

*Sources:* Derived from statistics included in the data bank *The Correlates of War Project* (University of Michigan), J. David Singer, Director.

that after 13 years of fascist government, Italy's unemployment rate was similar to those of the non-fascist economies with high unemployment. But the Italian situation was worsened by the fact that not only was 1935 the year in which Italy invaded Abyssinia, but artificial measures were also introduced to reduce unemployment. The October 1934 agreement between the Confederation of Fascist Industrialist and Industrial Trade Unions was aimed, among other things, to induce women, teenagers and retired people to leave their jobs and be replaced by adult males without being counted as unemployed (in 1934 the lower-bound unemployment estimate was 14.2% and the upper bound 35.8%).

It is evident, however, that the fascist parties in both Germany and Italy, as well as in other European countries, received an impetus from this artificial lowering of unemployment levels. Also we should not forget that in the fascist states military build-up and territorial expansion were not considered by the majority of the local population to be negative. Also, we should not forget that in the United States, the 'major' country of the 'capitalist' world, the industrial unemployment rate in 1935 was 30.2% (see Table 1.3) and as high as 27.9% in 1938, when Germany's rate had fallen to 3.2%. On the other hand, Germany's rapid economic growth was accompanied by an increase in occupational injuries and by a decrease in real hourly wages. But again, things are never simple; since this decrease in wages was accompanied by a larger increase in working hours, it meant a rise in total weekly wages.

So this rather short inter-war period, which lasted for less than half the post-World War II period until the present, was rich in events of which we have generally a distorted picture. The fascist economies were not as good as have been thought. The depression was much less severe than is generally assumed and, more important, it was not caused by protectionist measures. Such policies can, of course, lead to a slackening in economic activity; however, the consequences deriving from an adequate trade development policy are much more important than its short-term effects. Those problems are of prime importance for the Third World, and therefore the experience of the developed countries is crucial. This experience will be the main subject of the next three chapters.

## Notes

1 Liepmann, H., *Tariff Levels and the Economic Unity of Europe*, London, 1938.
2 League of Nations, *Quantitative Trade Controls*, Geneva, 1943, p. 10.
3 Miron, J. A. and Romer, C. D., 'A new monthly index of industrial production, 1884–1940', *The Journal of Economic History*, L, No. 2, 1990, pp. 321–38.
4 Kindleberger, C. P., 'Commercial policy between the wars', in Mathias, P. and Pollard, S. (eds), *The Cambridge Economic History of Europe*, Vol. VIII: *The Industrial Economies: the Development of Economic and Social Policies*, Cambridge, 1989, pp. 161–96.
5 Since this is the first time we are mentioning the large economic regions, it is worth giving the definitions used here, which are those used by most institutions. The developed countries or world (or future developed countries or world) include the following regions or countries: Europe (including the Asiatic part of the USSR but excluding the small European part of Turkey), the United States, Canada, Australia, New Zealand, Japan and South Africa. The Third World or developing countries, as the United Nations calls those countries, comprises the rest of the world. The qualification 'West' implies that the developed region referred to excludes the Eastern European countries (in their pre-3 October 1990 definition or, if one prefers, before German reunification), i.e. Albania, Bulgaria, Czechoslovakia, East Germany, Hungary, Poland, Romania and the USSR. The term 'Third World market economies' implies that China, North Korea, Mongolia and Vietnam are excluded.
6 Since, in order to improve the comparability of the data, I have corrected the GNP series (see source in Table 1.1), some of the figures presented in this section may differ from those in the original countries' sources. Due to the availability of new data, I have corrected some figures that were used in our original study.
7 League of Nations, *World Production and Prices 1938/39*, Geneva, 1939, p. 16.

8 Unemployment statistics, even today, are not strictly comparable. In the inter-war period this was much worse, even if, as mentioned earlier, we used relatively comparable series.

9 Silverman, D. P., 'National Socialist Economics: the *Wirtschaftswunder* reconsidered', in Eichengreen, B. and Hatton, T. J. (eds), *Interwar Unemployment in International Perspective*, Dordrecht, 1988, pp. 185–220.

10 Toniolo, G. and Piva, F., 'Unemployment in the 1930s: the case of Italy', *ibid.* pp. 221–45.

# 2

# Was there a Golden Era of European Free Trade?

The myth of protectionism as a cause of the 1929 crash and of depression in the 1930s brings us to a more general and much more important myth concerning the long-term history of commercial policies. This fallacy is almost a dogma among neoclassical economists and can be expressed in the following terms: 'Free trade is the rule, protection is the exception.' How many times have we heard of the Golden Era of free trade from which 1920s and 1930s protectionism departed? The fact that I have spent almost three years with GATT, 'the temple of free trade', has made me more sensitive to this myth. The truth is that, historically, free trade is the exception and protectionism the rule, so it is worth giving here a brief history of commercial policies that may convince the reader of this truth. This chapter will deal with Europe and Chapter 3 with the rest of the world.

## 1815: an ocean of protectionism surrounding a few liberal islands

Let us begin by putting the nineteenth century into an historical perspective. The sixteenth and seventeenth centuries were the golden age of mercantilism.[1] Precious metals were considered as crucial to a nation's wealth and power. Therefore a nation without access to gold or silver mines had to regulate its foreign trade in order to obtain a surplus of exports over imports. Furthermore, colonial possessions had to serve as protected markets for exports. In fact, the title of the book by Thomas Mun, the pre-eminent mercantilist, summarizes well this widespread theory: *England's Treasure by Foreign Trade* (1664).

The eighteenth century is generally seen as a period of transition. Trade policy during the first half of the century was still closely linked with mercantilism, but after 1760 important changes took place. First with the Physiocrats, then with the theories of Adam Smith, and, above all, with the Anglo-French commercial treaty of 1786, commercial liberalism, an integral part of *laissez-faire* economics, was established, if not all over Europe, at least in the trade between two of its leading powers. But the unrealized hopes of the treaty of 1786 and, above all, wars caused the eighteenth century to end with a return to protectionism.

The wars in the period 1790–1815, and, in particular, the English blockades of France that began in 1806, reinforced European tendencies towards protectionism in government commercial policy. As far as economic thought was concerned, however, liberalism made progress. Book IV of Adam Smith's *The Wealth of Nations* is essentially a defence of free trade at the international level. Smith's book (published in 1776) became the leading work in economics at the end of the eighteenth century. In England eight editions were published before 1800; and before 1796 it had been translated into almost all European languages. The direct or indirect successors to Adam Smith, which means, for most economists, all the founding fathers of modern economics, adopted a liberal position on international trade.

However, on practical grounds this supremacy of liberal economic thought in Europe did not eliminate the mercantilistic type of protectionism, still less prevent the development of a new one. This new-style protectionism was related to an increase in nationalism in the early nineteenth century, and still more important, was the result of awareness of the process of economic development resulting from the Industrial Revolution and of the advance of British industry. Friedrich List's most pre-eminent book, *The National System of Political Economy*, did not appear until 1841, but before this the pro-protectionist works of the American Alexander Hamilton (1791), the German Adam Müller (1809) and the Frenchmen Jean-Antoine Chaptal (1819) and Charles Dupin (1827) had appeared, List, however, had already risen to prominence in Germany in the 1810s, and can be considered as the major international figure in protectionist theory.

Protectionism for List (and for the mainstream of the protectionist school) was not a goal in itself but a temporary policy in order to allow a country to build up a strong economy through industrialization. Here arises the main point: a country must industrialize without being overpowered, in the early stage of this process, by the competition of more mature foreign industries. Therefore, the special requirements of each country should be taken into account, especially its degree of development. Even if this protective stage involves negative results, these should be considered as industrialization learning costs. This was later called the 'infant industries' argument. For List, once industries have grown sufficiently to support international competition, free trade should be the rule. He was even convinced that industrialization was only possible in temperate regions, and that tropical countries should concentrate on the production of primary goods of which they had a natural monopoly. It should be noted that this point of view is absent in contemporary protectionist thinking.

In Europe, at the beginning of the nineteenth century, the most effective opposition to trade liberalization did not come from protectionist theorists but from a wide range of representatives of different sectors of the economy who, rightly or wrongly, considered it harmful to their own particular interests.

## *1815–46: towards liberalism in the United Kingdom, but not before 1842 and not elsewhere*

In practical terms, trade policy in the various European states in the 1815–25 period can be described as an ocean of protectionism surrounding a few liberal islands. Table 2.1 gives a comparative outline of the state of trade policy in the main European countries at the time.

In the United Kingdom the political struggle between the supporters of free trade and those in favour of protectionism began more or less at the end of the wars with France in 1815. The aristocracy voted for a new Corn Law aimed at protecting domestic agriculture against foreign grain imports. It should be noted that Corn Laws were almost a permanent feature of the history of tariffs in most European countries. They had always aimed at a precarious balance between protecting local agriculture and preventing the price of bread from rising too steeply. In England the first national laws of this kind date back to 1436.

The Corn Law of 1815 prohibited the import of wheat until its price on the domestic market reached 80 shillings per quarter, which meant that the price of food and therefore also wages would be kept at a relatively high level. This did not please manufacturers, who wanted to expand their exports still further through a combination of mechanization (especially cotton spinning) and low wages. This law marked the beginning of conflict between the interests of agriculture, whose relative importance in economic life was declining, and those of manufacturing, which was becoming the main sector of economic activity. In the nineteenth century the balance of power between these two sectors and the degree to which their interests converged was to determine the changes in tariff policy not only in the United Kingdom but also in

**Table 2.1** Commercial policies in selected European countries around 1820

| | Imports of manufactured goods | | Protection of agriculture | Export duties | Internal duties | Navigation laws |
|---|---|---|---|---|---|---|
| | Prohibitions | Average level of duties (%)[a] | | | | |
| Austria-Hungary | Numerous | [b] | [c] | Yes | Yes | Liberal |
| Denmark | Rare | 30 | Moderate | [c] | Yes | Liberal |
| France | Numerous | [b] | Moderate | Rare | No | Protective |
| Portugal | No | 15 | Strict | Yes | [c] | Liberal |
| Prussia | No | 10 | Moderate | No | No | Liberal |
| Russia | Numerous | [b] | Moderate | Yes | [c] | [c] |
| Spain | Numerous | [b] | Strict | Yes | Yes | Protective |
| Sweden (Norway) | Numerous | [b] | [c] | Yes | Yes | [c] |
| Switzerland | Rare | 10 | Moderate | Yes | Yes | Liberal |
| The Netherlands (Belgium) | No | 7 | Moderate | Yes | No | Mildly protective |
| United Kingdom | Rare | 50 | Strict | Rare | No | Protective |

[a] Figures quoted are very approximate.
[b] Not at all significant in view of the importance of the prohibitions.
[c] Incomplete information or difficult to classify.

*Sources*: See Table 3.3.

practically all European countries.

The Corn Laws were not abolished until 1846. In other spheres, however, liberalism did make some progress. As early as 1825, Parliament again authorized the emigration of skilled workers, which had been forbidden since 1719, an Act motivated by fear of foreign competition. On the other hand, the efforts of some engineers to remove the ban on the export of machinery were not successful. In 1833 reductions in some import duties were introduced.

During this period, British industry was increasing its lead over its rivals, a lead which was already considerable. Even if calculations are made for the whole of the United Kingdom, which reduces the average level of industrialization since Ireland had few industries, this lead was remarkable. The United Kingdom, containing about 8–10% of the population of Europe, in 1800 produced 29% of all pig iron in Europe, a proportion that reached 45% in 1830. More significant is the fact that the per capita level of industrial production in 1830 exceeded that of the rest of Europe by 250%, compared to 110% in 1800.[2] From this we can easily understand the efforts of industrialists and their supporters to establish a more effective system of free trade.

The main obstacle to effective free trade, however, was still the substantial protection of agriculture. Since this led to high food prices and hence lower real wages, the strategy of the manufacturers, especially those in the cotton industry, was to use the poverty of the workers to strengthen their attack on the Corn Laws. The free traders also emphasized the point that, by reducing the import of foreign foodstuffs from countries with an agricultural surplus, the Corn Laws were thus decreasing the chances of exporting British manufactured goods to those countries. The Anti-Corn Law League was founded in September 1838 in Manchester. Although this was a pressure group of manufacturers, the League was led by sincere men: John Bright and, in particular, Richard Cobden, who was to be the true 'apostle' of free trade. The League quickly became very active; in fact it can be regarded as the first example of an economic lobby.

An important step was taken in April 1842. Prime Minister Robert Peel introduced a fairly liberal tariff reform which reduced import duties appreciably and, most important, completely revoked the ban on exporting machinery which had been in force since 1774. However, no significant changes were made to the Corn Laws even if there was some adjustment in the rates of duties for cereals. In short, the main obstacle to a complete system of free trade remained, although somewhat weakened. Ultimately it was because of the very wet summer and autumn of 1845, together with the disastrous potato crop in Ireland, that the Corn Laws were repealed (the law of 15 May 1846, also abolishing many duties on manufactured goods). As Morley wrote in his life of Cobden, 'It was the rain that rained away the Corn Laws'.[3]

The date 15 May 1846 is rightly held to mark the beginning of the free trade era in the United Kingdom, and, by one of those historical coincidences, that year (six months later, in November) was also that of the suicide of the ill and financially harassed apostle of protectionism, Friedrich List. If the weather was the immediate cause of the repeal of the Corn Laws, it merely accelerated a trend in trade policy that was, in any case, inevitable. For if around 1810 agriculture's contribution to the GNP in Britain still exceeded that of the secondary sector of the economy by 70%, around 1840 it was industry that exceeded agriculture by 60%. But one should not forget that 1846 means almost a century and a half after the beginning of the British Industrial Revolution.

At the same time that Britain was becoming aware of its industrial lead and drew the logical conclusions from this by adopting a free trade policy, the rest of Europe was becoming conscious of its industrial backwardness and was seeking a way of catching up in a new form of mercantilism more defensive than offensive – in short, what was, from the 1840s, to be called protectionism. It should be noted that for the first time in history people began to argue in terms of levels of development to be reached more or less quickly rather than in terms of taking the largest share of total wealth; a bigger cake instead of a larger slice of it.

## 1846–60: the theoretical influence of British liberalism on the Continent

While liberalism was gaining a stronger hold in the United Kingdom, protectionism was being maintained on the Continent in spite of free trade propaganda. The fact that the British continued to advance economically was a great advantage to the supporters of free trade: the most highly developed country had become the most liberal, which made it easy to equate economic success with a free trade system, whereas in fact this causal link had been just the opposite. After 1846, the United Kingdom continued to pursue a liberal trade policy, becoming increasingly an open economy.

The period 1846–60 witnessed a number of events which, although partly exogenous to economic life in the strict sense, had important consequences for the economy, especially for the flow of trade. These included the significant reduction in transport costs following the introduction of the steam engine to railways and shipping; the very rapid expansion of the stock of precious metals as a result of discoveries in North America and Australia; and the beginning of farm mechanization in the United States.

The liberalization of British trade directly and indirectly fostered foreign trade in the rest of Europe. The Continent's volume of exports, which had grown by 1.9% per annum between 1837/9 and 1845/6, increased by 6.1% per annum between 1845/7 and 1857/9. For this reason, these years were one of the three most favourable periods for export growth in the nineteenth century. In addition to this positive evolution of international trade in Europe supporters of free trade did not fail to draw attention to the British example. The Association Belge pour la Réforme Douanière published a manifesto for tariff reform in 1855 which began as follows: 'Inspired by the results of economic science and by the experience of real facts, especially that of England, where, since the introduction of Sir Robert Peel's reforms, agriculture, navigation and industry, far from declining, have flourished in force and energy in the most unexpected way.'[4]

It was generally at the instigation of these national pressure groups, and also sometimes under the more direct influence of the British, that tariff reductions were made by the majority of large European states. They were not, however, very important until 1860, and only weakened slightly the thoroughly protectionist character of the tariff laws of the major powers of Continental Europe.

To summarize, it can be said that before 1860 only a few small Continental countries, representing only 4% of Europe's population, had adopted a truly liberal trade policy. These were the Netherlands, Denmark, Portugal and Switzerland, to which we may add Sweden and Belgium (but only from 1856–7 onwards), and even then these maintained some degree of protectionism.

## 1860–79: the European free trade interlude

The fundamental breakthrough of free trade began in 1860 with the Anglo-French trade treaty. The concentration of the efforts of English free traders on France can largely be explained by the fact that France was not only one of the main European trading partners of the United Kingdom but was also the country with which Britain had the highest trade deficit.

What the French supporters of protectionism (that is, the majority of deputies in the *parlement*) called the new *coup d'état* was revealed by a letter from Napoleon III to his Minister of State. This made public the secret negotiations which began with the meeting in Paris in 1846 between Richard Cobden and Michel Chevalier, a former disciple of Saint-Simon and a professor of political economy. The commercial treaty between the United Kingdom and France was signed on 23 January 1860, and was to last for ten years. A way was found of avoiding the passage of the bill through *parlement*, which would probably have been fatal to the project. Hence, a group of theorists succeeded in introducing free trade into France, and thus indirectly to the rest of the Continent, against the will of most of those in charge of the different sectors of the economy. The minority in favour of free trade were strongly supported by Napoleon III, who had been converted to free trade ideas during his long stays in Great Britain and who saw the political implications of this treaty.

The Anglo-French treaty, which was very quickly followed by further treaties between France and many other countries, led to tariff 'disarmament' in Continental Europe, mostly as a result of the most-favoured-nation clause. This is a formula by which each of the two signatories to a treaty agrees to grant the other any advantage, favour or privilege with regard to trade or navigation that it granted at the time of signing, or that it would grant in the future to any other nation. In May 1861 a treaty was signed between France and Belgium. Between 1861 and 1866 practically all European countries entered into what is generally called the 'network of Cobden treaties'. Table 2.2 shows the tariff situation for manufactured goods in 1875, which was the height of liberalism on the Continent.

Here it should be stressed that, for agricultural products, the tariff 'disarmament' was all the more complete because in this respect the theories of free traders and protectionists coincided. Free traders were, in principle, skilled in free imports of agricultural products. List did not envisage a protectionist 'learning' period for agriculture as the protectionist theory implied for manufacturing. The objective of this learning period was to allow less advanced countries to acquire the general and technical know-how of all aspects of manufacturing to be able to compete in international markets. List and other protectionist writers clearly stated that was not the case for agriculture, where physical factors (quality of the soil, climate, etc.) are dominant.

Seen from a European standpoint it might appear that in the 1860s a Golden Era of free trade began for the world, but outside Europe, tariff history in the developed countries took a quite different course. This was especially the case in the United States. One should first be reminded that the modern protectionist school of thought, the one connected with the 'post-Industrial Revolution' period, was actually born in the United States. In fact, globally, as we shall see in Chapter 3, the 1860s were a period of increasing protectionism in the United States. But first let us follow the changing story of European trade policies.

**Table 2.2** Average levels[a] of duties on manufactured goods in 1875

|                              | Percentage |
|------------------------------|------------|
| Austria-Hungary              | 15–20      |
| Belgium                      | 9–10       |
| Denmark                      | 15–20      |
| France                       | 12–15      |
| Germany                      | 4–6        |
| Italy                        | 8–10       |
| Norway                       | 2–4        |
| Portugal                     | 20–25      |
| Russia                       | 15–20      |
| Spain                        | 15–20      |
| Sweden                       | 3–5        |
| Switzerland                  | 4–6        |
| The Netherlands              | 3–5        |
| United Kingdom               | 0          |
| Continental Europe[b]        | 9–12       |
| Europe[b]                    | 6–8        |
| United States                | 40–50      |

[a] Probable level of average, but not extreme ranges.
[b] Weighted averages (by value of 1869/71 imports).
*Sources:* See Table 3.3.

## 1879–92: the gradual return to protectionism on the Continent

Germany was the first important European country to make substantial changes to its customs policy, which it did with the new tariff of July 1879. This was an important event. Just as the Anglo-French treaty of 1860 was the beginning of the European free trade period, this new German tariff marked its end and the beginning of a gradual return to protectionism on the Continent. This was an outcome of Bismark's *Realpolitik*, since the elections of 1878 brought a protectionist majority to the Reichstag.

It should also be noted here that nearly all tariffs which came into force in the period 1879–1914 provided for specific duties (relating to specific quantities; for example, $2 per ton and not *ad valorem*, a percentage of the value). This trend was partly implemented because specific duties were much easier to collect (and there was less risk of fraud) since it was only necessary to establish the nature of the product in order to calculate the duties payable. Specific duties imply changes in the degree of protection when import prices vary. From 1874 until 1897–8 the international price level showed a falling trend, with a decline of about 35% in export prices and about 40% in import prices; therefore the use of specific duties implied an increase in the relative importance of duties.

In Continental Europe the triumph of protectionist ideas was very largely the result of the coalition between agricultural interests and those of industry. Farmers, who were disappointed by the slow growth in sales to the United Kingdom and seriously handicapped by the imports of grain and other foodstuffs from overseas, thus supported those manufacturers who had never really been convinced of the advantage of free trade.

As the title of this section indicates, the period 1879–92 saw a gradual return to protectionism in Europe. This means that if Continental Europe as a whole is considered, a large part of this period can still be said to have been characterized by predominantly liberal trade policies, using the term in its nineteenth-century sense. The real end of the liberal period can be dated from 1892. This year saw the adoption of the so-called Méline protectionist tariff in France, and was a watershed for tariff reform since most treaties expired then (the majority in February).

## 1892–1914: increasing Continental protectionism, but liberalism in the United Kingdom

These years can undoubtedly be described as a period of increased protectionism in Continental Europe, but not all countries changed their policies at the same rate, especially during the first ten years. The two major trading powers on the Continent showed a substantial contrast in their policy developments between 1892 and 1902. In Germany, the policy of tempering to a certain degree the high tariff barriers through commercial treaties, which had begun with the treaty concluded with Austria-Hungary in 1891, was continued until 1902. Between 1891 and 1896 treaties with six other countries were signed. These led to a certain reduction in protectionism, especially with regard to agriculture. France, on the other hand, became more and more protectionist. But after 1902, Germany also reinforced its protectionism.

As can be seen from Table 2.3 all the large countries (except the United Kingdom) had very protective trade policies in 1913. The case of small countries was different. Indeed, the development of trade policies in the smaller European countries was more uneven that in the large ones. It is true that the general trend was the same, but their protectionism took a less radical form, and there is also the case of the Netherlands, which did not follow the same pattern at all, remaining faithful to a liberal policy.

Let us now return to Britain, to what was still, at least around 1890, the world's leading economy. The reversal in the trends of commercial policy in Continental Europe and also in Canada caused inevitable repercussions in the United Kingdom, where the impact was enhanced by the new

**Table 2.3** Some indicators of import tariff levels around 1913 (percentage of total)

| | Import duties as % of special total imports (1909/13) | League of Nations indices[b] | | Liepmann's indices[a] | | British manufactures (1914) | Import duties on wheat |
|---|---|---|---|---|---|---|---|
| | | All products[b] | Manufactures | All products[b] | Manufactures | | |
| Austria-Hungary | 7.6 | 18 | 18 | 23 | 20 | 35[c] | 35 |
| Belgium | 15.8 | 6 | 9 | 14 | 9 | 10 | 0 |
| Bulgaria | 15.1[d] | - | - | 23 | 22 | - | 3 |
| Denmark | 5.8 | 9 | 14 | - | - | 18[c] | 0 |
| Finland | 12.1[d] | - | - | 35 | 28 | - | 0 |
| France | 8.7 | 18 | 20 | 24 | 21 | 22 | 38 |
| Germany | 7.9 | 12 | 13 | 17 | 13 | 17 | 36 |
| Greece | 26.6 | - | - | - | - | 19[c] | 37[c] |
| Italy | 9.7 | 17 | 18 | 25 | 20 | 18 | 40 |
| Norway | 11.4 | - | - | - | - | 12[c] | 4 |
| Portugal | 23.7 | - | - | - | - | - | Prohibited |
| Romania | 12.1[d] | - | - | 30 | 28 | 14[c] | 1 |
| Russia | 29.5[d] | - | - | 73 | 84 | 131[c] | 0 |
| Servia | 14.8 | - | - | 22 | 20 | - | 27 |
| Spain | 14.3 | 33 | 41 | 37 | 34 | 42 | 43 |
| Sweden | 9.0 | 16 | 20 | 28 | 25 | 23 | 28 |
| Switzerland | 4.4 | 7 | 9 | 11 | 8 | 7[c] | 2 |
| The Netherlands | 0.4 | 3 | 4 | - | - | 3 | 0 |
| United Kingdom | 5.6 | 0 | 0 | 0 | 0 | - | 0 |

[a] Potential indices in the sense that these indices are calculated on a standard list of 144 goods imported (thus including some products not normally imported).
[b] Excluding alcoholic drinks, tobacco and mineral oils (in general, very high duties).
[c] 1904, and not strictly comparable with 1914 figures; in general, they have to be reduced by 30% to be more comparable.
[d] General imports.

*Sources:* Import duties as percentage of imports: author's estimates derived from various sources.
Average level of duties: League of Nations, *Tariff Level Indices*, Geneva, 1927; Liepmann, H., *Tariff Levels and the Economic Unity of Europe*, London, 1938.
British manufactures: 1914: Great Britain Committee on Industry and Trade, *Survey of Overseas Markets*, London, 1925, p. 543; 1904: Board of Trade, *British and Foreign Trade and Industrial Conditions*, London, 1905.
Import duties on wheat: author's computations based on duties provided in Board of Trade, *Foreign Import Duties, 1913*, London, 1913, pp. 1065– 6. Assumed uniform import prices of wheat of $36 per ton (based on average import prices for selected European countries).

trends in the economy: from 1875 to 1877 onwards British economic growth slowed considerably.[5] Finally, and perhaps most importantly, during the 1870s the total value of British exports to Europe and the United States fell, whereas those to the rest of the world, and especially to the British Empire, increased noticeably.

The combination of the above factors inevitably created a climate of opinion which favoured a certain degree of protectionism and especially a retreat to the Empire. This reaction crystallized in 1881 with the creation of the Fair Trade League, which had a very strong influence on British public life. Its demands were fairly moderate and were designed to restructure commercial policies. The League wanted to impose retaliatory import duties as a prelude to negotiations for reciprocity. In particular, manufactured goods imported from countries which did not allow free entry to British manufactured goods would be liable to duties of 10–15%. Imported products which competed with those coming from British colonies would also be taxed. However, at the beginning of the 1880s the arguments put forward by those in favour of a realignment of commercial policy towards protectionism encountered a very convincing, because very simple, argument on the part of the Liberals. It was the fact that Britain exported almost five times more manufactured goods than it imported.

It was not until the early twentieth century that a new pressure group in favour of a change in British commercial policy emerged. The ratio of 5 to 1 in favour of British exports of manufactured goods had meanwhile been replaced by a ratio of only 2 to 1. Moreover, even this situation was essentially the result of the large surplus of manufactured goods exported to the British Empire. In extra-European markets, where British influence was still very strong, British products faced serious competition from European rivals. If we consider only the ten countries outside Europe in which about 82% of British capital was invested, we find that the UK share in the total imports of these countries fell from 50% in 1869/71 to 29% in 1913.[6]

It is in this context that Joseph Chamberlain's campaign for tariff reform in the first years of the twentieth century should be seen. Paradoxically, 20 years earlier, when the Fair Trade League was active, Chamberlain's task as President of the Board of Trade was to lead the counterattack, and he adopted a very liberal position, but progressively he shifted towards a policy of a preferential system for the British Commonwealth. However, since he did not succeed during his time in office in introducing a true preferential trade system with import duties on grain in particular, he gradually moved towards a more protectionist position. His speech in Birmingham on 15 May 1903 marked the beginning of what was to be a real crusade for tariff reform. This reform was to further three aims: to increase revenue (in order to finance social policies); to give some protection to industry; and to set up a preferential system for the benefit of the Empire. This far-reaching speech had a great impact and was followed by others giving further details of what was to become the doctrine of the Tariff Reform League, which amounted to a very mild form of protectionism incorporating a reciprocal preferential system for the Empire.

In 1903 the Liberals' counterattack took shape in a report by the leading British economist, Alfred Marshall, made at the request of the Treasury. After an argument on the difficulties for England to enact 'reprisals against hostile tariffs', Marshall wrote that:

> On the other hand, it is not merely expedient – it is absolutely essential – for England's hopes of retaining a high place in the world, that she should neglect no opportunity of increasing the alertness of her industrial population in general, and her manufacturers in particular; and for this purpose there is no device to be compared in efficiency with the plan of keeping her markets open to the new products of other nations, and especially to those of American inventive genius and of German systematic thought and scientific training.[7]

From 1900 to 1904 economic stagnation, a noticeable drop in real wages and a relative reduction in exports lent support to those pressing for tariff reform. The events of 1905, however, which led to the general election on 12 January 1906, were favourable to the Liberal Party which was in favour of free trade. In this year the total value of exports rose by 9.7% and the volume of GNP by 3.0%. The Liberal Party had an overwhelming victory in the election. Six months afterwards, Chamberlain suffered a stroke, never really returned to active politics and died on 2 July 1914.

Even if tariff reform gained more support in the 1906–10 period, the improvement in the economic climate allowed action to be delayed. It may be said that certain of the Tariff Reform League's ideas began to be adopted from 1916 onwards, but these were war measures, and 1932 was the real date of the abandonment of British free trade. Since by 1913 most of the non-European developed countries had also opted for protectionist policies (see Chapter 3), the characterization of world trade policy in 1815 as 'an ocean of protectionism surrounding a few liberal islands' is even more valid for 1913. Inside this ocean, Continental Europe was, to a large extent, less protective than the overseas developed countries, and certainly much more liberal than the United States.

Before leaving Europe it should, however, be stressed that all the indicators presented in Table 2.3 (as well as in Table 3.2 in the next chapter) are not sufficient to give a real picture of the degree of protectionism of each region or country. Unfortunately, we do not have any valid estimates of the levels of effective protection. Indeed, the same average level of duties can imply quite different levels. A simple example can demonstrate this. Two countries each have, say, a 20% average level of duties on manufactured goods. In country A this average results from a uniform 20% on all manufactured goods whatever their stage of elaboration. In country B this average results from a 5% rate on raw materials, a 10% rate and a 45% rate on finished goods. The result is obvious. Furthermore, as is the case even today, in 1913 there were no adequate measures of non-tariff barriers such as sanitary regulations, internal taxes, labelling requirements, etc.

## Notes

1 Even this may be challenged as a partial myth. See Piuz, A.-M., 'Note sur l'acceptation ancienne de Free Trade (XVIe-XVIIe siècles)' in Schneider, J. (ed.), *Wirtschaftskräfte und Wirtschaftswege. Festschrift für Hermann Kellenbenz*, Vol. IV, Nuremberg, 1978, pp. 585–97.

2 Bairoch, P., 'International industrialization levels from 1750 to 1980', *The Journal of European Economic History*, **11**, No 2, 1982, pp. 269–333.

3 Morley, J., *The Life of Richard Cobden*, London, 1882, p. 215.

4 *Congrès International de réformes douanières réuni à Bruxelles (22–25 September 1856)*, Brussels, 1857.

5 In Canada the major turning point came when the Conservatives adopted a 'National Policy' based on protectionism as their election platform in 1878. Their victory led to new tariff legislation in 1879 protecting both agriculture and industry; we shall return to this in Chapter 4.

6 Bairoch, P., *Commerce extérieur et développement économique de l'Europe au XIXe siècle*, Paris, 1976, pp. 215–16. The ten countries are: Argentina, Australia, Brazil, Canada, Chile, China, Egypt, the United States, India and the Union of South Africa.

7 Marshall, A., 'Memorandum on the fiscal policy of international trade' in Keynes, J. M. (ed.), *Official Papers by Alfred Marshall*, 1926.

# 3

# *Was there Free Trade in the Rest of the World?*

The European commercial expansion resulting from the Industrial Revolution had very different consequences on the trade policies of the rest of the world. In simplified terms, this can be divided into two spheres. In those parts of the world which gradually became part of the developed world, protectionism was the dominant commercial policy. This was especially the case in the United States, which, far from being a liberal country as many think, can be characterized as 'the mother country and bastion of modern protectionism'. In the second sphere, the future Third World (and especially those countries that were colonized), liberalism prevailed, but it was not by choice; it was enforced liberal commercial policy.

I shall outline a brief history of these developments, but first it is worth giving a schematic overview of the trade policies of major non-European civilizations before the nineteenth century.

## *Non-European traditional trade policies before the nineteenth century: a sharp contrast over time and space*

Contrast over time? Let us just give two, but major, examples: China and Japan. Here we can speak almost of a fallacy of protectionism. Both countries are generally described historically as very closed economies. This was indeed true for centuries and especially for the first centuries of closer, or at least more frequent, contact with Europe (from the beginning of the sixteenth century to the beginning of the nineteenth).

30

But this has not always been the case. In China's Sung dynasty (AD 960–1279), maritime trade increased greatly and provided the basis for the very substantial growth of some coastal cities.[1] The Europeans' image of a China closed in on itself, meeting foreign traders with distrust as they came into direct contact with the Celestial Empire at the beginning of the sixteenth century, has no bearing on these three centuries. Commercial relations with the outside world were not only tolerated but actively sought and encouraged. Thus the edict of 1137 issued by the Emperor Kao Tsung declared, among other things: 'The profits from maritime trade are very great. If they are managed adequately, they can bring in a million [of monetary units of the period]. Is this not better than to tax the people?' Foreign merchants were not only welcomed but were sometimes fêted and authorized to establish themselves in many cities. Moreover, China itself dispatched trade missions abroad and participated directly in international exchange. This open policy, which also meant Chinese commercial and maritime expansion, received a further impetus under the Mogul Dynasty (AD 1280–1368).

However, after a little more than five hundred years of what could be called liberal trade policy, China closed its doors. This took place in 1490, just two years before Columbus reached the New World in his search of a direct sea link to Asia. Two and a half centuries later (in 1757), China further reinforced its 'protectionism'. But these two measures had very different origins. The first case was mainly an expression of arrogance towards the less-developed 'barbarians' making up the rest of the world; in the second case, it was more a defensive measure against an intruding and vigorous West.

Japan, which between 1639 and 1854 was probably one of the most closed societies (only one Western boat could enter a Japanese harbour every year), also had a period of openness. In fact, it was a side-effect of this openness that led to the strict reaction of 1639. From the 1550s onwards, the Jesuits, followed by other religious orders, succeeded in converting many of the population in some regions of Japan, and those regions were also more prone to contact with the West. In the first years of the seventeenth century the number of Christians is estimated to have reached some 700,000 (or 3% of the population). An order prohibiting Christianity was promulgated in 1612. The predominant role played by Christians in the uprising of 1637 led in 1639 to an almost total ban on foreign trade, which was viewed as a vehicle of foreign ideas and ideologies. Thus in very broad terms, the 'liberal' period lasted some 250 years, from the fifteenth century to the middle of the seventeenth.

Sharp contrast in space? Indeed, during those centuries when China and Japan were very 'protectionist', another large non-European empire was very 'liberal': the Ottoman Empire. It is interesting to note that the ardent nineteenth-century free trader, J. R. McCulloch, begins his outline of the commercial policy of the Turks in his *Dictionary of Commerce* as follows: 'It is singular that as respects commerce, the policy of the Turkish government, whether originating in design or carelessness, is entitled to the highest praise.'[2] Indeed, this policy could be praised by a free trader since the Ottoman Empire was very open to imports. Import duties were lower than most internal duties. This liberal policy can be traced back to 1536, the date of one of the first 'commercial treaties' between the Ottoman Empire and a European country (France). More specifically, it can be seen to originate in the 1790 'capitulation'. The term 'capitulation' does not derive from the word 'capitulate' (surrender), even if during the nineteenth century it led to such a situation. It comes from the Latin *caput*, meaning 'head' and also 'chapter'. In its origins the capitulation was an act granting economic privileges by the Ottoman sultans to a subject of friendly non-Muslim states. The 1673 and 1740 capitulations (which were supposed to be perpetual) implied only 3% import and export duties, and some internal trade taxes that were higher than that. In fact, if those capitulations were not perpetual, they were abrogated only by the treaty of Lausanne in July 1923.

It is interesting to note that if the trade policy of the Ottoman Empire was praised by a British free trader, it was also called as evidence by an opponent of many aspects of British free trade policy: Disraeli. He intervened during the great debate on the abolition of the Corn Laws (February 1846) which was, in fact, 'the' debate on protectionism and free trade. After giving the example of Spain as that 'of the injury done by prohibitive protection' he cited the example of Turkey as 'an instance of the injury done by unrestricted competition'. For the Ottoman Empire he declared:

> There has been a complete application for a long time of the system of unmitigated competition, not indeed from any philosophical conviction of its policy, but rather from the haughty indifference with which a race of conquerors is too apt to consider commerce. There has been free trade in Turkey, and what has it produced? It has destroyed some of the finest manufactures of the world. As late as 1812 these manufactures existed; but they have been destroyed. That was the consequences of competition in Turkey, and its effects have been as pernicious as the effects of the contrary principle in Spain.[3]

## The United States: mother country and bastion of modern protectionism (1791–1860)

The long protectionist history of the United States is forgotten more often than that of Continental Europe,[4] even though as early as the nineteenth century the relative economic importance of the United States among the non-European developed countries was very large. To give just one example: in 1860 the US population was 32 million compared to 5 million for the total of the rest of this group (Australia, Canada and New Zealand).

As noted earlier, one should not forget that modern protectionism was born in the United States. In 1791, Alexander Hamilton, the First Secretary of the Treasury (between 1789 and 1795) in the first US government, drew up his famous *Report on Manufactures*, which is considered to be the first formulation of modern protectionist theory. I have briefly outlined in Chapter 2 the main elements of the protectionist theory as presented by Friedrich List. The major contribution of Hamilton is the emphasis he put on the idea that industrialization is not possible without tariff protection. He was apparently the first to have introduced the term 'infant industries'. Even if the 'infant industry' argument was already present in mercantilist theories, Hamilton put it to the forefront of economic thinking.

At the end of the nineteenth century, Callender could write, with no exaggeration, that:

> Next to currency problems no purely economic subject has aroused so much interest in the United States, and played so great a part in political discussion both in and out of Congress as the tariff policy of the federal government. From the first measure of 1789 until the present time no generation of the American people has escaped the tariff controversy.[5]

A legislator in the state of Pennsylvania suggested that man should be redefined as 'an animal that makes tariff speeches.'[6] Further, it is no exaggeration to say that the tariff question had been one of the causes of the American Revolution.

The first tariff of 1789 is often described as moderately protectionist; in fact, analysis of the levels of import duties shows it to be a liberal tariff. It is true that, compared with the previous situation, this tariff was a step towards protectionism, and, in addition, the remoteness of the United States from other world economies constituted a natural, protective barrier. This first American tariff, which, according to its preamble, was aimed at protecting local industry, provided duties for manufactured goods averaging about 7.5–10%. After two successive revisions, the tariff of 1792 increased duties on most categories of goods by 50%. On many subsequent occasions various duties were increased, leading to the 1816 tariff, where import duties were about 35% for almost all manufactured goods.

The opposition between the South, which as an exporter of agricultural products (cotton, tobacco) was liberal, and the North, which was industrializing and hence protectionist, emerged during this period. The protectionist movement – supported by economists such as Daniel Raymond and, later, Henry C. Carey – was encouraged by pockets of unemployment and by cyclical crises. From 1819 onwards, associations were formed to press for industrialization to be achieved as a result of protectionism. This movement was also well supported by publications.

From then on it is possible to divide nineteenth-century American commercial history into three relatively distinct periods. The first, which can be called a protectionist phase, lasted from 1816 to 1846. From 1846 to 1861 came a period which is sometimes said to have been liberal, but should more accurately be described as one of very modest protectionism. The final phase, which lasted from 1861 to the end of our period (and in fact to the end of World War II), was one of strict protectionism. Let us examine this in more detail.

After some congressional vicissitudes, a series of modifications adopted between 1824 and 1832 further strengthened the protectionist nature of the 1816 tariff. Import duties on woollen manufactured goods were 40–45% and those for clothing 50%; but import duties on all manufactured goods averaged 40%. Some duties on agricultural products were also increased: on many these amounted to more than 60% of their value. On the basis of the importance of import duties relative to import values – not a perfect indicator – the tariff in force after 1829 showed American protectionism at its height (see Table 3.1).

This development led to a serious crisis because of opposition from the South and certain states declared the federal laws on these matters null and void. The crisis was resolved in 1832 by the adoption of the Compromise Bill, which provided for a progressive reduction in the highest import duties, leading to a relatively unified level of 20% in 1842. This liberalization of trade policy reached its peak with the tariff of 1842, which reduced import duties on manufactured goods to an average of 25% and increased the number of products that could enter freely. However – and this was characteristic of American tariff history – this rather liberal tariff remained in force for only a very short period: two months. The emergence of the Whig Party (which was highly protectionist) and the political crisis of 1841–2 (linked to the death of President William Harrison one month after his inauguration in 1841) led to the tariff of 1842, which more or less restored the high tariff levels of 1832.

The return of the Democrat Party in 1844 resulted in the tariff of 1846, which reduced import duties by about 10–20% and generalized the system of *ad valorem* duties. The average *ad valorem* duty on the 51 most important categories of imported goods was 27%. There were scarcely

**Table 3.1** Ratio of import duties to imports in the United States for significant trade policy periods and recent data, 1823/4–1988/90

| | Ratio of duties calculated to imports (%) | |
| | Total imports (free and dutiable) | Dutiable imports |
| --- | --- | --- |
| 1823/4 | 43.4 | 45.8 |
| 1829/31 | 50.8 | 54.4 |
| 1842/6 | 25.3 | 31.9 |
| 1857/61 | 16.3 | 20.6 |
| 1867/71 | 44.3 | 46.7 |
| 1891/4 | 22.9 | 48.9 |
| 1908/13 | 20.1 | 41.3 |
| 1914 | 14.9 | 37.6 |
| 1923/7 | 14.1 | 37.7 |
| 1931/3 | 19.0 | 55.3 |
| 1935/8 | 16.4 | 39.8 |
| 1944/6 | 9.5 | 28.3 |
| 1968/72 | 6.5 | 10.1 |
| 1978/82 | 3.5 | 5.8 |
| 1988/90 | 3.6 | 5.4 |

*Sources:* US Bureau of Census, *Historical Statistics of the United States, Colonial Times to 1970*, Washington, 1975, p. 888. US Bureau of Census, *Statistical Abstract of the United States*, Washington, various issues.

any major modifications until the tariff of 1861, and this is the phase we have called modest protectionism.

The year of Napoleon III's liberal *coup d'état*, 1860, is in the United States the year in which Abraham Lincoln was elected and which marked the beginning of the Southern states' secession. The long and bloody American Civil War, which ended in April 1865, signified the victory not only of the abolitionists of the North over the pro-slavery South but also the triumph of the protectionists of the Northern industrial states over the free marketers of the South, whose main export was raw cotton. As can be seen in Table 2.2 (in the preceding chapter) around 1875, at the height of economic liberalism in Europe, whereas in Continental Europe the average level of duties on manufactured goods was 9–12% the rate in the United States was 40–50%. To these figures one must still remember to add the natural protection resulting from geographical distance of European exporters.

If in 1791 the new-born United States was a very small economic entity, things were very different by 1860. To give some idea of the rapid changes, let us first note that in 1791 the US population had just passed 4 million, which represented 2% of Europe's population (including Russia), and US manufacturing capacity represented probably 1% of that of Europe. In 1860 the US population had reached 32 million which not only represented 11% of that of Europe but put the United States on a level with the greatest European states. At the time France had 37 million inhabitants; Germany, 36 million; Austria-Hungary 35 million; the United Kingdom 29 million; Italy 25 million; and Spain 16 million. Only backward Russia had a much larger population (probably 78–84 million). In 1860 the volume of United States' industrial production represented 13% of that of Europe, and only 20 years later the ratio would rise to 24%. This means that from 1870 to 1880 onwards tariff events in the United States became events of world importance.

## The United States: from 'infant industries' arguments to the protection of American wages (1861–1914)

As noted earlier, at the beginning of the 1860s the turning points in tariff history in Europe and the United States were very different, and it is during the 1860–90 period that the contrast between European and American trade policies became most marked. The 1861 tariff was the beginning of a policy that was to be followed in the United States until the end of World War II. Import duties were increased again during the American Civil War, and victory by the North brought further protectionism. The tariff in force from 1866 to 1883 provided for import duties averaging 45% for manufactured goods (the lowest rates of duty were about 25% and the highest about 60%).

The way in which the United States caught up with, and even overtook, European industry rendered obsolete the 'infant industries' argument for United States protectionists. The Republican Party therefore based its case for introducing the McKinley Tariff of 1890 on the need to safeguard the wage levels of American workers and to give the agricultural sector more protection. This tariff implied a distinct increase in effective protection, due to a general increase in import duties, a combination of specific and *ad valorem* duties (with sliding scales) and an enlargement of the number of tariff items.

During the 1890–1913 period there was a series of tariff modifications which alternately reduced and increased import duties by small amounts, according to the results of elections. The principle of reciprocity, which was already central to United States' trade policy, was retained. In his message to Congress in 1901, Theodore Roosevelt wrote:

> Reciprocity must be treated as the handmaiden of Protection. Our first duty is to see that the protection granted by the tariff in every case where it is needed is maintained, and that reciprocity be sought for so far as it can be safely done without injury to our home industries.[7]

**Table 3.2** Indicators of tariff levels in 1913 in different types of country

| | Import duties as % of special total imports (1908/12) | Approximate average level of import duties on manufactures | Level of duties on wheat |
|---|---|---|---|
| **Developed countries** | | | |
| Continental Europe | 10.4 | 19 | 25 |
| United Kingdom | 5.7 | 0 | 0 |
| Australia | 18.2 | 16 | 22 |
| Canada | 18.7 | 26 | – |
| Japan | 9.1 | 25–30 | 18 |
| New Zealand | 16.6 | 15–20 | 3 |
| United States | 21.4 | 44 | 0[a] |
| **Non-developed countries** | | | |
| Selected independent (in 1913) countries | | | |
| Argentina | 21.6 | 28 | 0 |
| Brazil | 37.4 | 50–70 | – |
| Colombia | 49.1[b] | 40–60 | 20 |
| Mexico | 33.7[b] | 40–50[c] | 42 |
| Selected semi-independent (in 1913) countries | | | |
| China | 3.3 | 4–5 | 0 |
| Iran | 8.0[b] | 3–4 | 0 |
| Siam | 2.7[d] | 2–3 | 3 |
| Turkey | – | 5–10 | 11 |

[a] With 10% for wheat originating from countries where US wheat is imposed.
[b] To total imports.
[c] 1910.
[d] 1910/13.

*Sources:* Percentages of import duties: author's computations based on various national sources.
Average level for manufactures:
Ranges: author's estimates on basis of individual tariffs.
Other figures: see Table 2.3 and national sources.
Level of duties on wheat: see Table 2.3 for method of calculation. Additional sources were used for this table.

On 4 October 1913 a serious (but very temporary) break with previous policy occurred. This change in direction was made possible by the victory of the Democratic Party in the 1912 elections. The so-called Underwood Tariff of 4 October 1913 led to a large increase in the categories of goods allowed free entry and to a substantial drop in average import duties. According to calculations by the League of Nations, the average duty on imports fell from 33% to 16% and the average duty on manufactured goods from 44% to 25%.[8] This still remained one of the highest tariff rates in the world (see Table 3.2).

This interlude of moderation in US protectionist policies did not last long. World War I prevented the tariff of October 1913 from having any important role, and following the return to power of the Republican Party in May 1921 new 'emergency' tariff legislation came into force on 22 September 1922. This involved a distinct increase in protectionism compared with the 1913 tariff. Although import duties did not return to the high levels of the tariffs in force in the 1861–1913 period, the percentage effectively paid on manufactured goods rose by 30%. So strong is the idea of the United States as a leader in free trade policies that, despite the fact that the October 1913 tariff had almost no practical meaning, often we find that it is generally accepted as an indicator of the US level of duties for the pre-World War I period.

## British dominions: tariff independence brings protectionism

The fact that tariffs played an important role in the rejection by the United States of British rule was an important factor in Britain's early decision to grant a large measure of tariff independence to what were later (at the end of the century) to become the self-governing colonies, in other words, essentially those with large European populations (Canada, Australia and New Zealand). In the nineteenth century the trade policies in these countries went through two main phases. The first, which, depending on the country, lasted until 1867–88, was a period of liberal policies justified mainly by the export opportunities for agricultural products favoured until the early 1850s by the British preferential system. During the second phase (between 1867/88 and 1913), all these countries sought, to some degree and with varying amounts of success, to encourage their industrial sectors through protectionist tariff policies. The geographical position of these countries was an important influence on their policies: the isolation of Australia and New Zealand contrasted with the proximity of the United States to Canada.

In Canada, the repeal of the Corn Laws in Britain (in 1846) and the abolition of other preferences on Canadian goods led to the necessity of a drastic reorganization of Canadian trade policy, since from 1840 to 1846 60–70% of Canadian exports went to the United Kingdom. The Canadians naturally turned towards their southern neighbour, and this led to the reciprocity treaty of 1854 with the United States which resulted in free trade in agricultural products between the two countries in exchange for fishing and navigation rights for the Americans.

However, the major turning point came when the Canadian Conservative Party adopted a 'National Policy' based on protectionism as their election platform in October 1878. The new tariff legislation of 1879 protected both agriculture and industry. For agricultural goods, average import duties were between 20% and 50% *ad valorem*, and manufactured goods about 20–30%. This was only the beginning of a series of increases in duties which continued to 1887, raising the degree of effective protection in most sectors of industry. By 1887 the average import duties on manufactured goods were around 25–35%. This protective policy did not exclude the 'motherland', but in 1898 a unilateral preference of 25% for British goods was introduced.

Australia or, more precisely, the colony of Victoria (accounting at the end of the nineteenth century for about 46% of the population of the six separate colonies which formed the Commonwealth of Australia), was the first British colony to introduce a trade policy intended to promote industry by means of a protectionist tariff. This policy, which dates from 1867, can be largely explained by the unemployment in this region at the beginning of the 1860s. The unemployment was itself the result of the extremely rapid influx of population[9] resulting from the discovery of rich gold seams in 1851. After 1856 gold production began to drop, thus creating a large unemployed workforce composed mainly of townspeople.

The first Australian federal tariff in 1902 represented a compromise between the protectionism of Victoria and the liberalism of the other states. This truce did not last long: the 1906 Australian elections returned a protectionist majority. In 1906 the Australian Industries Preservation Act was passed, which was an anti-dumping law. The new tariff of 1908 aimed at protection and provided for a doubling of import duties on most categories of goods, while retaining preferences for British products. On the whole, the degree of protection in 1913 (see Table 3.2) was lower than that prevailing in Canada, and lower even than the average level in Continental Europe. But Australia's extreme remoteness from Europe must be taken into account. Further, the tariff reform of 1914 provided for an increase in import duties on manufactured goods of about 25%. Even though this increase was a war measure, it should be noted that the tariffs adopted after the war reinforced protectionist tendencies.

Throughout the entire nineteenth century New Zealand had a more liberal tariff than either Australia or Canada. This can be explained by the size of the country (fewer than 500,000 inhabitants in 1880, as opposed to 2,500,000 in Australia and 4,300,000 in Canada) and by the dominant importance of agriculture in the New Zealand economy. Except for some processing industries linked to agricultural exports, the local market was too small to permit real industrialization. However, even in New Zealand the depression of the 1880s caused a change in attitude towards the tariff system, which had until then been regarded purely as a means of raising revenue. In much the same way as had happened in Australia, the decrease in gold production resulted in the

**Table 3.3** Average tariff rates on manufactured products in selected developed countries, 1820–1987 (weighted average; in percentages of value)

| | 1820[a,b] | 1875[b] | 1913 | 1925 | 1931 | 1950 | 1980 | 1990 |
|---|---|---|---|---|---|---|---|---|
| **EUROPE** | | | | | | | | |
| Austria[c] | * | 15–20 | 18 | 16 | 24 | 18 | 14.6 | 12.7 |
| Belgium[d] | 6–8 | 9–10 | 9 | 15 | 14 | 11 | 8.3 | 5.9 |
| Denmark | 25–35 | 15–20 | 14 | 10 | – | 3 | 8.3 | 5.9 |
| France | * | 12–15 | 20 | 21 | 30 | 18 | 8.3 | 5.9 |
| Germany[e] | 8–12 | 4–6 | 13 | 20 | 21 | 26 | 8.3 | 5.9 |
| Italy | – | 8–10 | 18 | 22 | 46 | 25 | 8.3 | 5.9 |
| Netherlands | 6–8 | 3–5 | 4 | 6 | – | 11 | 8.3 | 5.9 |
| Russia | * | 15–20 | 84 | * | * | * | * | * |
| Spain | * | 15–20 | 41 | 41 | 63 | – | 8.3 | 5.9 |
| Sweden | * | 3–5 | 20 | 16 | 21 | 9 | 6.2 | 4.4 |
| Switzerland | 8–12 | 4–6 | 9 | 14 | 19 | – | 3.3 | 2.6 |
| United Kingdom | 45–55 | 0 | 0 | 5 | – | 23 | 8.3 | 5.9 |
| United States | 35–45 | 40–50 | 44 | 37 | 48 | 14 | 7.0 | 4.8 |
| Japan | * | 5 | 30 | – | – | – | 9.9 | 5.3 |

* Numerous and important restrictions in importation of manufactured products, which make all calculations of average tariff rates not significant.
– Not available.
[a] Very approximate rates.
[b] Range of average rates, not extremes.
[c] Before 1925 Austria-Hungary.
[d] In 1820: the Netherlands.
[e] In 1820: Prussia; after 1931 Federal Republic of Germany.

*Note:* The data for one period are not strictly comparable to those following it, with the exception of 1820/75, 1913/ 25 and 1978/87.

*Sources:*
1820 and 1875: Author's calculations. See Bairoch, P., *Commerce extérieur et développement économique de l'Europe au XIXe siècle*, Paris and The Hague, 1976; except United States and Japan: Bairoch, P., 'European trade policy, 1815–1914', in Mathias, P. and Pollard, S. (eds), *The Cambridge Economic History of Europe* (Volume VIII, *The Industrial Economies: The Development of Economic and Social Policies*), Cambridge, 1989, pp. 1–160.
1913 and 1925: League of Nations, *Tariff Level Indices*, Geneva, 1927; except for Japan: Bairoch, P., 'European trade policy, 1815–1914', *op. cit.*
1931: Liepmann, H., *Tariff Levels and the Economic Unity of Europe*, London, 1938. Except for the United States and Japan: Bairoch, P., 'European trade policy, 1815–1914', *op. cit.*
1950: Woytinsky, W.S. and Woytinsky, E. C., *World Commerce and Governments*, New York, 1955.
1980 and 1990 (or pre and post Tokyo round): GATT's Secretariat.

strengthening of a protectionist trend which was already noticeable in 1873. Again, as in Australia, the workers' parties strongly supported the protectionist movement. This pressure came to a head in 1888, and the tariff adopted in that year involved a policy based in principle on the protection of certain sectors of industry.

Thus, as we have seen, it is no exaggeration to claim that, with the exception of Britain, the developed world was an ocean of protectionism. It was an ocean that did not recede until after World War II (see Table 3.3).

## In the future Third World: liberalism enforced

If we move outside the ocean of protectionism that washed the developed world there is no doubt that the future Third World was an ocean of liberalism. But it was compulsory economic liberalism, an economic liberalism of two main types, one for real colonies, and another for nominally independent countries for which certain customs regulations had been suggested (or imposed).

As far as the colonies were concerned, the general rule consisted of free access to all the products of the mother country (occasionally charged with low duties for fiscal reasons). In certain colonies, particularly the British ones, in the second half of the nineteenth century all goods, whatever their place of origin, were freely allowed in but with disguised measures for giving precedence to products from the mother country. These measures consisted mainly of formal or informal pressures on public or semi-public sectors, such as railways, to use the 'motherland's' products.

Furthermore, in some cases when import duties were imposed on manufactured goods for fiscal reasons, they were minimal and often counterbalanced by local fiscal measures. This was notably the case of India when, after 1859, the British government reintroduced modest duties (5%) on textile goods. As the result of a 'legitimate' protest by British manufacturers, local Indian producers of those goods were subject to a tax of the same magnitude in order to put the two types of production on the 'same footing'.

As for the Third World countries which were independent or not real colonies in the nineteenth century, that is, the most important parts of Latin America, China, Thailand and the Middle East as a whole, Western pressure had imposed on most of them treaties that entailed a more or less total elimination of customs duties on imports. Generally, it was the '5% rule' that applied, that is, a tariff regulation under which no duty could rise above 5% of the import value of the goods.

Most of those treaties, rightly called 'unequal treaties', were signed between 1810 and 1850, mainly initiated by British pressure. The political independence of almost all Latin American countries (which took place mainly between 1804 and 1822) had been largely helped by British intervention. This led to numerous trade treaties, one of the earliest of which was with Brazil in 1810. All these treaties opened those countries' markets to British and European manufactured products. Before their independence, it should be remembered that almost all Latin American countries were under Spanish or Portuguese domination; i.e. by the least industrialized countries in Europe.

A tariff treaty with the Ottoman Empire was signed in 1838, opening still further what was already a very open economy, as we have seen. The Opium Wars (1839–42), which in fact aimed at making the vast Chinese territory available to British trade, ended with the Treaty of Nanking on 29 August 1842. This was the first step towards China's loss of tariff independence, which went as far as the appointment of a British citizen (R. Hart) as Inspector-General of customs, who remained in office from 1863 to 1908. The most comprehensive treaty with Thailand, leading to a real open economy, was signed in 1855, but this was preceded by others in 1824, 1826 and 1833.

If certain countries, particularly the large ones of Latin America, were able to modify their customs policies from 1880 onwards, we will see in Chapter 8 that others had to wait until World War I and even later to free themselves from these restraints. For example, China regained independence in this field only in 1929, and Turkey in 1923.


At the beginning of Chapter 2 I described the trade policy of Europe around 1815 as an ocean of protectionism with a few liberal islands. To a very large extent, the same description holds true for the entire world around 1913. In the developed part of this world there were only two islands of liberalism. The most important one was indeed an island in real terms: Britain; and the other country is very open to the sea: the Netherlands. The combined exports of these two countries then represented 21% of those of all the developed countries (this was also the share of Germany and Belgium). In the Third World the independent (or semi-independent such as China) liberal countries' combined exports represented only 22% of Third World exports, and this was enforced liberalism. The rest of the Third World's exports came from colonies which even had more liberal tariffs. Therefore, the Third World was an ocean of liberalism without any island of protectionism. Between 1815 and 1913 only Europe had a short period of real liberalism lasting, on average, no more than a fifth of this time span. Since we must wait until the early 1960s to see the beginning of a new liberal period, the liberal interlude was reduced to a seventh of the time span, not counting the mercantilist centuries that preceded 1815. Therefore, from 1815 to 1960 it is very difficult to speak, as is often done, of a past Golden Era of free trade!

## *Notes*

1 Ma, L. J. C., *Commercial Development and Urban Change in Sung China*, Ann Arbor, 1971.
2 McCulloch, J. R., *Dictionary, Practical, Theoretical and Historical of Commerce and Commercial Navigation*, new edition, London, 1844, p. 373.
3 Quoted by Holland, B., *The Fall of Protection, 1840–1850*, London, 1913, p. 265.
4 A few years ago, I listened to a Voice of America programme on American radio in which a debate was held between a 'free trader' and a 'protectionist' on the necessity for a change in United States' trade policy on manufactured goods. One of the major and 'devastating' arguments of the 'free trader' was to ask his opponent the following question (I am quoting from memory): 'What would have happened in the past if this country had adopted a protectionist policy; would the United States have reached such a high level of industrialization?' The most astonishing fact was that, apparently, the 'protectionist' representative was not aware of the United States' long history of protectionism.
5 Callender, G. S., *Selection from the Economic History of the United States, 1765–1860*, Boston, 1909; quoted by Taylor, G. R. in Taylor, G. R. (ed.), *The Great Tariff Debate, 1820–1830*, Boston, 1968, p. v.
6 Eiselen, M. R., *The Rise of Pennsylvania Protectionism*, Philadelphia, 1932, p. 7.
7 Ashley, P., *Modern Tariff History: Germany-United States-France*, 3rd edn, London, 1920, p. 238.
8 League of Nations, *Tariff Level Indices* (International Economic Conference, Geneva, May 1927), Geneva, 1927.
9 In 1850 Victoria had 76,000 inhabitants, but by 1860 there were 538,000 (representing an annual growth rate of 22%).

# 4

# *Has Protectionism Always had a Negative Impact?*

Analysis of the economic impact of nineteenth-century commercial policies is certainly not easy. Obviously, this is also the case for any attempt to isolate one factor among the complex mix of factors playing a role in economic development. But in the case of commercial policies there are many preconceived ideas which have become almost dogma. Only recently (in the last two to three decades) have there been sufficient macroeconomic data to question the dogma that protectionism has necessarily a negative impact on an economy.

I will concentrate here on six main aspects that are linked to the most important changes in tariff history, even if some are not directly the topic of this chapter. I will begin with the impact of the first case of trade liberalization, that of the United Kingdom after 1846, which for that country meant a confirmation of liberal theories. Then I will move on to the difficult problem of free trade in Europe and the great European depression of 1870–2 to 1891–3; this is difficult mainly for liberal theories, since the depression started when trade policies reached their most liberal stage. The third section will deal with the impact of Continental Europe's return to protectionism after 1892. This return 'paradoxically' coincided with economic expansion in Europe. The fourth section is entitled 'Protectionism and the expansion of foreign trade', although this may be considered provocative by some readers. The fifth and sixth sections will consider the non-European developed countries, especially the United States, which will confirm the positive impact of protectionism. The final section will be concerned with the impact of the compulsory liberalism on the Third World; liberalism that was to be the road to underdevelopment.

44

## Liberalism and economic growth in the United Kingdom after 1846

The major question is whether British trade liberalization had a positive impact on the trade and economic growth of that country itself. Analysis of annual statistics on exports and GNP shows that this major change in tariff policy was accompanied by acceleration not only in the growth of foreign trade but also in the rate of economic growth. But was this the result of trade liberalization?

The expansion of exports was already extremely rapid in the 10–15 years before 1846 (about 5% per annum), and it accelerated further after that date. From 1843/7 to 1857/61 the volume of British exports increased by just over 6% per annum. It is worth emphasizing that this growth (for such a time span) was the most spectacular since data was available on the subject (1697).

Economic growth was equally exceptional in this period. Between 1843/7 and 1857/61 the annual growth in the volume of GNP was 2.4%. Since this period was marked by a very slow population growth (0.2% per annum) due to a fall in Ireland's population, the per capita growth of GNP was 2.2%, which is the highest recorded for a period of this length, certainly between 1800 and 1945, and probably from the Industrial Revolution to 1945.

The share of British cotton manufactures sold abroad, which had begun to fall before 1846, now rose again. From the point of view of the international cotton trade this meant a further rise in the importance of the United Kingdom, which was already predominant in the field. As far as iron was concerned, Britain's share of European production rose from 54.2% for 1838/42 to 58.5% for 1851/62.

It is thus clear that the global balance sheet was extremely favourable to Britain. British industry, which had a very important technological lead, had found a much larger market. But this market was essentially outside Europe. The value of exports to Europe increased by 4.5% per annum between 1839/41 and 1859/61, while those to the rest of the world increased by 5.1%. This expansion of imperial trade reduced the importance of Europe. In 1830 exports to Europe accounted for about 48% of British sales, and in 1860 for no more than 34%.

These last percentages highlight the fundamental difference between the geographical structure of British exports and those of the rest of Europe. Towards 1860 Continental European exports to other European countries represented 82% of the total.[1] The relatively small proportion of British exports to Europe explains the attempts to convert the

Europeans to liberalism in the 1850s and is itself explained by the protectionism of Continental Europe.

Therefore, globally speaking, the first free trade experiment was a positive one, and this had, as we have seen, an important impact on the policies of most European countries after 1860. But one should not forget the uniqueness of the British situation around 1846. Not only was Britain the birthplace of the Industrial Revolution, but this revolution had reached its centenary in Britain while most other countries had been industrialized for less than fifty years. This implied, as mentioned earlier, a very important technological lead. Last but not least, this lead had been achieved behind high and long-lasting tariff barriers.

## Free trade and the great European depression

As we saw in Chapter 2, the liberal phase of European trade policies lasted from 1860 to 1892 while the period when free trade reached its height in Europe in the nineteenth century was undoubtedly during the twelve years from 1866 to 1877. In the middle of this period (around 1870–73) there began what has been called the great depression of Europe.

As far as the volume of European trade was concerned, the reversal of the trend began in 1873. Partly as a result of the rapid expansion of British foreign trade, the volume of European exports grew very rapidly in the 1846–60 period. The first decade (1860–70) of the free trade period had already been marked by a noticeable slackening in this growth, but there was almost no deceleration for Continental Europe. From 1873 to 1893/4, however, the volume of European sales grew only by about 2.3% per annum, compared to 5–6% in the preceding decades. For Continental Europe this slowing down was even more pronounced (see Table 4.1).

This serious decline in the growth of trade is only one aspect of the depression. In the case of economic growth, the turning point came a little earlier: in 1868–70. The European per capita growth rate of GNP declined from an annual rate of about 1.6% for the 1850s and 1860s to 0.6% for the next two decades. In other words, during this depressed phase European economic growth was even lower than it had been even in 1830–40 (when it was about 1%; see Table 4.1).

### Free trade = Depression? Protectionism = Recovery?

The important point to note here is not only that the depression started at the peak of liberalism but that it ended around 1892–4, just as the return to protectionism in Continental Europe had become really effective. This asks important questions about the influence of tariff policy on economic

**Table 4.1** Annual growth rate of different sectors according to tariff policies and economic periods, 1830–1913 (%)

| | Exports | GNP | Industry | Agriculture[a] | Population |
|---|---|---|---|---|---|
| **Tariff policy periods (Europe)** | | | | | |
| Protectionist 1830–1844/6 | 3.5 | 1.7 | 2.7 | (0.8) | 0.6 |
| British liberalism 1844/6–1858/60 | 6.0 | 1.5 | 2.3 | (0.9) | 0.7 |
| European liberalism 1858/60–1877/9 | 3.8 | 1.7 | 1.8 | 0.5 | 0.8 |
| Shift to protectionism 1877/9–1890/92 | 2.9 | 1.2 | 2.2 | 0.9 | 0.9 |
| Protectionism 1890/92–1913 | 3.5 | 2.4 | 3.2 | 1.8 | 1.0 |
| **Economic periods** | | | | | |
| Europe | | | | | |
| Slow growth 1829/31–1842/4 | 3.5 | 1.6 | 2.5 | (0.8) | 0.6 |
| More rapid growth 1842/4–1868/70 | 5.0 | 2.0 | 2.3 | (0.9) | 0.7 |
| Depression 1868/70–1891/3 | 2.8 | 1.1 | 1.9 | 0.7 | 0.9 |
| Rapid growth 1891/3–1911/13 | 3.8 | 2.4 | 3.4 | 1.7 | 1.0 |
| Continental Europe | | | | | |
| Fairly rapid growth 1829/31–1868/70 | 4.3 | 1.8 | 2.0 | (1.0) | 0.7 |
| Depression 1868/70–1891/3 | 2.9 | 1.0 | 2.0 | 0.8 | 0.9 |
| Rapid growth 1891/3–1911/13 | 4.0 | 2.6 | 3.8 | 1.5 | 1.1 |

[a] For agriculture based on seven-year annual averages.

*Notes:* Figures in parentheses have a higher margin of error than other figures for the same periods. The first starting dates have been chosen for reasons of availability of data.

*Sources:* Bairoch, P., *Commerce extérieur et développement économique de l'Europe au XIXe siècle*, Paris, 1976; and data assembled for this study.

development. How and to what extent could free trade have caused a depression in the European economy, and how could protectionism have led to a recovery?

A first clue to the role of trade policy can be found in the fact that the depression was less pronounced in the United Kingdom, and that economic recovery benefited mainly those countries that had reverted to protectionism. Thus, during 1870–90, compared with 1850–70, the decrease in the growth rate of GNP per capita was 30% in the United Kingdom (or from 1.6% to 1.1% per annum) and 80% for Continental Europe (or from 1.1% to 0.2% per annum). Moreover, whereas during its protectionist phase the economy of Continental Europe grew at an annual rate per capita of about 1.5%, in the United Kingdom this growth rate continued to decline and was only about 0.7%.[2]

The second clue, which tells us much more about the impact of changes in trade policy on economic development, is to be found in an analysis of the evolution of the major sectors in Europe in general and in Continental Europe in particular. As can be seen in Table 4.1, for Europe as a whole, the slowing down in the growth of GNP was mostly the result of a decline in the growth of agricultural production. For Continental Europe, there was even a drop in production per capita of about 0.2% per annum between 1870/74 to 1888/92, compared to a growth of about 0.3–0.4%

during the previous decades. This agricultural crisis in Continental Europe can be almost completely explained by the influx of overseas grain, itself the result of a decrease in transport costs, and of the total abolition of tariff protection for grain which took place in Continental Europe between 1866 and 1872.

It should be noted here, as we saw in Chapter 2, that as far as agriculture was concerned, tariff 'disarmament' was all the more complete, because in this respect the theories of free traders and protectionists coincided. List did not argue for a protectionist 'learning' period for agriculture. The influx of American grain began at the end of the country's Civil War, and rapidly became very significant, even compared to total local European production. Even in France, which can be described as an agricultural economy, imports of wheat, which had amounted to 0.3% of domestic production in the decade 1851–60, rose to 19.0% in 1888/92. In Belgium, the level of imports rose from about 6% around 1850 to more than 100% around 1890. In the rest of Europe the figures were usually somewhere between these two extremes.

In this period grain accounted for some 35–40% of all agricultural production in the industrialized countries of Continental Europe (in other words, Belgium, France, Germany, Sweden and Switzerland). In such a situation, the substitution of 22% of grain production by imports in the space of 26 years represents, in very simple terms, a decrease of 3.3% per annum in the volume of total agricultural production, assuming that there was no exceptional increase in consumption due to greater availability of supplies. It does not seem that such an increase in consumption took place in these countries. In France, the country for which the most complete statistics are available, total consumption of grain per capita (including animal consumption but excluding seedgrain) increased by only 0.27% per annum from 1855/64 to 1875/84.[3] Thus the rapid influx of grain itself explains in large part the serious deceleration of growth in the total agricultural production of Continental Europe.

This influx of grain particularly affected farmers, because the low price of imports led to a drop in the domestic prices of grain and of agricultural products in general. It should be noted that the share of cereals in cash crops is more important than their share in total agricultural production. As a result, the standard of living of farmers in nearly all countries of Continental Europe remained static, or even fell.

The decline or stagnation in the farmers' standard of living clearly had important consequences not only within the agricultural sector but also outside it, because of the relative importance of this sector, which, at the time, accounted from some 60% of the total population in Continental Europe. This negative trend affected the overall demand for industrial products, and for the construction sector. Its consequences on the European economy were further exacerbated by the fact that in the 1870s and 1880s the United States had been the main supplier of grain to Europe. Because of US protectionist trade policies its additional grain sales to Europe did not lead to a corresponding increase in purchases of European manufactured goods, creating an unfavourable balance of trade between Europe and the United States. Around 1870, Continental Europe's trade deficit towards North America represented 5–6% of imports from that region. This reached 32% by 1890 and 59% around 1900.

## Similar evolutions but different consequences

The apparent contradiction between the negative effects of these increased imports of foodstuffs in Continental Europe and the positive ones of this same policy in the United Kingdom some 25 years earlier is to be explained essentially in terms of the different stages of economic development reached by the two at the time this policy was adopted. In the United Kingdom, the agricultural workforce represented only about 22% of the total working population in 1846, whereas those engaged in the manufacturing industry comprised about 37%. For the whole of Continental Europe in 1860/62 about 63% were in the agricultural sector and some 18–20% in manufacturing. Even in the industrialized countries of Continental Europe some 52% of the working population were still engaged in agriculture and only 19–21% in manufacturing.

These striking differences suggest that the transfer of labour from agriculture to industry should have taken place in Continental Europe at a rate at least twice as fast as that of the United Kingdom, and at a time when foreign outlets clearly could not play the same role as for the United Kingdom because of that country's more advanced stage. This did not and could not happen. Two other structural differences emerge between the two types of economy and the two periods. By 1846 the United Kingdom had a higher level of imports of foodstuffs than Continental Europe (and even than industrialized Continental Europe) had around 1860;[4] a situation (it is important to note) which was the result of a very slow process which had begun in 1770–80. This process had therefore allowed a gradual shift in production factors (labour and capital) from agriculture to industry. Second, around 1846 non-European grain was not yet available in large quantities, and, moreover, the high cost of transport made it less competitive. Therefore the impact on farm prices was more limited.

## *Protectionism and the expansion of foreign trade*

Despite its title, this section is not concerned with an explanation of the development of European foreign trade purely in terms of changes in commercial policy. Its primary aim is to present facts that constitute real paradoxes for the supporters of free trade. Not only did the period of the reinforcement of protectionism coincide with a more rapid expansion of trade but also, and even more paradoxically, the most highly protectionist European countries experienced the most rapid trade expansion. Even if this cannot be taken as proof that protectionism generates international trade, it does indicate that protectionism does not always necessarily hinder it.

On the other hand, trade expansion is not an aim in itself but merely a means of achieving economic growth. It could even be argued that, if identical levels of production of goods and services could be obtained either with or without foreign trade, the quantity of goods and services available for effective consumption would be greater (all things being equal) without foreign trade, since in this case less transport and fewer services would be needed to distribute those goods.

The data presented above, particularly in Table 4.1, show how far the protectionist period if not facilitated at least was concomitant with a recovery not only in the different sectors of the economy but also in trade. During the 20 years following the reintroduction of protectionist policies the annual growth rate of volume of GNP increased by more than 100% and the volume of exports grew by more than 35% (compared with the previous 20 years).

If the statistics in Table 4.2 show individual variations, according to country and period, it remains generally true that in all countries (except Italy) the introduction of protectionist measures resulted in a distinct acceleration in economic growth during the first ten years following a change in policy, and that this took place regardless of when the measures were introduced. In the next ten years, during which the protectionist measures were strengthened, there was usually a further acceleration in economic growth. In every country the years 1909–13 – which fall outside the analysis in Table 4.2 – were marked by an even higher growth rate. In the United Kingdom, on the other hand, where there was practically no change in trade policy, there was first a period of stagnation and then a marked decline in the growth rate. Furthermore, in Continental Europe the rate of growth reached its peak at the time all countries strengthened their protectionism.

As far as foreign trade is concerned, an almost universal slowing of expansion is noticeable in the first ten years after the abandonment of free trade, but in the second ten years the rate of growth in the volume of exports in nearly all the protectionist countries was faster than it had been in the ten years prior to the adoption of protectionism (see Table 4.2). Moreover, and this is important, during these two decades the expansion

**Table 4.2** Growth of exports and GNP by countries and periods in relation to changes in commercial policy at the end of the nineteenth century (annual growth rates based on three-year annual average[a])

| | Date of policy change | 10-year period preceding protectionist move | | Periods following protectionist move | | | |
|---|---|---|---|---|---|---|---|
| | | | | First 10 years | | Second 10 years | |
| | | Exports | GNP | Exports | GNP | Exports | GNP |
| **Protectionist countries** | | | | | | | |
| France | 1892 | 2.1 | 1.2 | 1.9 | 1.3 | 2.7 | 1.5 |
| Germany | 1885 | 3.0 | 1.3 | 2.4 | 3.1 | 5.2 | 2.9 |
| Italy | 1887 | 0.4 | 0.7 | 1.7 | 0.5 | 4.5 | 2.7 |
| Sweden | 1888 | 3.4 | 1.5 | 2.8 | 3.5 | 2.4 | 3.3 |
| **Semi-protectionist countries** | | | | | | | |
| Belgium | 1887 | 4.9 | 1.2 | 2.3 | 2.0 | 2.7 | 2.8 |
| Denmark | (1889) | 1.4 | 3.3 | 4.3 | 3.8 | 4.1 | 3.0 |
| Switzerland | 1887 | 0.4 | – | −0.6 | – | 3.8 | – |
| Continental Europe | (1889) | 3.0 | 1.1 | 2.6 | 2.3 | 3.7 | 2.3 |
| United Kingdom | (1889)[b] | 3.9 | 2.2 | 1.1 | 2.3 | 3.2 | 1.2 |
| Europe | (1889) | 3.4 | 1.3 | 2.2 | 2.3 | 3.6 | 1.9 |

[a] Average of three years preceding the period, including the year when the policy change was made.
[b] No commercial policy change at this date, but year used in the calculations of annual growth rates.
*Note:* Parentheses indicate approximate dates.
*Sources:* See Table 4.1.

of trade was much faster in the countries that had adopted protectionism than in the United Kingdom, which remained liberal. Even if a bias in the calculations of the volume of exports cannot be ruled out, the proof of a slower trade expansion can be found in the fact that the value of the United Kingdom's exports represented only 31.1% of those from Continental Europe in 1909/11, whereas they had accounted for 36.3% in 1889/91. As with economic growth, the expansion of trade became even greater when all countries increased their protectionism. This is also a partial proof that economic growth is more an engine of trade than vice versa. I will return to this in Chapter 13, where a section is devoted to this less important myth.

## Trade policies and economic development in non-European developed countries

We shall concentrate here on the case of the United States. During the entire nineteenth century and in fact until the end of the 1920s the 'mother country and bastion of protectionism' experienced one of the fastest rates of economic growth in the world. If we limit ourselves to the period from 1829/31 to 1909/11 (in order to avoid the unreliable data for the 1800–30 period and to exclude the very divergent impact of World War I) we have the following annual growth rate in the volume of the GNP per capita: United States 2.4%; Western Europe 1.2%; the fastest growing European countries 1.5–1.6%. In global terms the differences are even larger since the US population increased much more rapidly during this period from that of Europe.

Obviously the success of the United States was not due entirely to its tariff policy. At least three other factors contributed: in agriculture the high ratio of land to people; for industry the widespread availability of raw materials; and for the economy in general the massive influx of labour and capital from Europe. But since both Europe and the United States had different phases of commercial policies, let us see how this influenced the American economy.

## *The US success story is even greater in the more protectionist periods*

As far as contemporary opinions on this period are concerned, until very recently the dogma of free trade was so strong that I have not found any research published before the 1980s showing the impact of protectionism on US industry in the nineteenth century to be positive. The first paper to challenge that dogma is that of Mark Bils (which deals with the first half of the nineteenth century), whose main conclusion is that

> My finding could hardly conflict more with the consensus view on the economic importance of the tariff. The calculations above demonstrate that, as of 1833, removing protection would have eliminated the vast majority of value added in the cotton textile industry.[5]

Let us now see what happened during the less protectionist period, that between 1846 and 1861. Here too there is a lack of specific studies. According to its contemporary observers, this policy, half-way between a very mild form of protectionism and moderate liberalism, did not have any noticeable effect on economic life. Critics of the tariff legislation of 1846 cannot claim that it did more than slightly retard the industrial process in the United States; while its warmest supporters do not pretend that it did much to hasten it. In fact, its effect either way was probably only small.[6] The data available do not enable us to be much more positive; the statistics for the 1840s and the 1850s are still unreliable, and those for the period before 1840 belong to what has been called the

'Statistical Dark Age'.[7] The data available on the volume of GNP per capita shows an annual growth rate of about 2.1% from 1820 to 1840 and about 1.7% from 1840 to 1860. It is thus probable that economic growth slowed down, but this growth was still fairly rapid if one views the 1.7% per annum in relation to the growth rates of other countries at this period (the rate in Europe from 1840 to 1860 was about 0.9%).

The most interesting period is that of the years 1870–92, those of the 'Great Depression' that affected the European continent in its most liberal period. In those years the United States, which, as we have seen, was increasing its protectionism, went through a phase of very rapid growth. Indeed this period can be regarded as among the most prosperous in the whole economic history of the United States. Between 1830 and 1870 the best 20-year periods in terms of economic growth were those of 1850–70, when GNP per capita increased at an annual rate of 1.8%. Between 1870 and 1890, the rate was 2.1%. The next best 20 years are those of 1890–1910 (2.0%). Therefore the best 20 years of American economic growth took place in a period when its trade policy was protectionist while that of the United States' major competitors was liberal.

In Canada the story is somewhat different. As we saw in Chapter 3, Canada adopted a protectionist policy in 1879. If we compare the ten or twenty years before and after 1879, the balance is in favour of the liberal period. If, however, we take a 30-year period, the result is the opposite. Furthermore, the 1890–1910 period contained Canada's best and the third-best decade. Even more important is the fact that this protectionist period led to the foundation of Canadian industry. Canada's per capita level of manufacturing production, which in 1860 represented 40–45% of that of the developed countries, increased to 82–7% in 1913. The same also holds for Australia, where the protectionism tariff also brought industrialization.

I will not go further into these cases. My main objective was to show that outside Europe protectionism did not necessarily have a negative impact and also that in the world of economic history things are not simple.

## The negative impact of compulsory liberalism on the Third World

Since we ended Chapter 3 with the Third World, let us finish this chapter with an important point. There is no doubt that the Third World's compulsory economic liberalism in the nineteenth century is a major element in explaining the delay in its industrialization. Since the first

decades of the nineteenth century the large amounts of cheap manufactured products had led to a process of de-industrialization. To cite one
major example: after 1813 when the East India Company's trade
monopoly was suppressed, a monopoly which prevented imports of
textile goods into India, the influx of English textiles into India increased
considerably. About 1 million yards of cotton cloth were imported in
1814; 51 million in 1830; and 2,050 million in 1890. This influx was
certainly due to the substantial progress made by the English spinning
industry as a result of technological innovation. By 1830 the productivity
of an English worker using modern equipment was, for an average
yarn, some ten to fourteen times higher and for fine yarn even two
hundred to three hundred times higher than that of an Indian or other
traditional worker.[8] At that time the gap in incomes, and therefore also
of salaries, was limited. In England the real per capita GNP was probably
not more than two to three times higher than that in India. In view of
prevailing working conditions it is likely that the wage gap was even
smaller. This means that with such a difference in productivity, even
taking into account large profits and high transport costs, the end-user
price of British yarn in India (or elsewhere) was certainly only a fraction
of local production costs, and those production costs could not be
reduced significantly since wage levels were very low. Therefore if one
combines this with an open market policy, a substantial number of
imports becomes unavoidable.

India was only the first major casualty in a very long list. We should not
forget (see Chapter 3) that even politically independent Third World
countries were forced to open their markets to Western products, and this
also led to an influx of manufactured goods. By 1860, annual exports of
cotton goods from Britain, France and the United States to Latin
America represented the equivalent of 10.6 square metres for each
inhabitant; the figure for the Middle East was 7.9 square metres.[9] These
statistics explain the almost total disappearance of the textile industries in
those regions. The case of iron industries was even more striking; in this
sector the de-industrialization process was the most pronounced. I shall
deal with the problem of de-industrialization in the Third World in
Chapter 8.

It is difficult to find another case where the facts so contradict a
dominant theory than the one concerning the negative impact of protectionism; at least as far as nineteenth-century world economic history is
concerned. In all cases protectionism led to, or at least was concomitant
with, industrialization and economic development. Also, in the four
examples of liberalism, three had negative or very negative consequences. The exception is the British case of the post-1846 liberal

period, where this policy was probably an important factor in the acceleration of economic development that characterized the two to three decades following an almost total tariff disarmament. But this related to a country which, as a result of being the 'cradle of the Industrial Revolution', had by 1846 a substantial lead over the rest of the developed world. Furthermore, at that moment Britain had behind it at least a century and a half of protectionism.

## Notes

1 Bairoch, P., 'Geographical structure and trade balance of European foreign trade from 1800 to 1970', *The Journal of European Economic History*, **3**, No. 3, 1974, pp. 557–608.
2 For indications on the various sources used in this and the next two sections see Bairoch, P., *Commerce extérieur et développement économique de l'Europe au XIXe siècle*, Paris, 1976, and Bairoch, P., 'European Trade Policy, 1815–1914' in Mathias, P. and Pollard, S. (eds), *The Cambridge Economic History of Europe*, Vol. VIII: *The Industrial Economies: the Development of Economic and Social Policies*, Cambridge, 1989, pp. 1–160.
3 Toutain, J.-C., 'La consommation alimentaire en France de 1789 à 1964', *Cahiers d'l'ISEA*, **5**, No. 11, 1971.
4 Around 1840–45 the United Kingdom imported 530,000 tons of grain annually, which represented 4–5% of its own production. Around 1860 Continental Europe as a whole produced more grain than it required, and the same was true (though to a lesser extent) for industrialized Europe.
5 Bils, M., 'Tariff protection and production in the early U.S. cotton textile industry', *Journal of Economic History*, **XLIV**, No. 4, 1984, pp. 1033–45.
6 Ashley, P., *Modern Tariff History: Germany–United States–France*, 3rd edn, London, 1920, p. 175.
7 David, P. A. 'New light on a statistical Dark Age: US real product growth before 1840', *American Economic Review*, Papers and Proceedings LVII (1967), pp. 294–306. Weiss, T., 'Economic growth before 1860: revised conjectures', Working Paper No. 7 on Historical Factors in Long Run Growth, NBER, Cambridge (MA), October 1989, p. 35.
8 Derived from Batou, J., *Cent ans de résistance au sous-développement. L'industrialiation de l'Amérique Latine et du Moyen-Orient face au défi européen (1770–1870)*, Geneva, 1990, pp. 380–1.
9 *Ibid.*, p. 386.

# PART II

# *Major Myths on the Role of the Third World in Western Development*

From myths mainly concerning the history of the developed world, and which are found usually, but not only, in the work of many neoclassical economists, let us move to fallacies dealing with the historical role of the Third World in the West's economic development, which are found mainly, but not only, in that of many radical economists. This distinction does not rule out a 'common market' of myths. One of the most important myths is that colonialism played a crucial role in the development of the Western world. This idea is based mainly on three arguments: that the developed world depended for its industrialization on raw materials from the Third World; that the Third World was an important outlet for the manufacturing output of the West; and that colonialism played a major role in triggering the Industrial Revolution. Although they are incorrect in general terms, these arguments do have some basis in reality, which helps to explain their widespread acceptance.

# 5

# *Were Third-World Raw Materials Central to Western Industrialization?*

There is a widespread belief that the development of the Western world, especially its industrialization, was based for a very long period on raw materials from the Third World. In this framework the emphasis is put on energy, which is undoubtedly the most important raw material, and for which the West depended heavily on the Third World. In 1973 30% of the commercial energy used by the Western developed countries came from the Third World; for Western Europe this share was as high as 58%. In the case of some metals the developed Western countries obtained as much as 90% of their supplies from Third World countries; globally (in terms of volume) for all the metals, the deficit was close to 30%.

However, contrary to widespread opinion, all this is a fairly recent phenomenon. As late as the immediate post-World War II period, the developed countries (even in the West) were almost totally self-sufficient in energy. Until the end of the 1930s the developed world produced more energy than it consumed and had a sizeable export surplus in energy products, especially coal, while one of the major energy exporters was one of the most industrialized countries: the United Kingdom. In 1913 its net export of coal (and coal products) amounted to 78 million tons or 27% of its national production (and 6% of the world's production). It should be noted that, due to the fact that British, and generally European, imports from overseas comprised more bulky goods than their overseas exports, Europe's outbound freight was cheaper than its inbound. This helped the exports of coal, a very low-value product. In fact, it was only after the rapid growth of Middle East producers that, immediately after World War II, there was a real modification to this pattern of consumption.

The story is very similar as far as major minerals are concerned. In fact, the only type of important raw material for which the developed countries depended on a Third World production surplus was textile fibres, but even here the dependency was limited. But let us begin with the most important raw material – energy – and with a balance sheet on the eve of World War I. I will then deal with minerals and other raw materials.

## *Energy: a cheap and bulky good*

The history of international trade in energy products begins very late, even if we start with the Industrial Revolution. Long-distance trade in firewood was an economic impossibility in view of the low value of this product and the high cost of transport. To give an approximate idea of the parameters involved before the age of steam and railways, the following are some indications of prices and costs. In order to have a meaningful indicator of transport cost I choose, as is often done, to express it in terms of cereals.[1] The average transport cost per ton/kilometre was 3.9 kg of cereals for transport by cart; 0.9 kg for transport by river or canal; and 0.3–0.4 kg for sea transport. It can be estimated that the price of firewood in Europe was some seventy to one hundred times lower than that of cereals, therefore transporting pinewood over a distance of only 2–4 km on carts and of only 10–16 km on inland waterways would double the price of the wood. This could probably be extended to some 100 kilometres in favourable conditions (downstream), but even so this was a sufficient barrier to long-distance trade.

Therefore we have to wait for coal and the revolution in steam transportation to see the beginnings of significant international trade in fuel. Also, as mentioned earlier, paradoxically the main exporter of large quantities of energy was the most developed country, the United Kingdom, who even exported coal to the future Third World. A million tons of British coal exports was reached in 1837, 20 million in 1882, and in 1913, as we have seen, exports amounted to 78 million tons, representing 6% of the world's coal production.

This, together with Germany's high exports, led to a situation for 1909/11 (see Table 5.1) where Europe had a 3.6% surplus of coal. In fact, as a general rule (to which there are exceptions), since economic development was aided by the availability of coal, the less developed countries of Europe were generally characterized by an energy deficit and the more developed by a surplus. Therefore, if we take the six most industrialized European countries (Belgium, Germany, France, Sweden, Switzerland and the United Kingdom), their combined surplus of coal exceeded their consumption by 12% despite the fact that three of these countries were net importers of coal (Sweden, Switzerland and France).

**Table 5.1** Production and commercial balance sheet of energy products for 1909/11 (annual average; millions of tons of coal equivalent)

| | Production | Imports | International trade Exports | Balance | |
|---|---|---|---|---|---|
| | | | | Total | In % production |
| **COAL[a]** | | | | | |
| Europe | 546.2 | 90.7 | 110.2 | 19.5 | 3.6 |
| Russia | 26.3 | 4.8 | – | −4.8 | −18.2 |
| North America | 467.5 | 13.6 | 17.2 | 3.6 | 0.8 |
| Oceania | 12.0 | 0.2 | 1.9 | 1.7 | 11.9 |
| Japan | 54.3 | 0.1 | 3.0 | 2.8 | 5.2 |
| Total developed | 1,113.2 | 109.6 | 133.6 | 24.0 | 2.2 |
| **OIL[b]** | | | | | |
| Europe | 3.4 | 5.4 | 1.2 | −4.2 | −123.8 |
| Russia | 9.3 | – | 0.8 | 0.8 | 9.0 |
| North America | 27.3 | 4.5 | 4.8 | 0.3 | 1.1 |
| Oceania | – | 0.1 | – | −0.1 | – |
| Japan | 0.3 | 0.3 | – | −0.3 | 100.0 |
| Total developed | 40.2 | 10.4 | 6.8 | −3.6 | −9.1 |
| **COAL AND OIL[b]** | | | | | |
| Europe | 553.3 | 98.5 | 112.0 | 13.5 | 2.4 |
| Russia | 40.2 | 4.8 | 1.2 | −3.6 | −8.9 |
| North America | 527.8 | 20.4 | 24.2 | 3.7 | 0.7 |
| Oceania | 12.0 | 0.4 | 1.9 | 1.5 | 12.5 |
| Japan | 54.8 | 0.5 | 3.0 | 2.4 | 4.4 |
| Total developed | 1,195.0 | 124.8 | 143.5 | 18.8 | 1.6 |

[a] Including lignite expressed in coal equivalent.
[b] In coal equivalent.
*Sources:* Derived from Monney, D., *La production, le commerce et la consommation d'énergie primaire commerciale dans le monde autour de 1910*, Centre d'Histoire Economique Internationale, University of Geneva, 1990 (mimeo).

Trade in oil began even later in absolute terms but earlier relatively, since modern commercial oil production began in the 1860s, and the United States, then (and for over a century) the world's largest producer, began exporting oil in the 1870s. US consumption of energy petroleum products began to exceed local production only after 1957. On the eve of World War I (see Table 5.1) the developed countries had a 9% deficit in this source of energy, the main deficit region being Europe (excluding Russia), where local production met less than half of local consumption. But oil was a very minor source of energy during this period. In Europe its share of total commercial energy consumption[2] was less than 1% (and probably less than 0.5% in total energy). This means that, in global terms,

Europe, which is now one of the world's most dependent regions on oil, then had an excess of 2.4% of its production of commercial energy. For obvious reasons, as far as the non-commercial energy sources were concerned, there was an almost total self-sufficiency in almost every country.

If we take the total of commercial energy products, we can see (Table 5.2) that the developed countries' self-sufficiency in energy persisted during the inter-war period. In 1937 the Western developed countries had a slightly larger surplus than in 1909/11 (3.5% compared to 2.0%). In fact, as mentioned earlier, it was only after the rapid growth of Middle East producers that immediately after World War II, there was a real modification to this pattern of consumption. Even in 1950 the deficit was less than 4% for the Western developed countries. But in 1973, which marks a historical peak, the deficit was close to 50% and for Western Europe 140%, which means that only 42% of this region's commercial energy consumption was produced locally. Since non-commercial energy had by then become very marginal in global terms, it also implies that less than half of the energy consumption was produced locally.

The rapid increases in the energy deficit should not be regarded as a consequence of the developed countries' coal mines being depleted but rather as a result of a price differential. In the mid-1950s, for the first time in its short history as a major energy product, petroleum became cheaper than coal. I shall return to this point in Chapter 14, where I will present some unobserved turning points in history. Also, since oil is a liquid and leaves almost no ash after burning, its use expanded rapidly. Domestic heating and electricity generation rapidly became based on oil. To give one example, coal, which represented almost 100% of the energy used in producing thermal electricity in Western Europe in the early 1950s, decreased to 48% by 1973, but rose to 69% in 1987, due to the large increase in the price of oil. The dependency of the developed countries for commercial energy products was reduced between 1973 and the beginning of the 1990s (see Table 5.2).

## *Minerals: a wide difference according to the product*

Here, too, price considerations in relation to transport costs are of primary importance. Let us first give some examples from contemporary figures. The average price of ores (in 100% metal content) for 1989/91 was below $30 per ton for iron ore and above $352 for manganese ore. For metals we have figures ranging from above $10,000 for nickel to below $700 for lead.[3] This implies considerable differences in the impact of transport costs.

**Table 5.2** Production and trade balances[a] of total commercial energy, 1909/11–1989 (in millions of tons of coal equivalent)

|  | 1909/11 | 1929 | 1937 | 1950 | 1973 | 1980 | 1990 |
|---|---|---|---|---|---|---|---|
| **WESTERN EUROPE** | | | | | | | |
| Production | 469.8 | 728.7 | 714.6 | 507.3 | 617.5 | 816.4 | 928.1 |
| Trade balance | 12.1 | 31.5 | 10.4 | −67.0 | −846.3 | −741.8 | −705.3 |
| **NORTH AMERICA** | | | | | | | |
| Production | 527.8 | 873.3 | 847.4 | 1,195.9 | 2,453.6 | 2,326.6 | 2,466.5 |
| Trade balance | 3.7 | 15.3 | 33.4 | 8.7 | −168.1 | −292.1 | −287.2 |
| **JAPAN** | | | | | | | |
| Production | 54.8 | 45.1 | 61.4 | 44.1 | 38.0 | 42.3 | 47.6 |
| Trade balance | 2.4 | −1.8 | −4.9 | −1.9 | −340.0 | −392.7 | −464.5 |
| **ALL WEST DEVELOPED** | | | | | | | |
| Production | 1,071.2 | 1,592.8 | 1,554.5 | 1,795.8 | 3,285.4 | 3,397.6 | 3,801.8 |
| Trade balance | 20.9 | 40.7 | 31.7 | −68.5 | −1,348.0 | −1,414.1 | −1,362.3 |
| **EASTERN DEVELOPED COUNTRIES** | | | | | | | |
| Production | 123.7 | 60.5 | 176.8 | 470.9 | 1,907.8 | 2,379.5 | 2,749.3 |
| Trade balance | −2.2 | −12.7 | −11.4 | 24.2 | 20.8 | 319.5 | 307.6 |
| **ALL DEVELOPED COUNTRIES** | | | | | | | |
| Production | 1,195.0 | 1,653.3 | 1,731.3 | 2,266.7 | 5,193.2 | 5,777.2 | 6,551.2 |
| Trade balance | 18.8 | 53.4 | 43.1 | −44.2 | −1,327.2 | −1,094.6 | −1,059.7 |

[a] Calculated by comparison of production and consumption statistics; except for 1909/11: calculated on the basis of foreign trade.

*Sources:* 1909/11: see Table 5.1
1929 and 1937: derived from United Nations, *World Energy Supplies in Selected Years, 1929–1950*, Statistical Papers, Series J, 1, New York 1952.
1950 and 1973: derived from United Nations, *World Energy Supplies, 1950–1974*, New York 1976.
1980 and after: derived from United Nations, *Energy Statistics Yearbook*, New York, various issues.

Let us begin the story with the major mineral: iron ore. The term 'major' is in fact too weak since, expressed in weight, by 1910 iron represented 95% of the total of all metals produced. Before considering the data presented in Table 5.3, let us quote Yates, whose book on foreign trade in primary products is still unsurpassed for the period it covers (1913–53).

The iron ore trade before 1914 was primarily an intra-European activity, France, Spain and Sweden supplying the import needs of the United Kingdom, Belgium and Germany; Europe also obtained some ore from Algeria and Tunisia. This European commerce accounted for 28 million out of the 32 million tons in world trade. Most of the remainder was a modest shipment from Cuba to the United States of America plus some exchange between the United States of America and Canada. China also exported a small quantity to Japan. All these were, relatively speaking, local shipments; it did not pay, and at that time was not necessary, to move

**Table 5.3** Production and trade balances of iron ore, 1913–90 (million tons of metal content)

|  | 1913 | 1937 | 1950 | 1960 | 1970 | 1980 | 1990 |
|---|---|---|---|---|---|---|---|
| **WESTERN EUROPE** | | | | | | | |
| Production | 35.0 | 33.0 | 28.3 | 51.3 | 54.3 | 38.4 | 21.0 |
| Trade balance | −0.2 | −2.6 | −0.6 | −12.4 | −48.3 | −54.4 | −65.0 |
| **NORTH AMERICA** | | | | | | | |
| Production | 27.0 | 37.9 | 51.1 | 58.0 | 83.8 | 79.1 | 58.3 |
| Trade balance | −0.8 | −1.2 | −3.8 | −10.8 | −1.6 | 3.6 | 5.3 |
| **JAPAN** | | | | | | | |
| Production | – | 0.3 | 0.5 | 1.0 | 0.9 | 0.3 | 0.1 |
| Trade balance | – | −1.9 | −0.8 | −8.6 | −63.2 | −80.3 | −75.2 |
| **OTHER WEST DEVELOPED**[a] | | | | | | | |
| Production | 0.1 | 1.5 | 2.2 | 4.1 | 37.5 | 81.1 | 91.0 |
| Trade balance | – | 0.2 | – | 0.3 | 28.3 | 63.7 | 70.9 |
| **ALL WEST DEVELOPED** | | | | | | | |
| Production | 63.0 | 72.6 | 82.1 | 115.1 | 176.0 | 199.5 | 170.3 |
| Trade balance | −1.0 | −5.4 | −5.3 | −31.6 | −84.8 | −67.5 | −65.3 |
| **EASTERN DEVELOPED COUNTRIES** | | | | | | | |
| Production | – | 16.4 | 23.2 | 60.2 | 109.0 | 138.3 | 142.7 |
| Trade balance | – | −1.0 | −5.9 | −2.6 | −0.8 | −7.4 | 5.0 |
| **ALL DEVELOPED COUNTRIES** | | | | | | | |
| Production | 64.0 | 89.0 | 105.3 | 175.3 | 285.0 | 337.9 | 313.0 |
| Trade balance | −1.0 | −6.6 | −6.6 | −34.2 | −85.6 | −74.8 | −60.3 |

[a] Australia, New Zealand, South Africa.

*Note:* Data for 1913 are not strictly comparable with those of the later years.

*Sources:*
1913: Yates, P. L., *Forty Years of Foreign Trade. A Statistical Handbook with Special Reference to Primary Products and Underdeveloped Countries*, London, 1959, pp. 128–9. (The data have been converted into metal content on the basis of later data.)
1937–60: United Nations, *Le marché mondial du minéral de fer*, New York 1968, pp. 48–51.
1970 and after: United Nations, *Unctad Commodity Yearbook*, New York, various issues; and data communicated by UNCTAD's Secretariat.

iron ore over long distances . . . Forty years later requirements were nearly twice as large, and much of the increase was met by more intensive exploitation of home and nearby resources.[4]

As can be seen from Table 5.3, on the eve of World War I the developed countries' iron ore deficit was only 1.6%. During the inter-war period production for export increased rapidly in some Third World countries (especially North Africa), leading to an increase in the developed countries' deficit. However, even in 1950, this was only about 6%. But here too, as for energy, in the early 1960s the situation was very different from that of the early 1950s. By 1960 the developed world had a deficit of some 20% of its iron ore production and, since this deficit was limited to the Eastern European countries, it was over 27% for the Western developed countries (or 22% of its consumption). This increased to 33% consumption for 1970.

Contrary to the case of energy, the situation in Western Europe was not very different from that of North America. In fact, the only two divergent regions were Japan and developed countries in the southern hemisphere (mainly Australia and South Africa). Japan's deficit was very important and started very early. In fact, in the first years of the twentieth century Japan imported from the Third World not only iron ore but also raw iron and steel (in the case of iron and steel, from India). The Australasian countries became late but important net exporters of iron ore (mainly to Japan).

For the other metal ores the situation was different, their higher price allowing them to be transported over much larger distances. Copper and tin exports from the future Third World started even before the nineteenth century, mainly from Latin America. As can be seen in Table 5.4, the dependency of the developed countries on those two metal ores was already important on the eve of World War I. For tin, net imports represented almost 86% of consumption, and this share was 21% for copper. The situation was quite different for most other ores. For zinc, the developed countries probably had an excess; for bauxite, there was an equilibrium; and for lead, the deficit was limited (11%).

In terms of volume (and of metal content), since iron is so predominant, the total dependency rate of the developed countries on ores was very low on the eve of World War I: no more than 2% of their consumption. In other words, the developed countries produced 98% of the ores they consumed. During the nineteenth century this share was probably above 99%. Furthermore, compared to a deficit of some 1.4 million tons of metal ore, there was on the eve of World War I, as we have seen, an excess of 18.8 million tons of commercial energy products, which means that for those two groups combined there was an excess of 17.4 million tons, representing 1.4% of developed countries' consumption.

Before examining developments after World War I we should take into consideration the fact that the value of iron ore was much lower than that of the other ores, where the deficit was higher. Therefore, expressed in value, the global deficit in ores, before World War I, was of the order of 4–6%. The main element in this deficit was tin, whose high value made it responsible for almost two thirds of the deficit (in value) of all mineral ores. For ores and energy products combined we are faced with almost an equilibrium in value (either a deficit of 0.6% or a total equilibrium).

The story of the other ores after 1913 is more or less that of iron ore; the 1950s and the 1960s saw a rapid increase in the dependency of Western

**Table 5.4** Production and trade balances of the main ores for 1909/13–1990 (thousand tons of metal content)

| | All developed countries | | | Western developed countries | | | | |
|---|---|---|---|---|---|---|---|---|
| | 1909/13 | 1934/8 | 1953 | 1953 | 1960 | 1970 | 1980 | 1990 |
| Iron[a] | | | | | | | | |
| Production | 64,000 | 89,020 | 105,280 | 82,100 | 115,110 | 176,010 | 199,530 | 170,310 |
| Trade balance | −1,000 | −6,570 | −6,640 | −1,380 | −31,600 | −84,780 | −67,490 | −65,270 |
| Copper | | | | | | | | |
| Production | 802 | 986 | 1,641 | 1,309 | 1,709 | 2,653 | 2,563 | 3,218 |
| Trade balance | −217 | −620 | −996 | −1,239 | −1,939 | −2,859 | −3,711 | −3,329 |
| Lead | | | | | | | | |
| Production | 1,002 | 1,062 | 1,347 | 1,062 | 1,125 | 1,918· | 1,770 | 1,724 |
| Trade balance | −120 | −340 | −501 | −502 | −773 | −712 | −1,547 | −1,937 |
| Bauxite | | | | | | | | |
| Production | 110 | 520 | 1,330 | 840 | 1,363 | 4,040 | 7,884 | 11,000 |
| Trade balance | 0 | 0 | – | – | −2,875 | −4,116 | −5,320 | −5,020 |
| Tin | | | | | | | | |
| Production | 16 | – | – | 8 | 7 | 14 | 19 | 17 |
| Trade balance | −100 | – | – | −106 | −148 | −139 | −119 | −117 |
| Manganese[b] | | | | | | | | |
| Production | – | – | – | – | 2,012 | 4,496 | 7,991 | 5,905 |
| Trade balance | – | – | – | – | −4,073 | −5,592 | −3,311 | −1,300 |

[a] 1950 instead of 1953; 1937 instead of 1934/7.
[b] Gross weight; not metal content.

*Note:* For copper, lead and tin the trade balances have been calculated by comparing production figures of ore with metal at a relevant stage of consumption: refined copper; primary lead; primary tin.
This is justified by the low cost of processing, which implies that many ores are processed in the Third World. *However*, this tends to overestimate the importance of net import in the developed countries by 10%.

*Sources:* See Table 5.3. To which should be added: League of Nations, *Statistical Year-Book of the League of Nations*, Geneva, various issues.

developed countries. For copper, compared to an import rate of some 21% for 1909/13, the comparable figure is of the order of 45–50% around 1970. By 1970, the import share for bauxite and manganese was also of the same magnitude (see Table 5.4). However, as a general rule, from 1975–80 onwards the relative importance of the rest of the world to the supply of ores to the Western developed countries showed, as with energy, a moderately declining trend.

Before dealing with the other raw materials, especially textiles, we should not forget the wide range of non-metallic minerals which, as a rule, are found in many parts of the world and are locally produced and consumed. This is due to their wide availability, which leads to very low prices and therefore very high relative transport costs. Three important materials of this nature are those used in clay, cement and glass industries.

In terms of volume, the clay industries are the most important since they manufacture a wide range of products, from roof tiles to very expensive high-quality porcelain. I have not been able to find any valid figures for the volume of clay production, but for the pre-World War I period on the basis of very incomplete data, it can be estimated that clay products represented a volume at least twice as important as cement, or some 70–80 million tons. By 1910 the developed countries' production of cement had reached 34.2 million tons and that of glass 2.2 million tons. Therefore, globally, for those three products the total was 110–120 million tons, or twice as much as metallic ores, and all locally produced.

## The other raw materials

The list of other raw materials is a varied one, and includes the numerous textile fibres (cotton, wool, jute, silk, flax and hemp) and the dyes for these textiles, as well as rubber, hides and skin. In terms of volume and value, textile fibres are the more important, so let us begin with these.

Contrary to the preceding groups of raw materials, in this case the Third World played a more significant role, but not a dominant one. Developed countries' yearly consumption of textile fibres for the 1909–13 period was 7,200,000 tons, the most important being cotton (3,600,000 tons), but most of that cotton came from the United States, therefore net imports of the developed countries represented only 13% of their consumption.[5] Coincidentally, this is also the share for wool, the second product. For all fibres the import share was 22–3%, due mainly to the 100% import rate for jute. In terms of value, however, this proportion falls to 17–19%, in other words, a self-sufficiency rate of 77–8% in terms of volume and 81–3% in value.

There is also a number of other raw materials for which the developed countries depended partially or even totally on the Third World but they are very marginal compared to those mentioned above. Annual consumption for 1909/13 of rubber was 107,000 tons and obviously all was imported. A more important group of products were those used for fertilizers. Guano imports amounted to less than 60,000 tons. Much more important were the net imports of natural phosphates, which amounted to some 2,900,000 tons (or 41–2% of consumption). However, globally, for all fertilizer-related products the deficit was in the neighbourhood of 20% and represented less than 3 million tons.

Therefore, on the eve of World War I when the developed world already had a volume of per capita manufacturing production some seven to nine times higher than that of the world in 1750, 98% of metal ores used by the developed countries came from the developed world; 80% of its textile fibres; and, as we have seen, over 100% of its energy. In terms of the volume of the rest of raw materials (such as those used in glass, cement, paper and clay industries), the degree of local autonomy was over 99%. Furthermore, and we are still dealing with the situation of the eve of World War I, the excess of net coal exports represented a volume about five times larger than the net imports of the rest of the raw materials. This implies, in global terms, even an excess of the magnitude of 1% of the volume raw materials.

The situation in terms of value was somewhat different, since the value of most of the ores was higher than that of energy products, and of textiles much higher than those of energy products. In terms of value, the self-sufficiency of the developed countries in raw materials was about 94–6% around 1913, and, as we have seen, the situation did not change much until just after World War II.

On the other hand, it is obvious that on the eve of World War I manufacturing industries were characterized by a greater dependency on some raw materials than was the case in the nineteenth century. If we take the example of textile fibres around 1830, wool, flax and hemp, then all locally grown, represented 80% of textile consumption. There were no jute industries (in the developed countries) and 50% of the cotton came from the United States. This means a self-sufficiency rate of 90% compared to 80% for 1913. As a very approximate estimate of the self-sufficiency of the developed countries during the 1800–1913 period I would suggest 96–102% (the upper figure implying some room for export).

## But things look different when seen from the other side

It is obvious that if seen from the other side the picture seems very different. Primary goods represented more than 90% of Third World exports, and, furthermore, in most of the Third World countries almost 100% of the raw materials produced were exported to the developed countries. These are complementary factors, helping to explain the creation of the myth that the West's industrialization has been a result of raw materials originating from the Third World.

However, even taking the other side of the picture, *raw materials* should not be equated with *primary goods*. Primary goods can be defined as all goods that did not undergo any real transformation, and of which some can even be consumed without any processing (for example, fruit and salt). Raw materials are primary goods used by the manufacturing industries. If indeed during the nineteenth century primary goods

**Table 5.5** Product distribution of exports from the Third World for the 1815–1914 period

| | |
|---|---|
| Raw materials | 27.9 |
| For textile industries | 16.9 |
| For metal industries | 2.3 |
| Energy products | 0.9 |
| Other non-food products | 4.9 |
| Food products | 48.2 |
| Manufactured goods | 9.1 |
| Other | 9.9 |
| Opium | 2.8 |
| Gold and silver | 3.8 |

*Sources:* Based on Bairoch, P. and Etemad, B., *Commodity Structure of Third World Exports, 1830–1937*, Geneva, 1985.

represented more than 90% of exports from the Third World, raw materials were only a quarter of its total exports. The (weighted) average shares of the main products exported from the Third World during the 1815–1914 period are shown in Table 5.5.

The self-sufficiency of developed countries in raw materials, as we have seen, was greater during most of the nineteenth century; however, after 1913, it declined gradually. But this decline after 1913 was very slow for the three next decades. Even if transport costs had fallen the possibilities of exporting fuels and minerals from the Third World to the developed countries were limited by those costs. It is significant to note the conclusions of the League of Nations study on the possibilities of exporting such goods in the early 1930s:

> The raw materials for heavy industries – viz., coal and iron ore – can, if mining for local purpose is left out of account, be economically produced only in Europe, North America and within a zone of, say, about 100 km [about 60 miles] from the coasts in other parts of the world. . . . Within this zone also, phosphates may be considered as exploitable. The second zone, where oil production is actually possible from the point of view of accessibility to the market . . . is situated . . . in Europe, the greater part of North America, in some other economically developed or favorably situated regions, and, furthermore, within a distance of 250 km (about 150 miles) from all sea-coasts, except those of the polar seas. . . . production of manganese and chromium ores – to mention one example – is possible farther away from the coast than production of iron ore, the first-mentioned ores having a considerably higher value. Zinc and lead ores should probably be possible to exploit still farther away.[6]

As we have seen, even at the end of the 1930s the self-sufficiency of the developed countries in raw materials was around 96–8% in terms of

70        *Economics and World History*

volume and 93·6% in terms of value. But again, if we look on the other side, the inter-war period witnessed a rapid increase in the production of raw materials in the Third World. The annual production of copper ore (in metal content) between 1908/12 and 1937/9 increased rapidly from 160,000 to 900,000 tons; bauxite from 2,000 to 980,000; iron ore from 3,100,000 to 18,400,000. For other minerals the rise was slower: tin ore from 100,000 to 175,000 and lead from 180,000 to 500,000 tons. Petroleum production rose from 3,800,000 to 72,100,000 tons. The increase was greatest in Africa (copper ore from 11,000 to 400,000 tons). Almost all of this was exported to the developed countries, but in relation to these regions' consumption, as we have seen it, it was marginal.

By 1953 the per capita level of industrialization of the West was some twenty-two times higher than that of the beginning of modern development and global industrial production some eighty-five times higher. Therefore, if in fact from 1955 onwards the large dependence on raw materials from the Third World was a reality, before that period it was a complete myth. The developed countries were thus able to reach a very high level of industrialization on the basis of local raw materials and also on the exploitation of their local workforces, but that is another story.

## Notes

1  I used this approach in some of my earlier research (Bairoch, P., 'La baisse des coûts de transports et le développement économique', *Revue de l'Institut de Sociologie*, No. 2, Brussels, 1965, pp. 309–32) which was systematized by Clark, C. and Haswell, M. (*The Economies of Subsistence Agriculture*, London, 1970). The figures quoted here are based on Clark's data complemented by sources that appeared afterwards (see Bairoch, P., 'The impact of crop yields, agricultural productivity, and transport costs on urban growth between 1800 and 1910', in Woode, A. D. van der, Hayami, A. and Vries, J. de (eds), *Urbanization in History. A Process of Dynamic Interactions*, Oxford, 1990, pp. 134–51.
2  When dealing with energy products it is a rule to divide them into two groups. According to the United Nations definition, commercial primary energy include the following products: coal lignite, jet, oil shale, petroleum, natural gas and electricity generated from hydro, nuclear and geothermal sources. The non-commercial primary energy products are essentially wood, agricultural wastes and human and animal energy.
3  UNCTAD, *United Monthly Commodity Price Bulletin*, Geneva, March 1990. One should not forget the wide price fluctuations. For example, the $10,600 for nickel for 1987/89 takes account of $4,870 for 1987; $13,780 for 1988; $3,770 for March 1987 and $18,010 for April 1988.
4  Yates, P. L., *Forty Years of Foreign Trade. A Statistical Handbook with Special Reference to Primary Products and Under-developed Countries*, London, 1959, p. 127.

5 The data on consumption, trade and prices of textile fibres and rubber were derived from the following two publications of the Institut International d'Agriculture (Rome): 'Les questions agricoles, un point de base international' in *Société des Nations, Conférence Economique Internationale*, Geneva, May 1929, pp. 200–71, and *Annuaire International de Statistique Agricole, 1929/30*, Rome, 1930.
6 League of Nations, *Report of the Committee for the Study of the Problem of Raw Materials*, Geneva, 1937, pp. 46–7.

# 6

# *Were Colonial Outlets Crucial to Western Industries?*

Contrary to a widespread opinion there has been no period in the history of the Western developed world when the outlet provided by colonies or by the Third World was a very important one in global terms for their industries, the Third World was not even a significant outlet. In this case, the myth probably has one of its origins in the fact that for the majority of the Third World countries, from the beginning of the nineteenth century until recently (and in many cases until today), almost all the manufactured products consumed locally came from the developed countries, and this is one of the major causes of de-industrialization in the Third World. I shall return to the important question of de-industrialization in Part III, which deals with fallacies concerning the historical roots of under-development and the present situation in the Third World. Therefore let us concentrate here on the facts concerning the outlets; on the myth that the Third World was an important outlet for the industries of the developed countries. I shall begin showing that even as far as total exports are concerned the Third World had only a modest role as an outlet for the developed world.

## Total exports: a modest role

A modest role played by trade to the Third World in general? Yes indeed, for the developed countries as a whole, during the period from 1800 to 1938, only 17% of total exports were sent to the Third World and of those, only half to the colonies, which means that only 9% of total European exports went to the colonial empires.[1] Since during this period total exports represented some 8–9% of the GNP of the developed countries, it can be estimated that exports to the Third World represented only 1.3–1.7% of the total volume of the production of those developed countries, and exports to the colonies only 0.6–0.9%.

All these figures are rather higher if we limit ourselves to Europe instead of to all developed countries. Indeed, one should not forget that despite the fact that the United States was geographically nearer to the main Third World trading area of this period (i.e. Latin America), its trade with the Third World was less important than that of Europe. For 1909/11, when 21% of Europe's exports went to the Third World, the figure for the United States was 19%. Also, since the export share of the American economy was much lower than that of Europe, the United States accounted for only 15% of the developed world's total exports to the Third World. During the entire nineteenth century United States exports to the Third World represented only 0.5–0.9% of its GNP. Therefore Europe's exports to the Third World during the 1800–1938 period were 18% of total exports compared to 17% for all the developed countries. The difference is rather more important as far as the ratio of exports to the Third World as a share of the total volume of production is concerned: 1.4–1.8% compared to 1.3–1.7%.

Obviously, these figures for Europe, like any averages, conceal some variations, in this case regional and product differences. The main regional exception was the United Kingdom. For this country, exports to the Third World represented 40% of its total (during the period 1800–1938). This fact is probably one of the foundations of the myth, since in Marxist literature it was widely quoted. Furthermore, the share of exports in GNP was greater for the United Kingdom than for the average of the developed countries: some 12–13%. Exports to the Third World thus represented 4–6% of United Kingdom total production, which, while being a share that was three to four times larger than for the rest of the developed world, remains very modest after all. As we shall see later, however, this does not rule out the possibility that, for certain periods and industries, Third World outlets were important for the United Kingdom.

## Exports of manufactures: also a modest role

As the main exports to the Third World were manufactures, the proportion of manufactured goods exported by developed countries to the Third World was higher than that of exports in total production. For the period between 1899 and 1938, for which the data are reliable, it can be estimated[2] that 26–32% of manufacturers' exports of the developed countries were sent to the Third World (compared with 20% for total exports). For the same period, the overall share of manufacturing production that was exported may be estimated at around 20–25%. This implies that between 1899 and 1938 approximately 5–8% of total manufacturing production of the developed countries was exported to the Third World. Therefore even if one takes the upper limit, 8%, this represents a very marginal outlet.

Data are insufficient to calculate comparable percentages for the nineteenth century. I tried to approach the problem indirectly in a study on the levels of industrialization[3] and calculated the total volumes of production of both the developed world and the Third World. I also estimated the total domestic volume of the consumption of manufactured products in the Third World on the basis of various hypotheses on the growth of per capita consumption of those goods. It can be assumed that the difference between the estimated volume of consumption and the estimated volume of indigenous production was composed of imports from the advanced countries. In view of the declining living standards of Third World populations, it seemed unduly optimistic to assume that the per capita consumption of manufactured goods would have remained stable; an extremely pessimistic hypothesis allows for a fall of 30%. Leaving aside the two extreme hypotheses and allowing for a margin of error in the data, this approach would suggest that 6–14% (with an average of around 10%) of manufactured goods produced in the developed countries were exported to the Third World during the nineteenth century.

This suggests that the damage caused to Third World industries by colonialism through the influx of manufactures did not in fact have a correspondingly large positive effect on the developed countries. Taken as a whole, access to Third World markets was no more than a small stimulus to the developed countries' industries.

We must, however, also examine national characteristics. Certainly, as we have seen in the case of the United Kingdom, the relative contribution of the markets of Third World countries was much more important than for the other Western countries. As far as textiles in general are concerned, some 35% of British production was exported to the Third World at the turn of the twentieth century. For cotton textiles this proportion was even much higher: 67%. We shall return to this specific case in the next chapter.

However, even in the case of Britain, the contribution of Third World markets came only after five or six decades of modern industrial development. On the other hand, it is obvious that even a marginal additional outlet can have a sizeable influence on the profitability of an industrial sector. We should also remember that access to such outlets may also have certain negative repercussions: for example, since they

**Table 6.1** Share of the Third World market economies[a] in exports from Western developed countries, 1900–90 (%)

|  | 1900 | 1938 | 1955 | 1970 | 1980 | 1990 |
|---|---|---|---|---|---|---|
| **Share of Third World in total exports of:** | | | | | | |
| All Western developed countries | 13.5 | 22.7 | 27.7 | 18.4 | 23.3 | 18.7 |
| Western Europe | 14.2 | 21.4 | 25.5 | 13.7 | 17.3 | 11.7 |
| United States | 11.2 | 26.8 | 37.3 | 29.6 | 36.2 | 33.9 |
| Japan | 30.0 | 49.1 | 57.7 | 40.0 | 45.4 | 39.5 |
| **All Western developed countries: share of the Third World in some exports[b]** | | | | | | |
| Food, beverages, etc. | – | – | 21.2 | 18.0 | 24.1 | 21.0 |
| of which cereals | – | – | – | 30.4 | 33.5 | 45.8 |
| Manufactured goods (total) | – | – | 32.6 | 19.8 | 25.2 | 19.3 |
| chemicals | – | – | 36.8 | 23.0 | 25.1 | 22.2 |
| machinery and transport equipment | – | – | 35.4 | 21.8 | 29.3 | 21.3 |
| other manufactured goods | – | – | 29.5 | 16.3 | 20.8 | 16.7 |

[a] China and other 'non-market' economies of Asia excluded; but their role is a minor one. For example, in 1980 only 0.4% of developed countries' manufactured exports went to this region.
[b] The last column refers to 1989.
*Sources:* 1900: derived from United Nations, *International Trade Statistics, 1900–1960*, May 1962 (mimeo).
Rest of the data: United Nations, *Monthly Bulletin of Statistics*, New York, various issues.

were 'easy' markets they did not encourage new products or technological innovation. Although this was the case in the United Kingdom, this is not sufficient to explain the loss of vitality in British industry, which was already evident between 1880 and 1890. However, as we saw earlier (Chapter 4), other commercial factors also contributed to this.

Before moving on to the next point, I will give a brief overview of what happened in this area after World War II. For political and statistical reasons, we must restrict the 'developed countries' to Western developed countries and 'the Third World' to the Third World market economies. This leads to an increase in the relative importance of trade flows between the two. In any case, the Communist countries represented only 10% of world trade.

The share of the Third World in Western developed countries' exports (see Table 6.1), which had increased from 21–3% in the pre-war period to a peak of 28% in the mid-1950s, fell to 18% in 1972, its lowest point in the twentieth century. The rapid increase in oil prices in 1973 led to a considerable increase in the demand for manufactured goods in the oil-exporting countries resulting in a rise in exports from developed countries. Between 1974 and 1983, the share of the Third World in developed Western countries' exports of manufactures fluctuated around 22%. Since 1984, this share has declined and has returned to the levels of the early 1970s.

This decline was due largely to a rapid increase of intra-European trade and especially Common Market trade. For these reasons, the Third World's share in Western Europe's exports fell even more sharply: from a peak in the mid-1950s of 26% to 13% in 1972. But Western Europe, which includes the major former colonial powers, has traditionally had the largest absolute volume of exports to the Third World.

As far as manufactured goods are concerned, the share of the Third World, as for the nineteenth century, is higher than for total exports. But, even in this case, the peak reached in the mid-1950s meant that only a third of those exports went to the Third World and, in more recent times (see Table 6.1), this has fallen to a fifth. This means an even smaller share than for the 1899–1938 period (see above), even if we include the non-market Third World economies. Since we mention the non-market economies it should be noted that the quantities of manufactured goods exported from the developed non-market economies to the Third World was very limited. By 1970 these represented a volume some twenty times smaller than the comparable figure for Western developed countries.

Let us move on to the share of the production of manufactured goods exported to the Third World in the contemporary period. The only available estimate seems to be that made by UNIDO (United Nations Industrial Development Organization), which estimates that for 1987, exports of manufactured products from the developed market economies to the Third World represented 3.5% of the production in those developed countries.[4] UNIDO adds that there is probably an upward bias in the percentage. But again, this very low share, like all averages, conceals wide differences on country and product levels. They are, however, sufficient to express the overall reality of the limited importance even today of Third World outlets for the industries of the developed countries. This contrasts sharply with the much greater importance of the developed countries as a market for the Third World. If we take the situation around 1970 we have the following pattern. For the Western developed countries total exports to the Third World market economies represented a little less than 2% of their GNP. On the other hand, if we express the exports of the Third World market economies destined for the developed countries as a percentage of their GNP, the figure around 1970 was about 11%. Thus we are confronted with a pattern which, in global terms, places the Third World countries in an unfavourable situation, for although the Western market is of prime, even vital, importance to them, the place of the Third World countries in the trade of the Western world can, by contrast, be considered if not exactly marginal, then certainly far from being of major importance.

Finally, if we return to manufactures, and this is more valid for the contemporary period than for the nineteenth century, we should not neglect imports in the developed countries of manufactured products originating from the Third World. At the end of the 1980s the value of those exports from the Third World to the developed countries represented some 60% of the flow in the other direction. By 1970, this share was approximately 27%, and in 1955, 16%. This implies that, in terms of net exports, the relative importance of the outlets of the Third World must be reduced by the above percentages. The success story of the Third World's exports, as shown by the figures mentioned above, should be qualified. In fact, as we shall see it in the next chapter, the 'Four Dragons' (Hong Kong, South Korea, Singapore and Taiwan), which contain only 3% of the Third World's population, are almost entirely responsible for this success.

## *A paradox: colonial powers characterized by slower growth*

An additional element leading to a reassessment of the role of colonization in the industrialization and economic development of the West can be found in the following paradox. If one compares the rate of growth during the nineteenth century it appears that non-colonial countries had, as a rule, a more rapid economic development than colonial ones. There is an almost perfect correlation. Thus colonial countries like Britain, France, the Netherlands, Portugal and Spain have been characterized by a slower rate of economic growth and industrialization than Belgium, Germany, Sweden, Switzerland and the United States. The 'rule' is, to a certain extent, also valid for the twentieth century. Thus Belgium, by joining the colonial 'club' in the first years of the twentieth century, also became a member of the group characterized by slow growth. The loss of Netherland's colonial empire after World War II coincided with a rapid acceleration in its economic development.

It is obvious that this correlation is far from being proof that all colonial ventures had been economically counterproductive. However, nothing excludes such a possibility, since slower economic growth could be explained by a diversion of a large amount of entrepreneurial skills and a general dynamism in colonial ventures. Furthermore, colonial markets were easy ones and therefore a factor against innovation and invention, which always implies an effort if not a necessity. However, this correlation can be at least a partial proof that colonialism has not been such a powerful force for development and industrialization, since otherwise we would have been faced with an inverse correlation.

The only alternative explanation lies in the possibility that non-colonial powers benefited from colonial markets without having to share the costs of colonization. This was perhaps the case for Switzerland, whose exports to the Third World in the middle of the nineteenth century were apparently much larger than those of other non-colonial countries. But this was certainly not true in those other non-colonial countries which, as a rule, had a much smaller share of exports to Third World countries. Thus if we take the situation in 1860 we see that while the United Kingdom's share of total exports to the Third World was close to 40% that for Germany was below 10% and that of the United States was, despite its proximity to Latin America, only 14%. Spain's share was 30% while that of Belgium and Sweden about 5%.

As noted above, the only exception was Switzerland, whose exports to the Third World in the same period probably represented some 30% of its total exports. The cautious tone adopted here is due to the lack of reliable statistics. Around 1910, for which the data are more reliable, Swiss exports to the Third World then represented no more than 10% compared to over 40% for the United Kingdom.

This negative correlation between colonialism and economic growth and industrialization on a national level does not imply that colonial ventures were not profitable for specific individuals, regions or sectors. For example, British cotton textile regions certainly prospered in the early nineteenth century due to large amounts of exports to United Kingdom colonies and especially to India (see Chapter 7). The same is true, if we still limit ourselves to Britain, for the port of Liverpool, which flourished in the eighteenth century as a result of the slave trade. But sectorial or regional benefits do not imply national benefits, and, furthermore, it is worth remembering that the British cotton textile towns have been among the most depressed regions of Britain since the 1920s. More globally, it is very probable that one of the causes of the relative absence of Britain in the 'new' industries at the end of the nineteenth century can be traced to reliance on easy access to colonial markets.

## Notes

1 Based on Bairoch, P., *Commerce extérieur et développement économique de l'Europe au XIXe siècle*, Paris, 1976, and Bairoch, P., 'The geographical structure and trade balance of European foreign trade from 1800 to 1970', *The Journal of European Economic History*, 3, No. 3, 1974, pp. 557–608.

2 Based on data produced by Maizels, A., *Industrial Growth and World Trade*, Cambridge, 1965.
3 Bairoch, P., 'International industrialization levels from 1750 to 1980', *The Journal of European Economic History*, **11**, No. 2, 1982, pp. 269–333.
4 Data communicated by the UNIDO Secretariat.

# 7

# Was Colonialism Important in Triggering the Industrial Revolution?

This myth specifically concerns Britain. We should not forget that not only was Britain the first country to undergo the Industrial Revolution, it was also for 50–80 years the only one to benefit from it to a considerable extent. Furthermore, as we have seen, British exports were among the most colonially oriented.

## The timing of the Industrial Revolution and of colonization

In fact, it is very difficult to defend the position which assigns to colonialism an important role in the birth of the British Industrial Revolution. Britain began its Industrial Revolution (and the Agricultural Revolution, which was a major part) as early as 1680–1700 and the development accelerated between 1720 and 1760. Progress made in crop yields and rising agricultural productivity made possible a significant grain surplus, making Britain a major exporter of cereals in the 1730s. Even though most industrial innovations only came into widespread use after 1750, they existed much earlier. To quote only three major examples: Abraham Dardy's process for producing iron by the use of coal was developed in 1709; Lewis Paul's patent for a spinning machine was filed in 1737; and Thomas Newcomen's steam engine dates from 1712.

However, in the first half of the eighteenth century, Britain's colonial empire was very limited. The most important part was North America, and even there it was not until the Treaty of Paris in 1763, which ceded

80

**Table 7.1** The development of the British Empire, 1700–1913 (million inhabitants)

|  | UK population | Colonial population | Population of colonies in percentages of that of the United Kingdom |
|---|---|---|---|
| 1700 | 9 | 1 | 10 |
| 1750 | 10 | 2 | 20 |
| 1800 | 16 | 75 | 370 |
| 1830 | 24 | 225 | 830 |
| 1860 | 29 | 260 | 800 |
| 1900 | 41 | 360 | 780 |
| 1913 | 46 | 390 | 750 |

*Note:* Including self-governing colonies (Australia, Canada, New Zealand, South Africa).
*Sources:* Bairoch, P., 'Colonie' in *Enciclopedia Einaudi*, Vol. 3, Turin, 1978, pp. 365–87 (with additional data and corrections).

Canada and Louisiana to the British Empire, that Britain's American possessions assumed any real significance. Around 1720 the British Empire in North America had a total population of 0.5 million, most of whom lived under conditions of near-autarky. The total population of the small colonial enclaves scattered over Asia (Bombay, Madras, etc.) and in Africa (Accra, Sierra Leone, Cape Coast, etc.) did not exceed 0.3 million, and the West Indies (mainly Jamaica and Barbados) were only slightly larger, with a population of less than 0.4 million – a total of some 1 million inhabitants. At the same time, the combined Portuguese and Spanish Empires had more than 10 million.

In fact (see Table 7.1) the British Empire became significant only at the end of the eighteenth century, due to its expansion to India, which really began in the 1780s. By 1797 Britain controlled less than a quarter of India's territory, but by then the colonization process was more the consequence of British technological and economic development. At the end of the eighteenth century Britain was already 'the workshop of the world', to use Chambers' expression.[1] By 1790, England's per capita consumption of iron was at least six times higher than that of the rest of Europe and that of cotton at least twenty times. In 1790, the patents for James Watt's steam engine and Richard Arkwright's spinning machine were both 21 years old.

Furthermore, until the early 1780s British colonies were much less trade oriented than those of Spain or Portugal. The majority of those two countries' colonies were located in regions whose climate made it possible to produce agricultural goods for export to Europe. There are no reliable comparative data for eighteenth-century colonial trade. During the greater part of that century it can be estimated that the trade of the

Spanish and Portuguese colonies were some five to seven times larger than that of the British colonies. Therefore it can be estimated that during the first half of the eighteenth century the trade of the British colonies represented no more than 5–10% of that of the European ones.

The situation was completely different on the eve of World War I. In 1913 (see Table 7.2) British colonies accounted for 72% of total colonial trade and 80% of the total colonial population, and this despite the fact that these two totals had meanwhile multiplied thirty to fifty times. The combined Portuguese and Spanish colonies, in 1913, represented only 1% of its total colonial trade and only 2% of the total colonial population. This is, if needed, an additional proof that during the eighteenth and nineteenth centuries colonization was primarily a result of industrial development and not vice versa. But let us return to the onset of the British Industrial Revolution.

## The role of trade and profits from colonial trade

Even more important is the fact that analysis of British colonial exports and, generally, non-European markets during the crucial first phases of the Industrial Revolution shows that their role was a very negligible one. In a study published almost twenty years ago[2] I tried to assess the role of total foreign trade in the first stage of the Industrial Revolution, i.e. the period between 1720 and 1780–90. Before 1720, even if, as we have seen, events had already begun to change, the economy was still a traditional one, but after 1780 Britain could no longer be considered a traditional society. The process of development had passed the point of no return by then.

Let us give just a few examples of this. By 1720 England's production of iron was about 22,000 tons, all still produced in traditional wood-fuelled installations. By 1790 this production had increased to close to 70,000 tons, of which over 80% was produced in blast furnaces fuelled by coke. This represents 10 kg per capita a level that was reached by France only around 1850 and by Germany around 1860. By 1790, the cotton spinning industry was already largely mechanized, and the per capita consumption of cotton was that of Germany in 1870. Finally, without any sizeable food imports, England's agricultural workforce had fallen close to 40%, a level that France would reach only as late as 1920.

During this crucial period for the whole of the British economy, all foreign markets provided only 4–8% of total demand during those 60–70 years. Trade with non-European countries represented some 33–9% of total British trade, so that the contribution of the future less developed countries could have absorbed, at most, 2–3% of total demand.

**Table 7.2** Area, population and exports of mother countries and colonies, 1700–1963

| | Area (1000 km²) Mother country | Colonies | Population (million) Mother country | Colonies | Total exports ($US million) Mother country | Colonies |
|---|---|---|---|---|---|---|
| **Situation 1700** | | | | | | |
| Britain | 230 | – | 7 | – | – | – |
| France | 501 | – | 22 | – | – | – |
| Portugal | 92 | – | 2 | – | – | – |
| Spain | 504 | – | 8 | – | – | – |
| EUROPE[b] | 4,940 | – | 101 | 16 | – | – |
| **Situation 1913** | | | | | | |
| Belgium | 29 | 2,360 | 8 | 11 | 702 | 11 |
| France | 536 | 10,590 | 40 | 55 | 1,328 | 320 |
| Germany | 540 | 2,940 | 67 | 12 | 2,403 | 57 |
| Italy | 301 | 1,530 | 35 | 2 | 485 | 3 |
| Netherlands | 34 | 2,020 | 6 | 46 | 413 | 275 |
| Portugal | 92 | 2,080 | 6 | 8 | 37 | 35 |
| Spain | 504 | 350 | 20 | 1 | 204 | 7 |
| United Kingdom | 315 | 32,860 | 46 | 393 | 2,556 | 2,450 |
| TOTAL ABOVE | 2,050 | 54,800 | 228 | 528 | 7,460 | 3,155 |
| EUROPE[b] | 4,940 | 54,800 | 320 | 530 | 7,990 | 3,160 |
| Japan | 380 | 290 | 53 | 20 | 356 | 150 |
| United States | 7,840 | 310 | 97 | 10 | 2,429 | 70 |
| TOTAL COLONIAL SITUATION | 10,270 | 55,400 | 560 | 560 | 10,245 | 3,380 |
| **Situation Europe[b]** | | | | | | |
| 1700 | 4,940 | – | 101 | 16 | – | – |
| 1750 | 4,940 | – | 120 | 22 | – | – |
| 1800 | 4,940 | – | 152 | 115 | 640 | 90 |
| 1826 | 4,940 | 11,200 | 176 | 210 | 620 | 150 |
| 1876 | 4,940 | 26,500 | 237 | 300 | 2,700 | 860 |
| 1900 | 4,940 | (45,400) | 285 | 500 | 4,130 | 1,330 |
| 1913 | 4,940 | 54,800 | 320 | 530 | 7,990 | 3,160 |
| 1945 | 4,940 | 31,800 | 290 | 598 | – | – |
| 1950 | 4,940 | 25,300 | 302 | 160 | 20,470 | 3,200 |
| 1960 | 4,940 | 10,600 | 327 | 70 | 51,500 | 5,300 |
| 1963 | 4,940 | 6,500 | 337 | 30 | 63,700 | 3,400 |

[a] Including protectorates and (until 1913) self-governing (British) countries; but excluding Greenland and Arctic and Antarctic regions, as well as (until 1913) quasi-colonies like China and some Latin America countries.

[b] Excluding Russia and from 1945 onwards also Eastern European countries.

*Note:* The figures on colonial population are very approximate (margin of error of 10% for 1913; 20% for the mid-nineteenth century; 30% for 1800 and 50% for previous periods.

*Sources:* Calculated by the author from the following:

1700–1900: See Table 7.1 plus the following sources: Darby, H. C. and Fullard, D. H., *The New Cambridge Modern History Atlas*, Cambridge, 1970. Bairoch, P. and Etemad, B., *Commodity Structure of Third World Exports, 1830–1937*, Geneva, 1985. Woytinsky, W. S. and Woytinsky, E. C., *World Commerce and Governments*, New York, 1955.

1913: Bairoch, P., 'European trade policy, 1815–1914' in Mathias, P. and Pollard, S. (eds), *The Cambridge Economic History of Europe*, (Volume VIII, *The Industrial Economies: The Development of Economic and Social Policies*), Cambridge, 1989, pp. 1–160 (Table 13, p. 105 and Table 15, p. 127)

1946–1963: Author's calculations derived from United Nations, *Demographic Yearbook*, New York, various issues; and *Yearbook of International Trade Statistics*, New York, various issues.

For the two most important industrial sectors, textiles and iron, the contribution of foreign markets was more important but not decisive. For the iron industry, these absorbed 11% of total production. This share is somewhat higher (18%) if one bases the calculation only on the increase in production and exports that occurred during the 1720–80 period. For the woollen industry foreign markets declined in relative terms, but the new cotton industry, which was the first to be mechanized, absorbed 10–15% of total production and 15–20% of additional production in foreign markets between 1760 and 1790. Here again, Third World markets represented less than 40% of total foreign markets and can therefore have absorbed only 6–8% of the additional production of the iron and cotton industries (4–5% of total production).

While the figures for profits are even less reliable, some tentative estimates can be made. The profits derived from colonial trade, and therefore the possibilities of reinvestment, were not large. My own estimates agree with those made more recently by Patrick O'Brien:

> What this exercise in counterfactual history suggests is that if the British economy had been excluded from trade with the periphery gross annual investment expenditures would have fallen by not more than 7 per cent. All biases in these calculations [which refer to the decades after the onset of the Industrial Revolution] run in favour of the hypothesis that this commerce provided a large share of the reinvestible surplus; and Britain, to reiterate the point, traded with other continents on a far larger scale than other European countries. There is, moreover, no evidence in the admittedly poor data now available that 'average' rates of profit earned on capital in commerce with the periphery were 'supernormal'. Over wide areas of tropical trades competition between the merchants of several maritime powers operated to hold prices of commodities and the returns to capital below monopolistic levels. And the significance of the periphery cannot be inflated much beyond its share in the national product by reference to externalities or to imports, described as decisive for the growth of the core. Trade in tropical produce gave rise to far greater opportunities for consumption than possibilities for production, and the view that American bullion was indispensable for economic progress in Western Europe is almost certainly untenable.[3]

## Other times . . . other situations . . .

This very limited impact of colonialism on the first stages of the Industrial Revolution does not imply that the same was true for Britain during the entire nineteenth century. Beginning with the first years of that century, colonial markets provided very important outlets for British manufactured goods. According to the data elaborated by Deane and Cole,[4] as early as 1819/21 53% of United Kingdom cotton manufactures were exported. Of those exports, a large share went to future Third World countries, among them many British colonies. Also, one should not forget that cotton yarn was then a very important sector, in terms of both exports and employment. However, between 1780 and 1820 not only did the British textile industry undergo a complete transformation but, as we have seen, the British Empire expanded considerably. In contrast to its 1 million inhabitants in 1720, in 1820 they could be counted in the hundreds of millions. The population of British India alone was then in the neighbourhood of 200 million.

As we saw in Chapter 6, Britain was the country that based its nineteenth-century development the most heavily on overseas and especially colonial outlets. The fact that, for example, at the turn of the twentieth century 79% of British cotton textiles were exported and that more than half of those exports went to the Third World is probably the major explanation for the myth concerning the role of colonization in the British Industrial Revolution. In fact, there is almost an inverse relationship: British colonization, and more generally European modern colonization, can be largely explained by the Industrial Revolution.

It is obvious that the fact that colonization followed industrialization does not prove causality. Furthermore, as we shall see in Chapter 13, Europe was far from being the only colonial power, and European and even more so non-European colonization began long before the Industrial Revolution.

In fact traditional colonization whether European or not, was limited not by lack of will but by economic and military constraints. Pre-industrial Europe, like any other traditional pre-industrial society, could have only limited economic relations with its colonies, and could therefore sustain (or need) only a relatively limited colonial empire. 'Traditional' Europe implies a low standard of living and a level of per capita consumption close to that of the colonies. This standard of living and level of consumption, in turn, implied that products from the colonies (mainly tropical and some luxury manufactured goods) could represent only a very small fraction of total consumption.

Therefore we have to wait for the increase in the standard of living resulting from the Industrial Revolution to allow a high level of consumption of tropical products and therefore make profitable a large colonial empire. For example, the consumption of cocoa in France increased from 10 grams per capita around 1790 to 650 grams around 1910. Per capita consumption of tea in Britain increased from 10 grams in 1700 to 520 grams in 1790 and 2,350 grams in 1910. Sugar consumption in

Europe (excluding Russia) increased from less than 0.5 kg per capita around 1700 to 17.0 kg in 1910. In this case, local production of beet sugar also contributed to the increase of consumption. Furthermore, the population of the developed countries (excluding Japan) more than tripled between 1780 and 1913. This unprecedented increase was made possible by the Industrial Revolution, and meant greatly increased needs.

The technological innovations resulting from the Industrial Revolution gave Europeans the military capability to conquer and control large and remote territories through not only better armaments but also faster and larger ships and improved communications. The role of European gunboats has become very familiar since it gave rise to the term 'gunboat diplomacy'. In the case of Africa and of other regions, if

> The steamer increased mobility and fire-power . . . it had less obvious functions. Officials believed that steamers greatly increased their moral superiority and special status in the eyes of Africans. As the Gambian administrator observed in 1841, he needed his own ship to establish a prestige equal to or preferably higher than that enjoyed by local rulers in the neighbourhood of his jurisdiction, in order to establish proper respect for his person.[5]

Improved communications meant not only railways and steamers but also, from the 1850s onwards telegraphic lines. Last but not least, a higher level of development also meant the possibility of diverting more resources to colonial ventures.

If we return to the British case, as we saw earlier, despite the important role of British colonial markets in the nineteenth century, Britain, like all colonial countries, then had a slower economic growth than non-colonial ones. This brings us to another very important historical question: the economic balance sheet of colonialism.

## Notes

1 Chambers, J. D., *The Workshop of the World. British Economic History from 1820 to 1880*, Oxford, 1961.
2 Bairoch, P., 'Le rôle du commerce extérieur dans la Genèse de la révolution industrielle anglaise', *Annales, E.S.C.*, **28**, No. 2, 1973, pp. 541–71.
3 O'Brien, P., 'European economic development: the contribution of the periphery', *Economic History Review*, **35**, No. 1, 1981, pp. 1–18.
4 Deane, P. and Cole, W. A., *British Economic Growth, 1866–1957*, 2nd edn., Cambridge, 1969, p. 187.
5 Kubicek, R. V., 'The colonial steamer and the occupation of West Africa by the Victorian State, 1840–1900', *Journal of Imperial and Commonwealth*

*History*, **18**, No. 1, 1990, pp. 9–32. For a general overview of the role of technology in European colonization see Headrick, D., *Tools of Empire: Technology and European Imperialism in the Nineteenth Century*, New York, 1981.

# 8

# *The Balance Sheet of Colonialism*

An alternative title for this chapter would be 'If the West did not gain much from colonialism, it does not mean that the Third World did not lose much'. As mentioned in the introduction to this part, the limited positive impact of colonization on the West's economic development may lead the reader to conclude that since, on the one hand, there were no important gains, on the other, the costs were also limited. But the economy is not a 'zero sum game'. There is no doubt that a large number of negative structural features of the process of economic underdevelopment have historical roots going back to European colonization. Therefore to put matters into perspective, the other side of the picture must be shown. Among the many negative legacies of the European colonization I will limit myself to the negative aspects that are cruel realities: the Third World lost much.

## *The reality of de-industrialization*

This case is conclusive, even if more research is needed to establish the exact amount of de-industrialization, of the disappearance of industries, experienced by various countries. In case A was it 85% or 95%, and in case B was it 50% or 70%?

Case A could be India, which, however, was not the most extreme. There is no doubt that the influx of British-manufactured goods from 1813 onwards led to very large de-industrialization in India. Let us take the Indian textile industry which, as in any traditional society, was the most dominant among industrial activities, representing probably 65–75% of total industrial manufactures. Before the nineteenth century

Indian textiles, especially calicoes, were highly prized in Europe. In fact during the eighteenth century, calicoes, together with other manufactured textiles, represented 60–70% of India's total exports.[1] As hinted at in Chapter 7, in the first decades of colonization, as long as the East India Company had a monopoly of trade, very few English woollen textiles and no cotton textiles were imported into India, the policy of the company being even to export as much Indian textiles goods as Europe could absorb. But it was only 'as much as Europe could absorb', since during most of that period the import of Indian textiles, like that of other countries' textiles, was prohibited in Britain.

As we have seen in chapter 4, as soon as the East India Company's monopoly disappeared (in 1813) the influx of English textiles into India increased considerably. Approximately 1 million square yards of cotton cloth were imported in 1814; 13 million in 1820; 995 million in 1870 and 2050 million in 1890.[2] The influx was certainly due to the great progress made by the English spinning industry as a result of technological innovations. By 1830, as we have seen, the productivity of an English worker using modern equipment was for the best (fine) qualities of yarn some two to three hundred times higher; and for the most commonly used yarn in traditional societies some ten to fourteen times higher than that of an Indian artisan. The same comparison could also be made with European artisans, but in this case the consequences were different as a result of tariff policies. While Europe (and the United States) as a rule either totally prohibited the import of yarn and manufactured cotton or imposed duties ranging from 30% to 80%, British textile goods could enter the Indian market with no duties at all. In 1859, when for fiscal reasons the British government in India introduced modest import duties (3–10%) on those imports, this led to a strong reaction in Britain, as we saw earlier. As a result of 'legitimate' protests by British manufacturers, local producers were subjected to a tax of the same magnitude in order to put the two types of production on the same footing. Not until the early 1920s was a more balanced policy implemented for local manufactures.

It is easy to understand the causes of the local Indian textile industry's rapid disappearance under such circumstances. The difficulty of establishing a modern textile industry in the second half of the nineteenth century is also obvious. Imports probably covered 55–75% of total textile consumption. The only question is the precise extent of this process of de-industrialization. By 1870–80 were local industry and artisans able to provide 25% or 45% of local textile consumption (or a level of de-industrialization of 55–75%)? The same questions can be asked in relation to the iron industry: by 1890–1900 did it produce 1% or 5% of local consumption (or a level of de-industrialization of 95–9%)? A decade or two ago, the answer would have been clearly almost a total disappearance of all industries. But, as is always the case once a dominant point of view has been established, research is focused on exceptions. Indeed, new research has demonstrated that in some regions (mainly remote ones) a certain level of industrial activity survived for a long period, so the answer is now closer to a rather lower level of de-industrialization.

The process was similar or even worse in the rest of Asia, except for China. In that country local industry was better able to survive and also to reorganize because the influx of Western manufactured goods started later, there was a greater amount of local autonomy and also because of the sheer size of the country. But greater resistance did not imply a victory. In the Chinese case the question mark is around the 40% level: around 1890 did local Chinese textiles provide 50% or 70% of local consumption?

The African story is similar to the Asian one, except that the starting point was generally lower. Therefore it is difficult to speak of a real de-industrialization, even if there was a sharp decline in the importance of the production of manufactured goods. I mentioned the case of the Middle East in Chapter 3, where I quoted Disraeli's comment on the destruction of the Turkish industry by imports from the West. Let me repeat it here: 'There has been free trade in Turkey and what has it produced? It has destroyed some of the finest manufactures of the world.'

The Latin American story is rather different, since in this case modern neocolonization succeeded three centuries of traditional colonization. Another difference is that while, in the first years of the nineteenth century, most of Asia was in the process of being colonized, most of Latin America became independent. Paradoxically, this independence led to a phase of de-industrialization since it facilitated the penetration of products originating from countries more advanced than Portugal and Spain. We have seen (in Chapter 4) that, around 1860, exports of cotton goods from Britain, France and the United States to Latin America represented some 11 square metres for each of Latin America's inhabitants, which means that very little was left for local production.

However, this political independence of Latin America also contributes to the fact that in 1913, with only 7% of the Third World's population, the region had 21% of the Third World's cotton spindles. The explanation for this is that, as a result of the influx of European products in the 1820–70 period and also under the influence of North American trade policy, most Latin American countries altered their trade policies in the 1870–90 period, introducing protectionist tariffs to promote in-dustrialization. In the case of Mexico, this shift took place much earlier, in the 1830s. The Brazilian move to protectionism gave rise to an

**Table 8.1** Levels of industrialization in the Third World and the developed countries, 1750–1990 (United Kingdom in 1900 = 100)

|  | Total | | Per capita | |
|  | Third World | Developed countries | Third World | Developed countries |
|---|---|---|---|---|
| 1750 | 93 | 34 | 7 | 8 |
| 1800 | 99 | 47 | 6 | 8 |
| 1830 | 112 | 73 | 6 | 11 |
| 1860 | 83 | 143 | 4 | 16 |
| 1900 | 60 | 481 | 2 | 35 |
| 1913 | 70 | 863 | 2 | 55 |
| 1928 | 98 | 1,260 | 3 | 71 |
| 1938 | 122 | 1,560 | 4 | 81 |
| 1953 | 200 | 2,870 | 5 | 135 |
| 1973 | 927 | 8,430 | 14 | 315 |
| 1980 | 1,320 | 9,910 | 19 | 347 |
| 1990 | 2,480 | 12,090 | 29 | 412 |

*Sources:* Bairoch, P., 'International industrialization levels from 1750 to 1980', *The Journal of European Economic History*, **11**, No. 2, Fall 1982, pp. 268–333. With revised figures for 1980 and new data for 1990.

interesting situation. The first Brazilian tariff aimed at economic rather than revenue objectives was that of 1879. When it was decided to prepare (before 1879) a revision of the tariff, a mission was sent to Europe to study trade liberalization, but it came back converted to protectionism. Therefore the 1879 tariff was openly protectionist. Its creator claimed that 'protectionist measures are never wrong for new countries like ours, where industry is not strong enough to face foreign competition'.[3]

Incidentally, it is worth re-emphasizing that Latin America represented only a small share of the Third World's population, since often problems specific to that continent are taken as a general model of the Third World. In 1800 Latin America had less than 3% of the total Third World population. This means that the success or failure of Latin America had little influence on the Third World's evolution.

The global impact of the de-industrialization process is presented in Table 8.1, which shows the probable growth of Third World manufacturing from 1750 to 1990. The figures refer to totals of traditional and modern industries. The level of industrialization, which was equal to the production of manufacturing per capita, in 1913 was less than a third of its probable 1750 level. Meanwhile since in the developed countries the level of industrialization has been multiplied by almost seven the gap between the two regions became very large: 1 to 28. The Third World, which around 1750 produced some 70–6% of the world's manufactures, produced only 7–8% around 1913. If we restrict the data to modern industry, the Third World accounted for only 1–2% rather than 7–8% of world manufacturing production in 1913.

To what extent did political independence after World War II change the picture? The answer is 'radically', since one of the first economic objectives of almost all the newly independent Third World countries was industrialization. Clearly, to a very large extent this was a success story but it was a costly success, with many weaknesses. Let us consider the positive side first. Between 1953 and 1990 manufacturing production multiplied by more than twelve times. This is equivalent to an annual growth rate of 7% in total terms or of more than 4% per capita. It represents a rate of growth of more than twice (in total terms) that of the developed world during its first century of industrialization (more than 50% more rapid again per capita).

However, this industrialization entailed negative aspects. Emphasis should be put on the high cost of industrialization in terms of mismanagement and even more in depriving the vital agricultural sector of much-needed investments. Further, it should be noted that the industrialization of the Third World has at least three weaknesses. The first concerns regional inequalities. Most of the manufacturing is concentrated in five countries: Brazil, Taiwan, Singapore, South Korea and Hong Kong. These, which together represent today only 6% of the Third World's population, have 25–7% of the manufacturing capacity and provide close to 80% of the Third World's export of manufactured products. The case is even clearer if we exclude Brazil and thus limit ourselves to the 'Four Dragons'. In this case, these countries, which represent less than 3% of the Third World market economies' population, in 1990 provided almost two thirds of the total exports (excluding re-exports) of manufactured goods of the entire Third World.

The other two weaknesses are the growing multinationalization of manufacturing industry in the Third World and specialization in traditional sectors. By the 1970s almost a third of the Third World's industrial production was undertaken by enterprises belonging to Western multinationals, where the corresponding share for those Western countries was 10–12%. At the same time, the Third World, which represented 10% of world industrial production, provided 50% of cotton yarn but only 1–2% of artificial fibres; and 22% of cement but only 1–2% of electronics.

## The reality of a large expansion in exported crops

Exports of tropical produce to Europe began long before the Industrial Revolution. The pepper and silk trade between Asia and Europe began more than 2,000 years ago (some claim 5,000 years ago). This increased in volume after the sixteenth century, when direct maritime contact between the two continents was established. Total imports of spices, for example (coming almost entirely from Asia), can be estimated at some 2,400 tons around 1500 and at 6,500 to 8,500 tons around 1700.[4] An even greater expansion took place in European sugar imports. In the fifteenth century sugar was a luxury product in Europe. At that time in England sugar was twenty-nine times more expensive than butter, already an expensive product; by the end of the sixteenth century this ratio had been reduced to five times.[5, 6] Today in Europe sugar is about six to ten times cheaper than butter; or in relative terms some two hundred times cheaper. than butter around 1400. In terms of price expressed in wages of unskilled labour (a good yardstick of real income) it can be estimated that one kilogram of sugar represented 1–2 months' wages in the fifteenth century compared to 5–7 minutes' today in developed countries (or four thousand to five thousand times less!).

Total imports of sugar into Europe around 1500 were in the region of only a few tons since sugar was used mainly as a drug in Europe before the sixteenth century. 'By 1700 this had increased to about 70,000–90,000 tons, and in terms of volume sugar probably represented 75% of the total imports of agricultural products from non-temperate regions. According to my estimates and calculations, the total quantity of those goods around 1700 amounted to about 100,000–120,000 tons and 380,000–410,000 tons in 1790. In the years preceding World War I the volume of exports of agricultural products from the Third World had reached 18,500,000 tons or about 16.5 kg per capita (of the Third World population) compared to some 0.2 kg around 1700. In terms of per capita volume of exports, the peak was probably reached at the end of the 1920s (but with a figure only slightly above that of the period before 1914). Around 1980 it was close to 12 kg, the increase in the Third World's population having been more rapid than the exports of these agricultural products. However, and this is important in view of the limited amounts of land for expansion, in terms of total volume around 1970 (an absolute peak) these exports were almost twice as high as before World War I (or 34 million tons).

Even if in some cases this rapid increase in exported crops had a positive impact, the overall consequences were negative and very disrupting for the entire society in the majority of the cases. Often the best land was devoted to export crops, leading to less favourable conditions for food crops. Many plantations were owned by Europeans, resulting in an export of profits. In some cases forced labour was employed; in others, peasants had to produce crops for export in order to pay their taxes.

## A rapid population increase that began during colonization

There can be little doubt that the extremely rapid increase in population that characterized the Third World already in the 1930s, and especially after 1950, is one of the major causes of the problems of economic development encountered by the great majority of Third World countries. The impact of this population growth that took place after colonization will be discussed in Chapter 12. Here we shall consider to what extent the origins of this growth and its onset can be traced to the period of colonization.

Until the Industrial Revolution, the long-term increase in population in all societies was very small. Around 1700 the world population was some 600–820 million, compared with 230–400 million in AD 0. Even if one takes the higher limit in 1700 and the lower one in AD 0, this implies an annual growth rate of only 0.07%. However, since the trend has not been uniform, the greatest annual increase in a period of 30–60 years in a country of average size has been much higher, but not more than 0.6–0.8% per year. During the nineteenth century, as a direct result of colonization, in some colonies the population increased at a rate unprecedented in traditional societies. This was notably the case in Java, whose population increased from 9.6 million to 28.7 million between 1850 and 1900 (an annual growth of 2.2%). Such rates were exceptional and may well be overestimates, but in many cases during the second half of the nineteenth century 1% was exceeded. For example, Latin America's population between 1880 and 1913 increased at an annual rate of 1.8%, but this was due in part to the influx of European immigrants. More specific was the case of countries like Egypt and Indonesia. The populations of both countries between 1880 and 1913 increased by 1.4%. In the case of Indonesia, this rapid population growth had already begun in the 1840s.

However, if we take the whole of the Third World, population growth remained relatively modest until the 1930s but it was already higher than that of traditional societies. The annual rates of population increase were the following: 0.5% for 1880–1913; 0.7–0.8% for 1913–29; 1.1–1.2% for 1929–38; and 1.2% for 1938–50. The rate for the 1938–50 period was very rapid; in fact, as fast as that of the West during its phases of fastest population increase. However, compared to what happened between 1950 and 1990, this was still modest: during this period the yearly rate was 2.2%.

## The reality of a very large difference in income

In the next part of this book I shall deal with the myth of the large difference in income between future developed and future Third World

**Table 8.2** Levels of GNP in the Third World and the developed countries, 1750–1990 (in 1960 US dollars and prices)

| | Total (billions of dollars) | | Per capita (dollars) | |
|---|---|---|---|---|
| | Third World | Developed countries | Third World | Developed countries |
| 1750 | 112 | 35 | 188 | 182 |
| 1800 | 137 | 47 | 188 | 198 |
| 1830 | 150 | 67 | 183 | 237 |
| 1860 | 159 | 118 | 174 | 324 |
| 1900 | 184 | 297 | 175 | 540 |
| 1913 | 217 | 430 | 192 | 662 |
| 1928 | 252 | 568 | 194 | 782 |
| 1938 | 293 | 678 | 202 | 856 |
| 1950 | 338 | 889 | 214 | 1,180 |
| 1970 | 810 | 2,450 | 340 | 2,540 |
| 1980 | 1,280 | 3,400 | 390 | 2,920 |
| 1990 | 1,730 | 4,350 | 430 | 3,490 |

*Sources:* Bairoch, P., 'The main trends in national economic disparities since the Industrial Revolution' in Bairoch, P. and Levy-Leboyer, M. (eds), *Disparities in Economic Development since the Industrial Revolution*, London, 1981, pp. 3–17. With revised figures especially for 1970, and new data for 1980 and 1990.

countries before colonization. Here, I wish to stress that at the end of the colonization period, say 1950, the economies of the Third World had a standard of living much lower than those of the developed countries. This resulted from divergent trends in economic growth of the two regions given in Table 8.2.

In the developed countries, a century and a half of the Industrial Revolution resulted in a multiplication by more than five of the average standard of living. In the most successful parts of the West, this had been multiplied by ten. In the Third World there were regions in which the standard of living in 1950 was lower than that of 1800. This was probably the case in China. But even for the average Third World countries the 1950s level was practically that of 1800 or, at best, only 10–20% above.

In any case, in 1950 the real income per capita of the Third World was five to six times lower than that of the developed countries. I use the words 'real income' since the figures included here are adjusted for the differences in the purchasing power of currencies. Indeed, there was, and there still is, a wide difference between the purchasing power of almost all Third World currencies (and also of other countries) and their exchange rate. In other words, an American dollar could buy, on average, twice as many products in the Third World than in the United

States. This means that, in monetary terms the gap is even wider, the average per capita income of the Third World in 1950 was a tenth of that of the developed countries.

The fact that there had been hardly any increase in the Third World's average living standards between 1800 and 1950 implies that the 1950 standard was a very low one, similar to or even lower than that of pre-industrial societies. Let us give more details of this low living standard in 1950. The daily per capita food consumption was about 1,910 calories (compared to 2,940 for the West). Average daily meat consumption was of the order of 25 grams (compared to 140 grams). It should also be noted that the Western consumption level in 1950 was still influenced by the aftermath of World War II. Finally, let us give two important global indicators. The labour productivity in the Third World's agricultural sector in 1950 was some seven times lower than that of the West and 30–40% below that of the developed countries in 1800. As can be seen in Table 8.1, in 1953 the per capita production of manufactured goods of the Third World was 35–45% smaller than that of the developed countries in 1800.

## And some other negative consequences

As the title of this book suggests, here we are dealing mainly with economics, and the major negative economic and social consequences of European colonization have been presented above. Although socio-economic dimensions are very important, they are not the only ones, and in the large area of non-economic life, the negative consequences are important.

The most important of these was the loss of national independence. Even if this implied, in many cases, more personal freedom and that in some cases there were no nationalist tendencies, it should still be considered as an important negative consequence of colonization. I mentioned additional personal freedom, since in some regions colonization meant the abolition of slavery and the introduction of political rights, but in many other cases colonization implied additional political constraints, notably through the introduction of taxation. There was even the introduction of forced labour (notably in Indonesia and some African countries).

This leads us to the controversial issue of the transatlantic slave trade. Some 11–11.5 million slaves were shipped from the African continent to the European colonies. Although, as we shall see in Chapter 13, this was not the only slave trade and not even the most important one, the dramatic character of this transatlantic slave trade cannot be qualified.

Less negative but far from marginal was the alteration of numerous forms of civilizations and cultures and the consequences of negative forms of urbanization to which we will return in Chapter 12. The cultural impact of colonization lies outside my expertise, and I would refer the reader to a number of references since there is apparently no one general synthesis on this subject.[7]

## The West did not need the Third World; good news for the Third World

It may sound paradoxical or provocative to say that there is good news for the Third World in the fact that the development of the West was not due to exploitation of the Third World. But consider the following.

If the exploitation of the Third World had been the main cause of or even only a major factor in the Industrial Revolution and/or of the first century of the West's development, this would entail a very significant consequence. Indeed, if such had been the case, it would imply that economic development requires the exploitation of other large regions to succeed and, since the Third World could not fulfil these conditions today, it implies the impossibility of its economic development. Therefore it is very fortunate that the experience of the West shows that a process of development is possible without exploitation of other regions.

However, this does not imply that the road to economic development for the Third World is an easy one. I was already very pessimistic on the chances of rapid growth in the Third World some 30 years ago when I completed my PhD dissertation on those problems.[8] In 1971, I published a book with the title *Le Tiers Monde dans l'impasse* (*The Third World at an Impasse*).[9] In a revised and expanded edition which appeared in 1983, I did not change the title despite the fact that, for the first edition, I wondered whether I should put a question mark at the end of it. Furthermore, the book's negative conclusions have remained unchanged. Since then I have not modified my point of view substantially, which is that, for most of the Third World, economic development is a very difficult road, one of the principal obstacles being a rapid growth in population. The third edition appeared in 1992, revised and expanded, but very few of its negative conclusions were modified. We will return to this important subject in Part III.

## Notes

1 Chaudhuri, K. N., *The Trading World of Asia and the English East India Company, 1660–1760*, Cambridge, 1978.

2 Desai, M., 'Demand for cotton textiles in nineteenth-century India', *Indian Economic and Social History Review*, **8**, 1971, pp. 337–61.
3 Bandeira de Mello, A., *Politique commerciale du Brésil*, Rio de Janeiro, 1935, p. 66.
4 Wake, C. H., 'The changing pattern of European pepper and spice imports, 1400–1700', *Journal of European Economic History*, **8**, 1979, pp. 361–403 (especially pp. 392–5).
5 Lyle, P. H., 'The sugar industry', *Journal of the Royal Statistical Society*, **63**, 1950, pp. 531–43.
6 Lippmann, E. O., *Geschichte des Zuckers*, Berlin, 1929, pp. 324–99.
7 Adu Boahen, A. (under the direction of), *Africa under Colonial Domination 1880–1935*, Vol. 7 of *The General History of Africa*, UNESCO, London, 1985; Mannoni, O., *Prospero and Caliban. The Psychology of Colonization*, New York and Washington, 1964; Memmi, A., *Colonizer and the Colonized*, London, 1990; Pannikar, K. M., *Asia and Western Dominance*, 1st edn, London, 1953.
8 Bairoch, P., *Révolution industrielle et sous-développement*, Paris, 1963, 4th edn, 1974.
9 This book has been translated into six languages and an English edition based on the third edition will appear in 1993.

# PART III

# *Major Myths About the Third World*

The study of the problems of underdevelopment began relatively late but expanded very rapidly. It is interesting to note that the use of the term 'development' outside Marxist literature is very recent, dating from after World War II, even if in some exceptional cases it goes back to the 1920s.[1] The recent use of the term 'development' is strictly linked to, and originated from, an awareness of the problems of 'underdeveloped' countries, which became apparent in the post-World War II years. A combination of recent origins and rapid development of this area of research led, in some cases, to hasty conclusions; and these conditions laid the foundations for the creation of a number of myths.

## Note

1 Arndt, H. W., 'Economic development: a semantic history', *Economic Development and Cultural Change*, **29**, No. 3, 1981, pp. 457–66.

# 9

# *Was there a Large Income Differential before Modern Development?*

The long-term history of civilizations, as is well known, has been that of numerous rises and falls. From Gibbon to Toynbee and, very recently, Paul Kennedy,[1] speculation about the decline of empires gave a stimulating insight into world history. While it is certain that many civilizations have been overwhelmed by economically weaker invaders, it is no less true that there was more generally a strong link between a high level of economic and technological development and flourishing civilizations.

We shall, for obvious reasons, not go into those very interesting points here but shall restrict ourselves to another interesting and crucial problem: that of the level of development of Europe compared to other regions in a period when the process of modern economic development had not yet begun to have any significant impact. This can be situated in the eighteenth century, let us say around 1700–50. (For a discussion of the timing of the Industrial Revolution, see Chapter 7.)

For this period it is often claimed that Europe was already much richer, if not more 'developed', than the rest of the world. My reluctance to use the term 'developed' stems from the widely accepted view that the notion of economic development only applies to post-Industrial Revolution situations. In other words, countries that are rich today were already prosperous before the Industrial Revolution and the poor were already poor before they became the Third World. Such a position often implies that a mix of factors, both geographical and human, is inexorably responsible for those differences, which, in turn, implies a terrible fatalism: the poor will remain poor or will even become poorer.

101

## An overview of attempts to measure the difference

There is still not and there will probably never be any reliable data to give a precise indication of the level of GNP per capita of different countries in the eighteenth century. The lack of statistical sources explains the fact that the number of people involved in this area of research can be counted on two hands.

Without describing sporadic and partial attempts at analysis, I will begin this overview with the first comprehensive attempt, that of Zimmerman,[2] which is generally not mentioned in the literature. In 1962 Zimmerman calculated the 1860 per capita income in 1952/4 US dollars for the entire world divided into ten regions. If we aggregate his data we arrive at $48 for the future Third World and $175 for the future developed countries, or a differential of 1 to 3.6. To interpolate to the starting point, we can assume for the 1750–1860 period an annual growth rate of 0.45% for the developed countries and stagnation for the Third World.[3] This reduces the differential to 1 to 2.2.

In the same year I published a paper[4] in which I made crude estimates of the 'starting level' based on 1957 income data comparisons and some retrospective data. I arrived at $90 (in 1957 US dollars and prices) for poor societies before the Industrial Revolution, and $120–60 for Western society at the beginning of the nineteenth century, or a differential of 1 to 1.6.

The second comprehensive attempt was that of Simon Kuznets, the Nobel Prize winner.[5] He posed the problem very clearly: 'We may now turn to the question whether the wide differentials in per capita product in the world today are of recent origin or have prevailed over a long period.' Also, to a large extent, the reservation he made in 1966 remains valid:

> A detailed answer to this question would require estimates of per capita product for all or most countries in the world, including those presently underdeveloped, over a period at least as far back as the late eighteenth century (and for many interesting aspects even further back). Such data are available only for some of the presently developed countries, and even for some of these for too short a period. Past records are particularly scanty for the presently underdeveloped countries. The few that are at hand suggest that over long periods, the per capita product was either constant or rose moderately.

The outcome of Kuznets' calculations and assumptions was that around 1865 the per capita product (in 1958 dollars) was $70 for the average of

─less developed countries and $270–90 for the average developed countries.[6] Since Kuznets expressly mentioned that the figure for less developed countries is almost incompressible, and if we apply to the developed countries the average yearly growth used above, this brings us for 1750 to $175 for the future developed countries (and $70 for the future Third World) or a differential of 1 to 2.5 in 1700–50.

Kuznets took up this problem again in a later study[7] and for 1870 arrived at a differential 'fractionally lower' than his 1966 study, which would imply for 1750 a differential of 1 to 2.4. On the same year[8] I made a new estimate which I described as preliminary and containing a large margin of error. In order to reduce this margin I excluded the Communist countries. In terms of 1970 dollars and prices and for 1770, I arrived at $210 for the Western developed countries and $170 for the Western underdeveloped countries, or a differential of 1 to 1.24.

Appearing between the two Kuznets estimates we have that of David Landes,[9] who, on the basis of Deane's estimate for Britain and Marczewski's[10] for France and data for less developed countries around 1961, concludes that 'Western Europe . . . was already rich before the Industrial Revolution, rich in comparison with other parts of the world'. The figures he quotes implicitly lead to an income per capita of £60–70 in 1960 pounds for Europe and £25–30 for average countries of the 1960s Third World, an implied differential between 1 to 2.2 and 1 to 2.6.

So let us now consider the two more comprehensive attempts I made in 1979 and 1981. The first was to estimate on the basis of six different approaches the greatest spread of national income per capita before the Industrial Revolution; the second was to assess the relative situations of the future Third World and future developed countries at the 'starting point'.[11]

The first attempt gave the following results (expressed in terms of the probable maximum spread of national income per capita):

1. Data on real GNP per capita estimates for 13 countries at a stage of development preceding the Industrial Revolution or close to traditional societies: 1 to 1.4–1.6;
2. Determination of the minimal and the average cost of living in current prices for countries which, in the first half of the nineteenth century, had already reached a relatively high standard of living: 1 to 1.5–1.7;
3. Spread of European countries' real GNP per capita at the beginning of the nineteenth century: 1 to 1.4–1.6;
4. Long-term (more than two or three centuries) growth in real wages: 1 to 1.4–1.6;
5. Per capita income of European cities in the sixteenth and seventeenth centuries: 1 to 1.5–1.7;
6. Last but not least, the contemporary view of international inequalities

as assumed by seventeenth- and eighteenth-century pioneers in national accounting: 1 to 1.3–1.5.

From the above it is possible to conclude that, if we exclude a certain number of small countries which, for specific reasons, could benefit from exceptional resources, it appears that before the Industrial Revolution the income differential between the poorest and the richest country was certainly smaller than 1 to 2 and probably of the order of only 1 to 1.5. In terms of 1960 US dollars and prices (the yardstick used here) the lowest level for traditional countries was around US$130–50, the highest around US$190–240.

It appears very likely that the income differential was more important at a micro-regional level (defining a micro-region as a country or part of a country of less than 2 million inhabitants). Indeed, high per capita income could then only derive from exceptional factors, and the probability that such factors were present in all parts of a large region is close to zero. On the other hand, if instead of countries we refer to broader geographic entities such as Western Europe, India, pre-Columbian America, Africa or China, the differential was probably even smaller, of the order of 1.0 to 1.3 or even less.

My second attempt was to assess the relative situations of the future Third World and future developed countries at the 'starting point'. Its conclusion was that there was a parity of income per capita for the average future Third World and developed countries before the latter region started to undergo the process of modern economic growth. Let us see how I arrived at this.

The data available for European countries are sufficient to validate a retrospective estimate of the level of GNP per capita of future developed countries around 1750 for which I arrived at an unrounded figure of $182; or, if one prefers, $170–90. For the future Third World I made rather elaborate calculations for the period 1900–77.[12] These gave an unrounded figure of $192 for 1900; or, if one prefers, $180–200. The estimate for the situation around 1750 was based on two factors. The first relied on less complete data on the growth of each future Third World region. The second factor was based on the assumption that, due to the burden of 'poorer Europe' (Russia, east and south-east Europe) and the 'richer' Asiatic civilizations (China and India), there was at least parity in GNP per capita of those two regions. The final estimate was a level of income of the future Third World some 3–4% above that of the future developed countries; or at an unrounded figure of $188; or, if one prefers, $175–95 around 1750, thus a differential of only 1 to 1.02 or, more correctly, a parity.

Between 1981 and the present there have been, as far as I know, two new attempts to estimate the level of GNP in the future developed countries before the Industrial Revolution. Let us begin with that of Nick Crafts,[13] which is limited to 17 European countries, and among those only for two does his series go back to the beginning of the nineteenth century. Complementing Crafts' series with additional retrospective calculations[14] we can infer that the implicit figure for the whole of the future developed countries around 1750 stands at $190–210 (expressed in 1960 US dollars and prices) or 4–15% above my figure.

The other attempt or rather group of attempts are those of Angus Maddison.[15] The first deals specifically with the differential between future developed countries and the future Third World. In these retrospective calculations Maddison arrives at results very close to mine for the future developed countries. In 1965 US dollars and prices the 1760 level is around $200. Since prices in the United States increased by 7% between 1960 and 1965 this translates to $186 compared to my figure of $182 for 1750. But for the future Third World, Maddison arrives at a much lower figure than mine. On the basis of data for Brazil, China, India and Mexico, he gives an unweighted average of $113; the weighted average is $120 or $112 in 1960 prices, compared to my figure of $188, a differential between future Third World and future developed countries of 1 to 1.6.

Thus this lower income of the future Third World or, more precisely, the differential between those regions resulting from Maddison's estimate is more in line with mine than most previous attempts. Maddison's analysis, like most on this subject, refers to two estimates, those of Kuznets and Landes (described above), but he also adds that 'if we use the Kravis–Summers estimates at American prices instead of their preferred multilateral weights, the 1760 position would be virtually as Bairoch claims' (Maddison, 1983, p. 32).

Let us now turn to the latest of Maddison's papers. To a large extent, although he is not specifically addressing our present question in his paper, he suggests a rather lower differential at the 'starting point' than in his 1983 paper. If we calculate the averages (weighted by population) of his data, we obtain the following result for the future Third World (translated from 1980 to 1960 dollars). For 1913, for Africa (only data for Egypt and Ghana, representing some 11% of this region) $211; for Latin America (data for six countries representing 71%) $303; Asia (data for nine countries, but representing 97%) $155. This brings the weighted average for the Third World to $170. For 1870 and for Asia (China, India, Indonesia and Thailand, 88% of the region) $124. For 1830 (China, India and Indonesia) $121. Taking into consideration the fact that India's level around 1750 was probably at least a third higher than around 1830[16] and that, at that time (1750), China was richer than India and that Latin

America was probably 'richer' than Asia, while Africa was probably 'poorer', a starting level for the future Third World of some $170–90 seems a very conservative estimate. In other words, a figure very close, or at least similar, to my 1981 estimate.

For the future developed world, using the various 1830 and 1870 data and previous evaluations, Maddison's figures can lead to a level expressed in 1980 dollars of $550–600 for Europe (including Russia) around 1750.[17] This translates in 1960 dollars and prices to $180–215. Therefore 'implicitly' the differential between future developed countries and the future Third World at this starting point is, according to Maddison's most recent estimate, of the order of 1 to 1.1–1.3, compared to my 1981 estimate of 1 to 1–1.1.

## The wealth of the future Third World confirmed by 'eyewitnesses'

What therefore can be our conclusions? My present position is that, even if I do not rule out the possibility that the future Third World before the Industrial Revolution had a somewhat lower level of income than the future developed countries than I estimated at the beginning of the 1980s, Maddison's $112 per capita GNP for the future Third World appears to be too low in view of what was said in the beginning of this chapter. A gap of over 20% for large regions seems very improbable, and the absolute level of $112 (expressed in 1960 US dollars and prices) is too close to the physiological minimum of $80. This minimum assumes a food intake just sufficient to sustain life with moderate activity and zero consumption of other goods.[18] Finally, the $112 level is also well below that of 10% of the poorest countries around 1970 (based on Kravis *et al.*[19]), which is $156 and even below the level of the five poorest countries, which represent only 0.5% of the world population, and whose GNP figure (always in 1960 US dollars and prices) is $124.

If we restrict the 'starting point' comparison to richer parts of Europe (say, the total of England, France and the Netherlands) versus the average of the future Third World, my actual guess would be a 20–40% superiority in this part of Europe. But I am still inclined to think that there was no sizeable difference in the levels of income of the different civilizations when they reached their pre-industrial peak: Rome in the first century, the Arab Caliphates in the tenth, China in the eleventh, India in the seventeenth and Europe at the beginning of the eighteenth.

After all, one should not forget that, seen from Europe and certainly until the eighteenth century, the 'wonderlands' were located overseas. We should begin with the descriptions by Marco Polo coming from one of the richest cities of Europe (Venice) when he saw the 'marvels of the East', and especially of China at the end of the thirteenth century.[20] In fact, for a very long period the story was too good to be true and the validity of those descriptions was only gradually recognized.

The same feelings were expressed two centuries later by the Spanish Conquistadores when they encountered the important pre-Columbian cities:

> When we saw so many cities and towns built over the water, and still other great cities on the dry land, and the paved highway, laid so smooth and level, that ran straight to Mexico, we stood dumbstruck with admiration. We said to ourselves that it resembled the enchanted dwelling places described in the book of Amadis because of the great towers and temples and the edifices built over the water, all of them constructed of lime and stone; some of our soldiers even asked if this vision were not a dream.

This expresses the wonder of Bernal Diaz de Castillo, who accompanied Cortez when he first entered Tenochtitlán (Mexico City), a wonder that became greater when he realized the scale, wealth and organization of the city. His description, borne out by others and by archaeological remains found on the site of the city, removes any doubt as to the high level of the pre-Columbian civilizations before the arrival of the Europeans. It is the view of many students that the cities of the pre-Columbian New World were indeed larger, richer and better organized than those of Europe at the time.

The eighteenth-century Jesuits describing China were also almost as enthusiastic as Marco Polo four centuries earlier. But in the eighteenth century it is probable that the difference between the West and the mighty empire of the East was smaller. During those four centuries, Europe probably progressed further than China.

The 'wealth' of the Middle East should also be borne in mind. In the case of Persia (in 1660) we have even an appreciation of the countryside which is much more rare. Chardin, who was considered to be a very reliable eyewitness, writes the following: 'The peasants are quite well off, and I can assert that there are, in the most fertile countries of Europe, people who are incomparably more wretched.' From one of the great countries of the Islamic world, let us move to another two and a half centuries later. Even if the beginning of the nineteenth century was not a very prosperous period for Egypt, its standard of living was seen to be much higher than that of many poor and average European regions.

It is, however, true that it is possible to find more negative descriptions than those quoted above, but, on the whole, the positive descriptions greatly outnumber the negative ones. This is true for the period before

colonization but obviously not for the nineteenth century, when the two
major regions had begun to diverge considerably.

Furthermore, it is true that a form of capital accumulation diverted to
build ostentatious cities may lead to incorrect economic analyses in
comparisons of the wealth of cities. In my previous book there is a section
entitled 'Splendid but impoverished cities', where referring to pre-
industrial societies, I wrote the following:

> The modest gap between rich and poor nations, duplicated in slightly more
> exaggerated form at the regional level, raises an important question. How
> under these circumstances do we explain the testimony provided by the
> urban remains left to us from former times, a testimony pointing to great
> differences in wealth? The answer lies in the low cost of investments in
> tokens of urban power and prestige. Between a rich city with sumptuous
> monuments and a poor city without monuments of any kind, the difference
> in terms of investments would have amounted to no more than a few
> percentage points of national income. Quite independently of the choices
> individual societies might have made in this regard, even a slight rise in the
> standard of living would have permitted the erection of cities of great
> magnificence. Indeed it was enough to mobilize only a relatively small
> fraction of national urban revenues to set massive construction schemes on
> foot, an additional allocation of some 3–7 per cent to construction probably
> sufficing to build urban edifices that in later years signified prodigious
> wealth.[21]

However, in the comparisons between the civilizations mentioned
above, the positive appreciations probably have a real value for at least
two reasons. The very large number of 'rich' cities combined with a higher
level of urbanization of those civilizations compared to that of Europe
reduces the chances of a bias in this indicator. Second, if the standard of
living of the city dweller was appreciably lower than that of Europe as a
whole, it would have been mentioned in the literature. Therefore it is
highly likely that those comparisons that we based on cities corroborate
the other comparisons.

Therefore it is probable that before the upheavals of the Industrial
Revolution the average country in the future Third World was probably
not poorer than a similar region in the future developed world; and
certainly not much poorer, for example not as much as 20% poorer. This
is not a surprising conclusion since before the Industrial Revolution no
country or region could be really rich. The world's average standard of
living was not far from the minimum level; the frequent famines that
occurred in all continents are an additional proof of that. Richer regions
of the future Third World appear to have been richer than the average
countries in the future developed world, and vice versa.

# Notes

1 Kennedy, P., *The Rise and the Fall of the Great Powers. Economic Change and Military Conflict from 1500 to 2000*, New York, 1988.
2 Zimmerman, L. J., 'The distribution of world income', in Vries, E. de (ed.), *Essays on Unbalanced Growth*, The Hague, 1962, pp. 28–47.
3 According to my estimates the annual growth rate was 0.53% for the developed countries and an annual decline of 0.06% for the Third World.
4 Bairoch, P., 'Le mythe de la croissance économique rapide au XIXe siècle', *Revue de l'Institut de Sociologie*, No. 2, Brussels, 1962, pp. 307–31.
5 Kuznets, S., *Modern Economic Growth*, New Haven, 1966, pp. 390–1.
6 In fact, Kuznets provides the figures for the range and not the average. I calculated these figures on the basis of Kuznets' assumptions and included the Communist developed countries.
7 Kuznets, S., *Economic Growth of Nations. Total Output and Production Structure*, Cambridge, MA, 1971, pp. 24–8.
8 Bairoch, P., 'Les écarts des niveaux de développement entre pays développés et pays sous-développés de 1770 à 2000', *Tiers-Monde*, **XII**, No. 47, 1971, pp. 497–514.
9 Landes, D., *The Unbound Prometheus*, Cambridge (MA), 1969.
10 Deane, P., *The First Industrial Revolution*, Cambridge, 1965; Marczewski, J., 'Le produit physique de l'économie française de 1789 à 1913 (comparaison avec la Grande-Bretagne)', *Cahiers de l'I.S.E.A.*, Série A.F., No. 4, July 1965.
11 Bairoch, P., 'Ecarts internationaux des niveaux de vie avant la révolution industrielle', *Annales, E.S.C.*, 34e année, No. 1, 1979, pp. 145–71; Bairoch, P., 'The main trends in national economic disparities since the Industrial Revolution', in Bairoch, P. and Levy-Leboyer, M. (eds), *Disparities in Economic Development since the Industrial Revolution*, London, 1981, pp. 3–17.
12 Bairoch, P., 'Le volume des productions et du produit national dans le Tiers-Monde, 1900–1977', *Revue Tiers-Monde*, **XX**, No. 80, 1979, pp. 669–91.
13 Crafts, N. F. R., 'Patterns of development in nineteenth century Europe', *Oxford Economic Papers*, **36**, November 1984, pp. 438–58.
14 For more details see Bairoch, P., 'How and not why? Economic inequalities between 1800 and 1913: some background figures', in Batou, J. (ed.), *Between Development and Underdevelopment, 1800–1870*, Geneva, 1991, pp. 1–42.
15 Maddison, A., 'A comparison of levels of GDP per capita in developed and developing countries, 1700–1980', *The Journal of Economic History*, **XLIII**, No. 1, 1983, pp. 27–41; Maddison, A., *The World Economy in the 20th Century*, Development Centre Studies, Paris, 1989; Maddison, A., 'Measuring European growth: the core and the periphery', in Aerts, E. and Valerio, N. (eds.), *Growth and Stagnation in the Mediterranean World in the 19th and 20th Centuries*, Leuven, 1990, pp. 82–118.
16 To our knowledge, there are two sets of independent comparisons between the standard of living at the time of Akbar (turn of the seventeenth century), the 1930s and the 1960s. According to one estimate, real urban wages decreased by 60–80%; according to the other, by 30–40%. The 1930 and 1960 levels of GNP per capita of India are higher than that of 1830. Mukerjee, R.,

*The Economic History in India 1600–1800*, Allahabad, 1967; Desai, A. V., 'Population and standard of living in Akbar's time', *Indian Economic and Social History Review*, **9**, 1972, pp. 43–62.

17  Based on Maddison's 'lower' countries for 1830 and 1870 (1830: Finland 529, Spain 669, Germany 690; 1870: Portugal 568, Russia 678); and on adapting 'high' countries in 1830 to 1750 or 1700, UK 1133 was assumed to be 670 in 1700; France 784 to be 600 in 1750.

18  Bairoch, P., 'Ecarts internationaux des niveaux de vie avant la révolution industrielle', *Annales, E.S.C.*, 34e année, No. 1, January–February 1979, pp. 145–71.

19  Kravis, I. B., Heston, A. and Summers, R., 'Real GNP per capita for more than one hundred countries', *Economic Journal*, **88**, No. 350, 1978, pp. 215–42.

20  The references of the citations used in the text are the following: Chardin, J., *Voyages du Chevalier Chardin en Perse*, Amsterdam, 1732, Vol. III, pp. 343–4; Diaz de Castillo, B., *La conquête de la Nouvelle Espagne*, Lausanne, 1962; Polo, M., *The Book of Ser Marco Polo, the Venetian Concerning the Kingdoms and Marvels of the East* (translated by Sir Henry Yull), 2 volumes, London, 1903; Scott, C. R., *Rambles in Egypt and Candia, With Details of the Military Power and Resources of those Countries, and Observations on the Government, Policy, and Commercial System of Mohammed Ali*, 2 volumes, London, 1837 (Vol. II, p. 176).

21  Bairoch, P., *Cities and Economic Development. From the Dawn of History to the Present*, Chicago, 1988, p. 203.

# 10

# *A Long-term Deterioration in the Terms of Trade?*

This myth, which has been gradually disappearing over the last ten to fifteen years, can be considered a prototype of those surrounding the development of the Third World, so wide was its acceptance among economists specializing in problems of underdevelopment. Its origins can be clearly established, since most of the literature quotes the same source and can be traced to a United Nations study: *Relative Prices of Exports and Imports of Underdeveloped Countries* (New York, 1949). This was a widely used study in the 1950s and was in fact one of the first to address this important question. But this, in fact, only repeated the results of an earlier and well-known League of Nations study published in 1945, *Industrialization and Foreign Trade*. The findings of the secretariat of the League of Nations were popularized by Raul Prebisch's work on the deterioration of the terms of trade.[1] According to the secretariat, between the last quarter of the nineteenth century and the eve of World War II, or more precisely between 1876/80 and 1936/8, there had been a 43% reduction in the world price indices of primary products compared with the similar indices for manufactured goods. Since Third World exports are almost entirely primary products and imports almost totally manufactured goods, the conclusion that there has been a deterioration in the terms of trade for the Third World is a legitimate one as long as the above trend is correct.

However, on the evidence of the information available on productivity changes in various sectors during this period, it is almost impossible for economic historians to accept that the price of primary products decreased relative to that of manufactured goods. The major result of the first two centuries of the Industrial Revolution was a very rapid increase in manufacturing productivity; almost twice as fast as that of the other

111

sectors producing primary goods, and therefore causing a reduction in the prices of manufactured goods relative to those of primary goods. Therefore, first we must investigate the validity of these contradictory results.

Indeed, there is a series of problems and even biases in the League of Nations 1945 estimate. The first is related to the choice of the final phase, 1936/8. The Depression was a very atypical period, especially for the evolution of prices. If we compare 1876/80 to 1926/9, still using the same data, the deterioration in the terms of trade of primary products is reduced to half: to 20%. This, however, is only a partial explanation since it still implies a deterioration in the terms of trade of primary products.

Indeed, the major bias in the League of Nations world trade price indices derives from the fact that they used British price indices only, and that three-quarters of the prices in the British indices are import prices. Also measured are not only the British prices of products but also their transport costs, and these costs fell considerably during the 1876/80 to 1926/9 period. Since there are more import prices for primary products than for manufactured goods, and since for those products transport costs are of particular significance, this involves a major distortion of the prevailing trend. Another bias derives from the fact that British export prices of manufactures were used as a proxy for world exports of manufactures. Subsequent studies have shown that British export prices increased more rapidly during that period than those of the rest of the developed world. This increase was due mainly to the fact that the parity of sterling was fixed at too high a level after World War I. Incidentally, this was one of the major causes of the depression in Britain in the 1920s (see Chapter 1).

These shortcomings were seldom mentioned for a long time. It should, however, be noted that the League of Nations never presented their figures as valid indices for measuring international terms of trade, but they were quoted as such in many studies and so pseudo-facts became dogma. The dogma was so widespread among those dealing with the problems of developing countries that during the 1960s and 1970s, whenever a specific study was carried out on the nineteenth-century evolution of the terms of trade either of a specific less developed country or for a particular primary product,[2] the results were generally presented in the following terms: contrary to the general case . . . here we have an improvement of the terms of trade of . . .

However, economists dealing with foreign trade were less inclined to adhere to this myth. For example, Viner, in the early 1950s, noted the following:[3]

> For comparisons over long periods, moreover, the available data are largely irrelevant. The primary commodities whose average prices for

broad categories are used in the computations of the terms of trade are for the most part, for averages so computed, not superior in quality, and in some cases are perhaps inferior, to the corresponding commodities of earlier years. The articles whose prices are used are always a much smaller sample of the total exports of manufactures than agricultural products, and no weight is given to the gain in utility from the new commodities which have become available, such as the automobile, the tractor, and penicillin. Where the manufactures are nominally the same, moreover, they have over the years become incomparably superior in quality. It may perhaps take more pounds of coffee, or of cotton, to buy a lamp today than it did in 1900, but today's coffee and cotton are, I presume, not appreciably better in quality than those of 1900, whereas today's electric lamp is incomparably superior to the kerosene lamp of 1900. The decline in transportation costs, moreover, has made possible the seeming paradox of the commodity terms of trade improving simultaneously for both sets of countries.

On the basis of more reliable international export prices, resulting from research in the 1960s and 1970s, it can be deduced that between the 1870s and the 1926–9 period the terms of trade for primary products relative to manufactured goods improved by 10–25%, instead of worsening by about 20%, as had been calculated by the League of Nations.[4] On the other hand, I have assembled a set of over 50 individual export prices of primary goods exported from less developed countries. This study is not yet complete, but preliminary results confirm that the terms of trade improved during the nineteenth century and up to the end of the 1920s.

## But every rule has its exception

As always, a rule has its exception, and in this case there is an important one. It concerns sugar, which was, at the beginning of the nineteenth century, a major Third World export crop. Around 1830 sugar represented almost 25% of Third World exports and for Latin America this share was as much as 43%.

Sugar is the first important Third World product for which there appeared a competing product from the developed world. In fact, when we speak of sugar before the nineteenth century it implies cane sugar; and the competing product was beet sugar. Due to exceptional conditions (the English blockade of the Continent) beet sugar began to be manufactured in the early nineteenth century. Until the early 1840s the volume of beet sugar remained limited: its world production (mainly in Europe) amounted to 50,000 tons compared to 1,100,000 tons for cane sugar. But by 1880 it had reached 1,810,000 tons, which was close to that of cane sugar (1,860,000 tons). Around 1900 the figures were 6,060,000 tons for beet sugar and 3,800,000 tons for cane sugar.

Incidentally, it is interesting to note that sugar was one of the first important primary goods which was subject to an international agreement, involving almost all the important European beet sugar-producing countries. After 11 years of negotiation, the first real agreement was signed in 1898, and its aim was to stop the product's falling prices. Indeed, prices had fallen sharply. Around 1830 the export price of a ton of sugar was $100 dollars and it had fallen to below $60 dollars by 1910. This implies that the terms of trade for sugar compared even to manufactured goods deteriorated during the nineteenth century. As an approximate indication we can put forward a 10–20% price decline for manufactured goods between 1830 and 1910, which means that the terms of trade for sugar relative to manufactured goods deteriorated by 25–35%. This explains why the thesis of falling terms of trade was easily accepted, especially since Latin American economists were pre-eminent in this field and, for Latin America, sugar, as we have seen, was more important than for other Third World regions.

This brings us to another point: the belief that the role of Latin America in the history of the Third World in the nineteenth century has been overemphasized. It is true that in many cases Latin American history has prefigured that of the rest of the Third World, but this region, as mentioned earlier, represented only a small part of the Third world in the nineteenth century. Latin America's share of the total Third World population was some 3% in 1800 (and 6% in 1910). In terms of trade its role was much more important but still far from dominant, probably 50% of Third World exports in 1800 but only 35% in 1938.

## *The 'net barter terms of trade' do not tell all the story*

Not only did the terms of trade or, to be more precise, the 'net barter terms of trade' of the less developed countries improve from the nineteenth century to the early twentieth, there was also a significant improvement for many tropical food products *vis-à-vis* the major Western agricultural product: wheat. The combined effect of the increase in the agricultural productivity of the developed countries and the availability of land, especially in North America, led to a substantial decrease in the real price of wheat during the nineteenth century, especially during the second half. For example, the average export price of Egyptian cotton between 1876/80 and 1926/9 rose from $300 to $570 a ton, while that of

United States wheat increased from $44.3 to $50.8. This means that, whereas in 1876/80 a ton of Egyptian cotton was worth less than 7 tons of wheat, in 1926/30 the corresponding figure was more than 11. Incidentally, note that for 1987/91 the ratio is more than 40.

However, the fact that the net barter terms of Third World trade improved does not necessarily imply a positive development. This would have been the case if it had been accompanied by a rise in wages and other incomes in the Third World, as in the developed countries. While the real wages of producers of primary goods in the Third World probably remained stagnant or increased very little between the 1870s and the 1920s, those of the producers of manufactured goods in the developed world increased by some 100–160% in the same period. This implies that in 1926/9, on average, Third World workers could buy with their wages 10–25% more manufactured goods than could their grandparents around 1875. But this gain is modest compared with what happened in the developed world. Here workers could buy with their average wages 80–130% more primary goods originating from the Third World than had been possible for their grandparents. In technical terms, this means that the 'single factorial terms of trade' for primary goods from the Third World probably improved but the 'double factorial terms of trade' deteriorated.

However, such an evolution can be considered normal, since the gains in productivity for manufactured goods in the developed countries probably increased more rapidly than those made in producing primary goods in the Third World. The word 'probably' is used intentionally. There is indeed a high probability of such a difference, but the data for productivity gains in the Third World's primary sectors are lacking, especially for agricultural products. Data is unavailable not only for the 1870–1928 period but also for the contemporary years (see page 117).

## But yesterday's fallacy can be today's reality

The story for the 'net barter terms of trade' – usually called 'terms of trade' – was very different in the 1950s. This is probably the main reason why the myth of long-term deterioration was so easily accepted: economic history is too often neglected in the training of economists and still more so in that of political scientists and other students of current affairs.

From the early 1950s until 1961–2 there was a real deterioration in the terms of trade of primary products in general, and even more so of those primary products exported by the less developed countries. The growing importance of petroleum exports and the divergent and erratic movements in the prices of these products make meaningless the overall evolution of

**Table 10.1** Evolution of the terms of trade of Third World market economies, 1876/80–1989/91 (1963 = 100)

|  | All countries | Major petroleum exporters[a] | Other countries |
|---|---|---|---|
| 1876/80 | 66–77 | – | – |
| 1928/29 | 89–96 | – | – |
| 1938 | 80 | – | – |
| 1950/54 | 111 | 100 | 115 |
| 1960/64 | 101 | 101 | 101 |
| 1965/9 | 91 | 89 | 104 |
| 1970/72 | 90 | 98 | 107 |
| 1973/5 | 147 | 236 | 116 |
| 1976/8 | 171 | 300 | 111 |
| 1979/81 | 225 | 484 | 106 |
| 1982/4 | 235 | 549 | 100 |
| 1985/7 | 189 | 365 | 95 |
| 1989/91 | 175 | 310 | 90 |

[a] Twenty countries representing 17% of the population of Third World market economies.

*Sources:* 1876/80–1938: see text. 1930–1960/64: United Nations, *Yearbook of International Trade Statistics*, New York, various issues. 1960/64 and after: United Nations, *Unctad Handbook of International Trade and Development Statistics*, New York, various issues; and data communicated by UNCTAD's Secretariat.

the terms of trade since the early 1960s (see Table 10.1). For the non-petroleum exporters, which represent 83% of the population of the Third World market economies, the period from 1961/2 to 1979/81 is marked by relative stability in the terms of trade. But in view of the previous trends, even this stabilization can be regarded as a negative evolution.

Since 1979/81 there has been a significant deterioration lasting at least until 1992. Therefore, globally speaking, the negative evolution of the Third World's 'barter terms of trade' of non-petroleum-exporting countries began in the early 1950s. The paradox is that the beginning of this negative evolution coincided with a wave of political independence.

The causes of this evolution can only be briefly outlined here. Among the factors that explain this change in the long-term trend are a slow down in demand for a large range of primary goods, combined with an increase in their supply, development of synthetic products, measures to restrict the imports of some tropical goods (internal taxes), technological progress that has reduced the input coefficients of raw materials in manufacturing industry and, last but not least, a structural dichotomy which is generally presented as the Singer–Prebisch thesis.[5]

This thesis suggests that, due to a weaker organization, the unequal relationship between the developed and the underdeveloped world leads to a situation where, in the case of primary products, the gains in productivity are translated into a decline in prices, while in manufactures, these gains are translated into higher salaries and profits. The irony is that, to a certain extent, independence could mean a freer hand for large purchasing companies to press for lower prices since, in such a case, local situations were no longer of direct concern for the former colonial developed country.

Finally, another explanation of this new evolution is possible but has not yet been tested. Since the 1940s in the United States and the 1950s in Western Europe there has been a complete reversal of the relative rates of increase of productivity in agriculture and manufacturing (see Chapter 14). From those years until the present (labour) productivity has increased almost twice as fast in agriculture as in manufacturing, resulting in a deterioration in the barter terms of trade of agricultural products from temperate countries. If during the past 30 years the rate of increase in productivity for tropical agriculture has been more rapid than that of manufacturing, this could explain, at least in part if not completely, the 1950–90 evolution of terms of trade. For the moment, there are not enough data to allow a valid estimate of the evolution of the labour productivity of tropical agriculture, so an evaluation of this explanation must wait; it is one of the many grey areas in economics and economic history.

Where the post-1979/81 evolution is concerned, the intervention of the above-mentioned factors can only be very partial, since deterioration in Third World terms of trade was much greater than the probable effect of these structural modifications. Indeed, between 1979/81 and 1989/91 there was a 15% deterioration in the terms of trade of the Third World's non-major petroleum-exporting countries. This deterioration is largely a result of the rapid increase in oil prices which led to an equally rapid rise in the prices of manufactured goods as well as of some semi-manufactured items such as fertilizers imported by Third World countries.

## Notes

1 See especially Prebsich, R., *The Economic Development of Latin America and its Principal Problems*, New York, 1950.
2 Among these, see Bhatia, B. M., 'Terms of trade and economic development. A case study of India 1861–1939', *Indian Economic Journal*, **14**, 1969, pp. 414–33; Montesano, A., 'Il movimenti dei prezzi in Giapone dal 1878 at 1958', *Giornale degli economisti e annali economia*, November–December 1967; Owen, E. R., *Cotton and the Egyptian Economy, 1820–1914. A Study in Trade and Development*, Oxford, 1969; Morgan, T., 'The long-run terms of trade between agricultural and manufacturing', *Economic Development and Cultural*

*Change*, **8**, 1959, pp. 1–23. See also Spraos, J., 'The statistical debate on the net
barter terms of trade between primary commodities and manufactures', *The
Economic Journal*, **90**, No. 357, 1980, pp. 107–28, and Bairoch, P., *The
Economic Development of the Third World since 1900*, London, 1975, pp. 111–
34.
3 Viner, J., *International Trade and Economic Development*, Oxford, 1953,
p. 114.
4 For a more detailed account see Bairoch, P., *The Economic Development of the
Third World since 1900*, London, 1977, pp. 111–34.
5 Singer, H. W., 'The distribution of gains between investing and borrowing
countries', *American Economic Review*, **40**, May 1950, pp. 473–85.

# 11

# The More Tropical Products Exported, the More Food Imported?

As we have seen (Chapter 8), the rapid expansion of exported crops was a reality. From 0.4 million tons around 1790 they reached a peak of 34 million tons around 1970. Furthermore, it is certain that in many countries this development had many negative social and economic consequences for people in those countries. In some cases indigenous food supplies were reduced, leading to the regular import of cereals and even to famine. However, in view of the decline in prices of cereals during the nineteenth century (and more specifically during its second half) there was a general improvement in the terms of trade of tropical agricultural products as compared with cereals from temperate countries (see Chapter 10). Furthermore, those cereal imports remained rather limited until after the 1950s.[1] In fact, until the first few years after World War II, the Third World economies (even if we exclude Argentina, which, in this respect as in many others, does not belong to the Third World) were still exporting more cereals than they imported. But for the 1948–52 period this excess changed to a deficit. The annual average deficit was of the order of 4 million tons or 2% of their production.

## A very large increase in food imports

The net imports of all cereals amounted to 15 million tons yearly for the 1958–62 period, reached 24 million for 1968–72, 63 million for 1978–82 and 84 million tons annually for the 1987–91 period.[2] In terms of share of local production this meant 7% for the 1968–72 period and 16% for 1987–91. As always, these figures for the whole of the Third World market

119

economies (excluding Argentina) varied considerably from one region to another (not to mention national differences). The situation was most dramatic in the Middle East, where the net imports of cereals represented 45% of the local production for the 1987–91 period. The best situation in this respect was that of Asia (excluding the Middle East), whose comparable figure was 3%. For black Africa the deficit was 28% and for Latin America (excluding Argentina) 18%.

Countries that have been net cereal exporters for centuries or even millennia have become net cereal importers, and some, especially oil-exporting countries, have reduced their cereal and food production to such a low level that it provides only a negligible share of their consumption. Let us take only one example in each of those evolutions. Under the Roman Empire, Tunisia was an important cereal supplier to what was one of the first great cities in the world: Rome. Tunisia's role as an important cereal exporter lasted for almost twenty centuries. At the beginning of the twentieth century Tunisia's net exports of cereals represented a fifth of its local consumption. For 1986/90 local production was able to meet less than half of local consumption.

For the case of petroleum exporters, I will take not one of the extreme cases but that of Iraq, Babylon in ancient times. The region of Iraq was always considered very rich in agricultural terms. As late as the early 1960s, it was still self-sufficient in cereals but for 1986/90 local production only provided 34% of local consumption. The import ratio for other foodstuffs was also very high; for example, sugar, whose consumption amounted to 40 kg per inhabitant, was almost all imported.

The title of this section mentions food imports, and until now I have dealt only with cereals, for two main reasons. Cereals were in the past, and are still today, the Third World's major food item. In fact, they provide 60% of the populations' food intake. The second reason is even more apparent: the sharp increase in the deficit for that product. But what exacerbates the food situation even further is the fact that in the past twelve to seventeen years there has also been an increased deficit in Third World market economies in other food products. To the deficit of 84 million of tons of cereal (annual average of 1987/91) one should add over 3 million tons of milk products, close to 3 million tons of meat and meat products and more than half a million tons of pulses.

## But can this be explained by exports of tropical products?

In the 1950s and 1960s the simultaneous increase in exports of tropical products and imports of Western cereals led to what seems to many a very obvious conclusion: the causal linkage of these two events. The greater financial return on exports crops leads to neglect of more primary foodstuffs, which must therefore be imported. There is no doubt that, in some cases, there is a relationship between them, but the increase in exports of tropical products is responsible for only a small fraction of cereal imports.

Already on the regional level there is a discrepancy: the region where imports of cereals increased the most and reached the highest level, the Middle East, is also one with the lowest level of per capita export of tropical agricultural products. The following are average annual net per capita exports of the total of major tropical products[3] for the 1986–90 period: black Africa: $11, Latin America: $41; Asia (excluding the Middle East) $3; and for the Middle East a negative balance of $7.

There is also a discrepancy in the timing. The Middle East is one of the two regions whose exports of tropical products hardly increased (a 0.4–0.5% annual increase in volume between 1961–5 and 1979–81). The other very negative region, as far as food is concerned, is black Africa, and in this case, there was even a reduction in the volume of agricultural exports (a 0.8–0.9% annual decrease between 1961–5 and 1979–81). The region with the least negative evolution in its food situation witnessed a rapid increase in its exports of agricultural products: the Far East (a 2.8–2.9% annual increase in volume between 1961–5 and 1979–81).

Furthermore, as we shall see in Chapter 14, in 1981, for the first time in at least two centuries, the Third World's market economies (excluding Argentina) imported more food products than they exported. Traditionally, the Third World has exported more than double the food products than it imported.

Nevertheless, if we return to more global data, we are still faced with the fact that between 1948/52 and 1987/91 the modification of food flows (still for Third World market economies, excluding Argentina) implies, in terms of cereal equivalent, some 90 million tons of imports since this region experienced an increase in its deficit of food exports of 4 million tons to one of 92 million tons. During the same period the volume of exports of tropical products increased by only 10–12 million tons.

The best answer to the question of the real impact of tropical exports on the increase in food imports is to assess what amount of food could have been produced on the land used for tropical agricultural products grown for export, and to compare this with food imports. I have restricted my calculation to the Third World market economies and to the 1984–8 period. For each tropical product I calculated the share of production exported, and this was related to the total area cultivated with this product (see Table 11.1).

**Table 11.1** Estimates of the areas of land devoted to export crops in the Third World market economies for 1984/8 (annual average)

| | Total area devoted (1,000 ha) | Total production (1,000 tons) | Net exports (1,000 tons) | Net exports in % of production | Area devoted to exports (1,000 ha) |
|---|---|---|---|---|---|
| Bananas | (2,900) | 37,390 | 6,815 | 18.2 | (520) |
| Citrus | (4,000) | 34,000 | 1,940 | 5.7 | (200) |
| Cocoa | 5,328 | 2,110 | 1,301 | 61.6 | 3,290 |
| Coffee | 10,870 | 5,541 | 2,486 | 44.9 | 4,880 |
| Cotton (lint) | 19,170 | 6,464 | 672 | 10.4 | 1,990 |
| Jute[a] | 2,216 | 2,887 | 1,176 | 40.7 | 900 |
| Oilseeds[b] | (60,000) | 26,170 | 2,030 | 7.8 | (4,700) |
| Pepper | 290 | 154 | 69 | 44.8 | 140 |
| Rubber | 9,050 | 4,356 | 3,131 | 71.9 | 6,510 |
| Sisal | 593 | 408 | 119 | 29.2 | 170 |
| Sugar (cane and beet) | 16,200 | 53,560 | 8,620 | 16.1 | 2,610 |
| Tea | 1,222 | 1,560 | 369 | 23.6 | 290 |
| TOTAL ABOVE | 131,840 | – | – | – | 26,200 |
| TOTAL EXPORTS CROPS[c] | 134,000 | – | – | – | (26,800) |

[a] Jute and jute-like fibres; including jute manufactured goods.
[b] Oilseeds, oleaginous fruits and oils: production and trade in oil equivalent.
[c] Including the following export crops not shown separately: other spices, tobacco, other fibres, other fruits.

*Note:* The area figures in parentheses are more approximate resulting from previous and indirect data.
For the same region and the same period the land area was the following (in 1,000 hectares): cereals: 314,000; arable and permanent crop land: 680,000; permanent pasture land: 1,495,500.

*Sources:* Derived from the following publications:
FAO, *Production Year Book*, Rome, various issues; *Trade Yearbook*, Rome, various issues; and *Commodity Review and Outlook, 1989– 90*, Rome 1990.
United Nations, *Unctad Commodity Yearbook*, New York, various issues, and data communicated by UNCTAD's Secretariat.
IRSG, *Rubber Statistical Bulletin*, Wembley, various issues; and *Fruit and Tropical Products*, London, various issues.

I also calculated the total amount of net food imports (converting meat and dairy products into cereal equivalents). The amount of land devoted to exported crops can be estimated to cover some 27 million hectares. The total amount of annual net imports of food for 1984–8 can be estimated at 110 million tons of cereals equivalent. If the land devoted to export crops had been entirely used for cereals, and if we assume that the average yield of this land was similar to that of the total cereals (1.7 tons per hectare), the conclusion is that it could have produced 40–45% of the total food deficit.

This percentage is probably rather high, since almost a quarter of the land involved is devoted to rubber production, and it is very unlikely that this land would have been able to produce the average yield of cereals. The same question applies to the area used for the cultivation of coffee and some fruits, so a more plausible overall figure would therefore be 35–40%. This is not an insignificant proportion, but it cannot be considered to be the main cause of the high level of food imports. To this argument we should not forget to add those presented above concerning the geographical and chronological discrepancies of movements of imports of food and exports of tropical products. The main cause of the food deficit was a significant population increase combined with a very rapid urbanization process leading to great pressure on land. This produced a situation in which additional demand for food from urban populations generally led to an increase in imports. These imports were also largely stimulated by external causes. One was the programme of Food Aid, the other was related to the rapid increase in Western agricultural productivity. This increase has been so rapid that it led to the paradoxical situation where, despite much higher salaries, the production costs of cereals in developed countries were lower than those in the Third World. We shall return to this interesting aspect in Chapter 14. The Food Aid programme started in 1954 and consisted mainly of shipments of free cereals to areas of shortages. These shipments reached high levels in the 1960s and in many cases what started as a temporary relief operation led to a process of increasing foreign dependency on cereals, often as a result of a change in the traditional diet. Food imports were also stimulated by the fact that most large cities are located on or near the coast.

## Export crops bring greater financial returns

Finally, it should be stressed that even if, as noted at the beginning of this chapter, export crops could have a negative impact on the economic development of the Third World, they are also, in many instances, a worthwhile economic alternative to domestic food production. As we can see in Table 11.2, what can be called the 'financial value' or 'export value' of land cultivated for those products far exceeds its value for food production, especially cereals. Cereals, which still remain the staple food, have become very cheap, largely because of the increase in Western agricultural productivity.

Any area planted with coffee produces almost seven times more gross income than when planted with wheat and almost three times more than rice. Not all exports crops are so profitable. In the case of sugar the gross dollar yield is less than half that of coffee and a fifth that of tea, but it is still twice more than that of wheat. It should be noted that the gross dollar yield figures are approximate and do not reflect the differences in net

**Table 11.2** Estimates of approximate economic export values of cultivated land for 1984/8 (annual average)

|  | Yield ton per hectare | Export prices (dollars per ton) | Approx. corrective factor[a] | Gross dollar yield per hectare |
|---|---|---|---|---|
| Bananas | (12.90) | 239 |  |  |
| Cocoa | 0.37 | 1,990 | 100 | 1,440 |
| Coffee | 0.53 | 2,700 | 100 | 1,060 |
| Cotton (lint) | 0.34 | 1,400 | 100 | 4,760 |
| Groundnuts | 0.89 | 630 | 70 | 390 |
| Sugar (cane) | 58.47 | 410 | 8 | 1,910 |
| Tea | 1.40 | 2,130 | 100 | 2,970 |
| Wheat (Third World) | 1.69 | 138 | 100 | 230 |
| Wheat (developed Western countries) | 2.45 | 138 | 100 | 340 |
| Rice | 2.45 | 276 | 65 | 440 |

[a] This corrective factor, expressed as a percentage, is designed to adapt the export prices to the type of product referred to in the Yield column. For example, the yield for groundnuts refers to unshelled while prices refer to shelled groundnuts. Instead of export prices it would have been preferable to omit international average production prices.

*Sources:* Author's calculations derived from FAO, *Production Year Book*, Rome, various issues; and *The State of Food and Agriculture*, Rome, various issues; and *Trade Yearbook*, Rome, various issues.

income. Operating expenditures are very different from one crop to another. Regional differences are also wide, resulting from differences in yields and in prices received by farmers.

Before leaving this topic and to end this chapter, one negative aspect of specialization in exports of tropical crops should be mentioned: the very erratic fluctuation in prices does not always correlate with variations in production. To take again the example of coffee and wheat, if we limit ourselves to the 1960–90 period, the following extreme price relations can be found between those two products. For the 1983–7 average, as can be seen in Table 11.2, the price of coffee is 22.1 times that of wheat. This ratio was 48.1 in 1977 and 7.6 in 1974, and this was due almost entirely to fluctuations in the price of coffee. Incidentally, this year (1992) the price of coffee in real terms reached its lowest level in history – some 50–60% below the previous low ebb in 1938.

## Notes

1 Etemad, B., 'Bilan céréalier du Tiers-Monde 1900–1982', *Revue Tiers-Monde*, **XXV**, No. 98, Paris, 1984, pp. 387–408.

2 All the data in this chapter relating to contemporary agriculture are based on FAO sources, notably various issues of *Production Yearbook*; *Trade Yearbook*; *Food Outlook*; and *Quarterly Bulletin of Statistics*.
3 I arrived at the total for the following products: coffee, cocoa, tea, pepper, sugar, oilseeds and cake meal, citrus, bananas, pineapples, rubber, cotton, jute and tobacco.

# 12

# Population Growth: the More,
# the Better?

We saw in Chapter 8 that in the Third World a rapid increase in population had already begun during the period of colonization. In some countries this happened as early as the mid-nineteenth century, but for the whole of the Third World it did not start until the 1930s. Let us recall the main data. If between 1880 and 1913 the population increased by an annual rate of 0.5%, for the 1913–29 period it was already 0.7–0.8%, reaching 1.1–1.2% between 1929 and 1938 and 1.2% for the 1938–1950 period.

## A population growth without precedent

From 1938 to 1950 onwards the rate of growth began to increase rapidly: 2.1% in the 1950s and 2.5% in the 1960s. Due to a significant slow down in China, the rate of growth for the whole of the Third World declined thereafter: 2.3% for the 1970s and 2.1% for the 1980s. Even if we take the entire 40-year period between 1950 and 1990, we are faced with an annual growth rate of 2.24%, which means a doubling of the population over a period of 31 years. If we exclude China from the rest of the Third World, the annual increase in the Third World market economies has been 2.44% during the same 40-year period, which means doubling every 29 years. For Africa the rate reached 2.7% (doubling every 26 years) and for some countries it was above 3%: Iraq, Jordan and Tanzania (3.2%); Syria (3.3%), Libya and Zimbabwe (3.7%). Also, 3.7% per year means doubling every 19 years, multiplying by 10 in 63 years and by 38 in 100 years.

Never has any large region witnessed a population increase during a 40-

126

year period even half as rapid as the recent average for the Third World. If, to begin, we limit ourselves to the societies before the Industrial Revolution, the most rapid increase in Europe, China and India was about 0.4–0.6%. After the Industrial Revolution the 40 years of most rapid population growth for the developed countries was the 1870–1910 period, where it stood at 1.1%. But this was made possible by the largest migration in history, when between 1870 and 1913 some 33 million Europeans emigrated – most of them to North America. If we limit ourselves to Europe, the 1870–1910 annual increase was only 0.9%.

Western Europe took a century (between 1810 and 1910) to double its population; the Third World market economies took only twenty-eight to twenty-nine years (between 1950 and 1978/9) and while the European GNP per capita increased by 180–200% during the nineteenth century, the rise was only 60–75% in the Third World. Another, although minor, fact is that during the eighteenth century Western Europe's population increased globally by 45–55%, whereas for the Third World market economies between 1850 and 1950 the total increase had been 120–130%. All these comparisons prove the magnitude of this problem in the difficult task of Third World economic development.

## A nexus of myths and a paradoxical alliance

Despite this, a nexus of myths took shape. These were largely mingled with ideological and religious dogmas, and even led to a paradoxical alliance. The first component in this nexus of myths is the wrong assumption that during the first stages of Western development, population increase was a positive factor. As we shall see later, this was not so, but even if it had been, as we just have seen, there is no comparison in the respective rates of population increase between these two cases.

Another component of the nexus of myths concerning population is that one of the major arguments for delaying population-control measures was that 'development is the best contraceptive', and the example of the West is given as a proof. The major problem in this argument is that it took almost a century in the Western world for the birth rate to counterbalance the decline in the death rate. In Western Europe the death rate had already begun to decline at the end of the eighteenth century, whereas the birth rate in most countries did not begin to fall until the 1870s and 1880s. Another argument against family planning is the belief that birth control is a disruption of traditional values, and of 'natural' population evolution. The real disruption is the rapid decrease in infant mortality due to modern technology, and birth control is only a corrective measure against this disruption.

Finally, very often there is confusion between population increase and population density. The fact that some regions are regarded, rightly or not, as low-density populated leads to the wrong conclusion that in such cases population growth has no negative aspects.

In the 1950s and 1960s a very paradoxical informal alliance was formed between the Catholic Church and the Marxists. The Bible was, and still is, the origin of the Catholic Church's opposition to birth control. For the Marxists the 'theological' opposition to birth control goes back to the bitter feud between Marx and Malthus. Western efforts to persuade less developed countries to introduce birth control were presented as an 'imperialistic plot' against the Third World. Mao Tse-tung even suggested the 'absurdity' of birth-control measures through his slogan 'a mouth more to feed means two more hands to work', forgetting, or deliberately ignoring for political reasons, that a mouth has to be fed for years before the hands can work: and that without tools, fertilizer and, above all, additional land, often hands cannot increase food production sufficiently.

One of the paradoxes is that all less developed countries that adopted Marxism, from China to Cuba, had, most of the time, stringent family-planning policies, and in fact experienced the lowest population increase. Between 1950 and 1990, China's population rose at an annual rate of 1.8% compared to 2.4% for the Asian market economies; Cuba's population increased annually by 1.5% compared to 2.5% for the rest of Latin America. The coalition between Catholics and Communists was one of the major causes of the failure of the 1974 United Nations-sponsored World Population Conference to recommend the family-planning policies in the Third World, a failure that retarded such measures in many countries.

After all, one could expect such a nexus of myths and paradoxes when we are dealing with a problem that arouses so much emotion and which entails such complex interactions. What is more emotional than dealing with expected or existing children and, even more, with grandchildren (and a grandfather is writing, who is blessed by great joy provided by 6-year-old Alice, 3-year-old Jonas and a newly born Colin). Complex interactions . . . yes indeed, the problems of relations between population growth and economic growth are very complex.

## *Population growth and economic growth: a complex problem*

Some years ago I was asked to prepare a report on 'Population growth and long-term international economic growth' for the International

Population Conference in Manila, 1981 (organized by the International Union for the Scientific Study of Population). In the introduction, I wrote the following:

> Population growth and economic growth, what a wide and marvellous problem; but what a difficult one also. Marvellous and frightening at the same time, for it involves two of the most important aspects of human evolution for, in the last two centuries, and even more so over the last three decades, there has been an unprecedented increase in the pace of change of both of those aspects which may lead, in the case of the Third World, to dangerous food shortages. A difficult problem . . . yes, since it is obvious that the interactions of these two fundamental aspects are numerous, deep, and complex. Difficult, as it is also obvious, population growth is only one among many factors which can influence or be influenced by economic growth. It is also difficult because there are few questions which are so deeply related to religious or political dogmas.

Yet despite the wide interest in and profound implications of this problem, and probably because of its difficulty, what a United Nations report of 1973 said then is still valid today: 'The empirical and comparative study of the interrelation between population and economic growth remains one of the least explained areas in the field of demographic economic interrelation.[1]

Statistical analysis of growth in the populations of individual developed countries and economic growth during the last two centuries does not provide any indication that periods of accelerating population growth lead to more rapid economic growth. Whatever the relation between these two factors, it is not a very strong one. If one takes into account the quality of the data, to the very limited extent that a statistically valid conclusion can be reached, it shows a negative relation between population and growth. The results are similar if, instead of a chronological, a cross-spatial analysis is performed. Here too it appears that it is rather the countries with a slower population growth that achieved the better economic performance. More rapid population growth was rather negative, especially when the rate of growth exceeded 1% per year.

## The constraints of rapid population growth

One of the most negative results of too rapid a population growth lies in the great difficulty for an economy to absorb the numerous newcomers into its workforce. In the Third World market economies around 1960 we had the following parameters. An annual increase in the workforce of 2.4%; a workforce distribution where 77% were employed in agriculture, 10% in industry and 13% in services. In such a situation, in order to absorb the surplus agricultural labour, it implied that employment in the other sectors should be increased by an annual 8.0%, which is impossible. In Europe, around 1800, when the share of the agricultural workforce was close to that of the Third World in 1960, the comparable percentage increase was below 2% per year.

In the Third World this situation did not allow the rest of the economy to absorb the agricultural labour surplus. Therefore, we saw a continuous increase in the agricultural workforce which exacerbated an already negative situation in the land/workforce ratio. Since in most regions land suitable for agriculture was already in use by the mid-nineteenth century, the situation in the mid-twentieth was even more negative. Around 1950 in the Third World market economies there were only 2.4 hectares of agricultural land[2] per agricultural worker. In Europe, around 1910, which was the historical low point, this figure was 3.6 hectares. At the same time, it was 14.6 hectares in the United States and 5.1 hectares for the whole of the developed countries. Around 1990, for the Third World economies this ratio had fallen to below 1.8 hectares, and in some large Asian countries even below 1.0 hectare (Bangladesh, 0.4 hectare).

Even if we take into consideration the fact that, because there are two crops a year in most rice-producing countries, yields are higher than they were in Europe in the nineteenth century, and that thanks to the green revolution important progresses were made, this still implies low cereal production capacity. In Asia, where three-quarters of the Third World's population are concentrated, the average yield per hectare for all the cereals combined is now close to 2,600 kg compared to 950 kg for Europe around 1850. But, on average, each European farmer then had four or five times more land. This explains the low agricultural productivity in the Third World, which, in turn, is one of the factors that has led to the rapid increase in cereal imports (see Chapter 9). But, in addition to this important negative constraint of population growth, others are also present. Let us give a brief overview of these.

The first, and the most obvious, is the need for a high rate of investment in order to absorb the population increase. According to the best estimate of the capital output ratio, 4–5% of GNP must be invested in the Third World in order to obtain a 1% growth in the economy. This implies that to compensate for the 2.4% population increase, some 10–12% of GNP needs to be invested. Such an investment ratio was reached in Europe only after more than half of a century of development, at a time when its population increase was only a third of that of the Third World today, and, what is even more important, when per capita income was higher.

A high rate of population increase implies an even more rapid rise in school-age populations. This, in turn, implies the necessity for a very rapid expansion in school facilities in both physical and human terms, and both are not easy. Training a large number of teachers is not an easy task. Rapid population growth also implies very large families, which entails negative consequences for both parents and children.

To what extent are these constraints modified in less densely populated countries? The only difference, and it is not a marginal one, lies in the availability of agricultural land. This, for example, enabled Latin America to increase the amount of land per agricultural worker despite an increase in their number. Even if some poorer land had to be used for cultivation, this enabled Latin America to increase its agricultural productivity much more rapidly than the rest of the Third World.

This, however, was not enough to counterbalance the other negative constraints of too rapid a population increase, especially since Latin America's agriculture was less dominant globally. The economic performance of this region has been much worse than that of the rest of the Third World. In Latin America, GNP per capita exceeded that of the rest of the Third World market economies by 170% by 1950, but this figure was reduced to 100% 40 years later. Without giving too much significance to this, it is worth noting that if we rank the major regions by their rate of population growth in the last 40 years, this ranking is exactly the inverse of that of per capita GNP growth.

Finally, and this is far from being a minor aspect, rapid population growth is one of the major causes of Third World urban expansion, which is unprecedented in both its scale and modalities.

Its scale . . . Between 1950 and 1990 the number of people living in the Third World cities rose from 0.26 billion to 1.45 billion. This implies a rate of growth more than twice as fast as that in Europe during its greatest period of urbanization. The absolute increase during this period, close to 1.2 billion city dwellers, represents a number twice as high as the total world urban population in 1950.

Its modalities . . . This urban expansion took place virtually without economic development and led to a concentration of populations in very large cities. Furthermore, living conditions in those cities are deplorable, especially as far as housing is concerned, not to speak of services such as basic health care, water and sewage. There has been a proliferation of shantytowns whose population in 1980 represented 40–45% of urban inhabitants in the Third World economies. Worse still is the fact that practically all the qualities that made Western cities in the nineteenth century (and in traditional societies in general) a factor in their countries' economic development do not play a similar role in the Third World. Globally, today in the Third World, urbanization is more a burden than an asset.[3]

Undoubtedly awareness of the reality of the constraints imposed by rapid population growth has increased. The number of countries in the Third World supporting family-planning programmes rose from two in the mid-1950s to eight in the mid-1960s, to 33 in 1970 and to 113 in 1988, and the 1980s were characterized by a slowing in the rate of population increase.

All this does not imply that the measures have been strict enough (except for China) and that therefore the rapid population growth will disappear in the near future. According to United Nations projections (medium variant) published in 1991, the Third World market economies' population will rise from 2.8 billion in 1990 to 5.4 billion in 2025. This means that by then, compared to the mid-eighteenth century, when this region was already largely populated, the level of population will have multiplied by 15 (for the developed countries, by seven). Furthermore, this does not imply either that the myth that population growth does not have negative aspects has disappeared, especially in the lower densely populated regions. Therefore it is crucial to take into consideration the fact that population growth was never an asset, and is in every situation a great constraint. Even if a rapid population increase had no negative economic consequences, it still leads to a reduction in one of the most prized assets: space, and this is more than a sufficient reason for an international effort to reduce population growth.

## Notes

1  United Nations, *The Determinants and Consequences of Population Trends*, 1, New York, 1973, p. 554.
2  Agricultural land being the total of arable land and land under permanent crops. As far as permanent meadows and pastures are concerned the situation is in favour of the Third World. Around 1910, the situation was the following (hectares per agricultural worker): 2 hectares for Europe, 3.3 for the whole of the developed countries compared to 5 for the Third World. If we include China, this figure falls to 4 hectares.
3  For more on this subject see Bairoch, P., *Cities and Economic Development. From the Dawn of History to the Present*, Chicago, 1988 (especially Chapter 30, pp. 475–92).

# PART IV

# 'Minor' Myths and Unnoticed Turning Points

The final part of this book differs from the other three in at least two aspects. The first is obvious from its title, since we will be exploring not only myths but also some unnoticed historical turning points. I felt it worth pointing out the latter because they can be just as misleading as myths. The other departure is reflected in the word 'minor' in this part's title. I have put the word in quotation marks to draw the reader's attention to other acknowledged myths and misconceptions about history, economic history and even the social sciences in general.

One may ask if there is such a thing as a minor or less important myth, especially in a period when economics and history have become such a wide field. Over 1,100 academics attended the last (August 1990) congress of the International Economic History Association, and this represents only a fraction (but what fraction?) of the total number engaged in this field. The number of papers in economic history rose from 300 in 1900 to 4,400 in 1950, and probably to 31,000 in 1990.[1]

In such a context this means that a growing number of historians and economists specialize in increasingly narrow fields. But a narrow field is almost never a minor field. For example, the history of relative prices can be regarded as a narrow field. However, it can span very large areas in both time and geography and can cover a very wide spectrum of goods and services. Its results can lead to important insights into sectoral productivity differences and also into the social status of some professions, both historically and geographically. Therefore, by analogy, one can conclude that there is no such thing as a minor myth. Moreover, and this is more the case in history and social sciences than in other sciences, it is difficult to establish a clear hierarchy of the importance of events. As historians generally and justly consider it: true history is the narrative of events that have had important consequences. At the end of the 1960s prices began to increase; this was a very minor inflation that would probably not have had much impact on world history. But this led to the Tehran Agreement, in which, for the first time, the oil-producing countries agreed on the increase in oil prices. This increase now seems moderate, since it was only 27%, but it paved the way for the quadrupling of oil prices in 1973, which in turn upset world history.

## Note

1 Bairoch, P. and Etemad, B., 'La littérature périodique d'histoire économique, tendances de l'histoire économique contemporaine (1950–1979) et expansion des publications d'histoire économique (1900–1985)', *Annales, E.S.C.*, No. 2, March–April 1987, pp. 369–401.

# 13

# *Some Less Important Myths*

I shall deal here with the following seven myths:

1. Foreign trade is generally considered to be an engine of economic growth; but history shows that this is hardly the case.
2. In many instances the years preceding World War I are described as a period of depression; as a result of more comprehensive data we have now shown that this was certainly not so.
3. The fact that the exports of almost all Third World countries consisted almost entirely of primary goods led to the conclusion that export of primary goods is a road to underdevelopment. The reality is much more complex, since some of today's more developed countries have been major exporters of primary goods in the past.
4. The myth that in the developed world the nineteenth century was a period of rapid economic growth is probably less accepted than ten to twenty years ago. But it is seldom realized how slow this growth really was.
5. A number of studies give a view of the traditional world as being little urbanized. Recent research has demonstrated that this was not the case. In fact for many centuries before the Industrial Revolution the world was three to four times more urbanized than was previously believed.
6. The history of the Third World, which is mainly composed of former European colonies, led to the false belief that Europe was the only major colonial power.
7. Finally we will see that the even more tragic fate of Africans sent to be slaves in European colonies tended to obscure the fact that Europe was not the only or largest slave trader. At least one other slave trade was larger than that of Europe.

## Was trade an engine of economic growth?

In Chapter 4 I suggested that events in the late nineteenth century were a partial proof that economic growth is more an engine of trade than vice versa. In fact, the entire nineteenth century yields similar evidence: economic growth leads to international trade and not vice versa. Let us be more explicit and begin with the first half of the nineteenth century. The data begin to be reasonably valid from 1835 onwards, and from this year until the beginning of the free trade period (1860) the volume of European exports and GNP shows divergent patterns. For the 1836–48 period GNP increased more rapidly than exports, and, despite a relatively strong increase in the growth of exports, the economy slowed down. During the free trade period (1860–92), as we have seen in Chapter 4, the slowing during the 'great European depression' affected economic growth earlier than foreign trade. The same pattern is seen in the recovery period and is even more clearly defined on the level of individual countries.

As far as the inter-war period is concerned, the most important event was the Great Depression of the 1930s which saw also the collapse of international trade. The fact that these two events took place in the same decade can lead us to assume a central importance for the role of international trade. But things are not so simple. In fact, the collapse of international trade accompanied or followed a decline in production at least in the country causing the crisis: the United States. US industrial production had already declined (by over 2%) in October 1929, while during the same month the value of US total exports increased by 20% and the exports of manufactures by 5%. On the world level, according to indices published by the League of Nations, in 1930 there was a 14% decline in the world's (excluding Russia) industrial production. During the same year, the volume of world trade – of which manufactures represented almost 50% – declined by only 7%. For 1931 the comparable figures are −13% for industry and −8% for trade; for 1932, which was the low point, −15% for industry and −13% for trade. However, to a large extent, the fall in world trade, and even more so the fall in prices, preceded the decline in production of primary goods in the Third World. But that is another story, a story of dependence.

If we now pass to the post-World War II period, it is necessary first, to quote Denison's study,[1] which has become a classic, on the factors of the economic growth in the United States and Western Europe from 1950 to 1962. According to this analysis, the impact of trade liberalization in the United States was negligible, while in Western Europe its contribution to a positive growth in production amounted to between 1% and 6%, according to individual countries, with a weighted average of 2% (which means that 98% of growth can be explained by other factors). More recently, Kendrick,[2] investigating a longer period, reaches conclusions that do not differ greatly from those of Denison on the increase of GNP in the United States. On the other hand, Kendrick is extremely sceptical as to the possibility of measuring the various factors of productivity increases at an international level. As far as Japan is concerned, one of the most penetrating studies of the factors of growth was by Ohkawa and Rosovsky.[3] According to these authors, the growth rate of Japanese exports has been high, much higher than the world average because the growth rate of the Japanese economy and industry in particular has been higher, much higher than, on average, the rest of the world and not vice versa. These authors are of the opinion that the most important factor in the increase of exports was not the advantage of low salaries but the possibilities for rapid technological progress, together with, obviously, the flexibility of the workforce. Yes . . . but what would have happened if during the 1950s and the 1960s Japan's industry had been confronted with a large influx of manufactured goods from much more productive and innovative countries?

Of course, this does not exclude the possibility that free trade in the Western world could have contributed significantly to rapid economic growth as a result of competition or even of expected greater competition. Maddison,[4] for instance, stresses the part played by trade liberalization in the growth of the West after World War II. But this does not rule out the converse, because competition can also eliminate certain lines of business without creating new ones. Even if we do not completely eliminate other factors, it must be admitted that lack of research on the negative role of free trade makes such an analysis difficult. This lack can be explained, on the other hand, by existing dogmas on the subject. Indeed, the type of analysis I have described above does not allow one (and does not attempt) to measure the positive effects of more restrictive policies such as those of Japan.

For most Third World countries it appears that here too the trade engine failed. It failed without any doubt during the nineteenth century, when rapid expansion in exports of primary products was more a factor of underdevelopment than of economic growth, and even less of real economic development. For the developed countries in the nineteenth century, as suggested earlier, in most cases economic growth has been an engine of trade and not vice versa. The only major exception among the large countries, which together represented more than 90% of this region's economy, was the United Kingdom during the first half of the nineteenth century. But even in the last decades the story is not much different. In a recent survey entitled *Trade as an Engine of Growth: Theory and Evidence*, James Riedel,[5] gives the following title to his conclusions: 'What is left of the "Trade Engine"?', and states that:

> In fact, there is little left of the assumptions which generated the
> mechanistic conclusions of the theory of the 'trade engine of growth' . . . In
> short, the 'engine' for foodstuffs has no fuel, while there is no fixed gear for
> other products, especially manufactures. The economic relationship be-
> tween developed and developing countries cannot be described meaning-
> fully in simple mechanical terms. The 'stylized facts' that underlie the
> theory of the 'trade engine of growth' turn out on close examination to
> belittle more than myths.

It is obvious that the problems are different for small countries. For
those, international trade plays a much greater role. The fact that exports
represent for them a much higher share of GNP already implies a greater
impact. For example, in 1910, if we limit ourselves to European
developed countries, we see the following approximate shares of exports
in GNP: small countries: Belgium 36%, Denmark 28%, Switzerland
24%; large countries: Germany and France 15%, United Kingdom 17%.
Even if, as a rule, the small European countries experienced a more rapid
economic growth during the nineteenth century, being small was not a
sufficient condition. To cite the most important case: Portugal's performance during the nineteenth century was a very negative one. The rate of
growth of its GNP per capita was probably one of the slowest of all
European countries.[6]

Finally, even if one considers that in small countries, trade can be an
engine of growth, small countries are only a marginal part of the world.
Defining today's small countries as those with less than 10 million
inhabitants, they represent 6% of the developed countries and 5% of the
Third World.

## *Did a depression precede World War I?*

This is a fallacy mainly, but not only, present in Marxist literature. A false
analogy is also sometimes made with the period preceding World War II,
in which indeed, as we saw in Chapter 1, many countries were
characterized by depression. The situation was very different in the years
preceding World War I. Let us consider the facts.

The first important fact is that the medium-term period preceding
World War I (1900–13) was one of the best ever recorded. As we saw in
Table 1.1, world per capita economic growth during the 1900–13 period
reached 1.5% compared to 1.2% for 1890–1900 and 0.5% for 1830–90.
However, in the developed countries, the 1890–1900 period saw a slightly
higher rate of economic growth, but this was due largely to a slower

population growth (1.1% per year for 1890–1900 and 1.3% for 1900–13). Therefore, in terms of overall economic growth, the 1900–13 period was better than the preceding one and the best up to that time.

What I have said about medium-term economic growth also holds true for industrial production and international trade, so let us now pass to the years just preceding 1914. In Europe, if 1910 can be regarded as a recession year, 1911, 1912 and 1913 were very good ones, with a total annual economic growth around 5%. In the United States, which is less relevant since the war broke out in Europe, these years were even better especially since there was no recession in 1910.[7]

Let us see now what happened in industry, for which the figures are less comparable on the international level than those of GNP. For the whole of Europe, the annual growth rate for the 1910–13 period was 5.2% compared to 3.3% for 1900–10, 3.6% for 1890–1900 and 2.2% for 1830–90. If 1913 was not the best year of the 1910–13 period, it was far from being a poor one, since the growth rate was 3%.

For the three main countries involved in World War I (France, Germany and the United Kingdom) the years immediately preceding the war, as well as the entire 1900–13 period, were very favourable. As far as economic growth is concerned, for each of those countries the 1909–13 period probably represented the best four years until then. Except in France, where 1913 was characterized by slow growth, this was a very good year, one of the best of the century (4.5% annual total growth in Germany; 3.4% in the United Kingdom, but 0.6% in France). France's poor performance was due entirely to a 3.1% decline in the volume of agricultural production.

Finally, let us deal with trade, which perhaps provides the greatest deflation of the myth of a depression preceding World War I, implying that the need for conquest of other countries and acquisition of their markets plays a major role. The volume of European exports increased in the 1910–13 period at an annual rate of 4.7% (5% in 1913) compared to 4.3% for 1900–10 and 2% for 1890–1900. As we saw in Chapter 4, the decades preceding 1890 were very negative.

Therefore World War I, unlike World War II, began during a phase of rapid economic expansion. The same was true for the major Western war in the nineteenth century, the Franco-Prussian War of 1870. The 1859–69 decade was the best since then in terms of both economic growth and international trade.

Furthermore, it is obvious that the two World Wars had very important long-term political and short-term economic consequences. The long-term economic consequences were, however, not simple. What political scientists dealing with the type of consequences, especially Organsky and Kugler,[8] have called the 'Phoenix effect' appears to be very valid. After the war the countries that lost it regained over ten to fifteen years their former economic power and international ranking. This does not contradict the fact that during the two and a half centuries of 'modern economic growth', to use Simon Kuznets' definition,[9] there has been a slow but important process of upheaval in the world's economic rank ordering. The most striking examples are the two most important countries of the Anglo-Saxon world: the decline of the United Kingdom and the rise of the United States.

## Are exports of primary goods a road to underdevelopment?

The origin of this myth is very simple. Since all Third World countries are (and, more so, were) primary goods exporters and most developed countries export manufactured goods, there must be a causal link between these two characteristics. Even if the export structure is more a consequence than a cause of economic underdevelopment, the emphasis is correctly put on the fact that very often, especially in the nineteenth century, in the Third World the interests of primary goods exporters dictated a country's economic policy. So the myth gradually took shape.

The reality is much more complex. The most important fact is that, on the eve of World War I, among the eight to nine richest countries in the world, five were exporters of primary goods, and one of those five countries was then, as today, the most developed in the world: the United States. Indeed, during the nineteenth century not only were more than two-thirds of that country's exports composed of primary goods, but a large share of these were raw materials, principally cotton. In the 1821–60 period US raw cotton exports provided almost three-quarters of Europe's needs.

The other rich primary goods exporters were Australia, Canada, Denmark and New Zealand. In these countries, as for the United States, not only were primary goods exported but also raw materials. After the 1850s New Zealand's and especially Australia's wool accounted for a large share of European imports of this fibre. In the first half of the nineteenth century Canada was an important supplier of timber to the United Kingdom. At the turn of the century, in addition to timber, Canada became a major exporter of nickel, asbestos and corundum. At that time and up to the 1920s manufactures represented less than 10% of total exports (for Australia and New Zealand this share was even smaller). Denmark concentrated on food exports and after the 1860s moved from cereals to butter, cheese and bacon. Agricultural products represented over 90% of Denmark's exports.

Since history does not end with World War I, I have to add the following note to this section. Practically all those primary exporting countries which are today also rich countries had already initiated in the nineteenth century an industrialization policy through protectionist measures. The only exception was New Zealand, which even today has few industries apart from those linked to agricultural exports. As we have seen (Chapter 3), such a policy reorientation was very early in the case of the United States (at independence) and rather late for Canada and Australia (last quarter of the nineteenth century). In the case of Denmark it was even later (the 1890s), and the protectionist moves were less comprehensive.

Therefore there is no doubt that specializing in exports of primary goods does not by itself lead to underdevelopment. It can result in a high standard of living providing that the export sector as well as the rest of the economy increases its productivity, which has been the case in all the countries mentioned above. However, at a certain stage, industrialization becomes an almost necessary option to achieve a higher level of development. Even if this is only a marginal proof, it is worth noting that New Zealand (the least industrialized of the five countries), which was around 1880 the sixth- to eighth-richest country in the world, in 1990 declined to the eighteenth to twentieth (even excluding the rich oil-exporting countries).

Another interesting case is that of Argentina, which, as a result of its large exports of agricultural products, was the tenth- to fifteenth-richest country in the world by 1910. The combined effects of a slow growth in its agricultural productivity and the limited level of industrialization led to a sharp decline in its relative position. By 1990, Argentina had declined to the forty-fourth–forty-ninth rank. A still better proof of the positive impact of industrialization is found in the fact that all the countries that chose to industrialize became rich as opposed to those specializing in exporting primary goods. To summarize: if exporting primary goods was not always a road to underdevelopment, the best road to development was industrialization.

## Was there rapid economic growth in the nineteenth century?

As mentioned in the general introduction, this was the subject of my second published paper, which appeared in 1962. There are numerous reasons for such a myth. The most important are related to the fact that the first stages of modern economic growth have been described by superlatives: 'Industrial Revolution', 'Take-off', 'The Unbound Prometheus'.[10] Indeed, I would be the last to deny the significant character of this fundamental turning point in history.

Further, there is no doubt that, compared to preceding centuries, the rate of economic growth achieved during the nineteenth century represented a large step forward. Even if we limit ourselves to Europe, which between 1500 and 1800 was on an upward trend, the annual rate of per capita growth was certainly below 0.2% and probably even below 0.1%. Compared to this, the 0.9–1.0% growth of the nineteenth century can unquestionably be described as rapid. But for the economists of the 1960s or 1980s even a 2.5% growth was considered to be slow. It is significant that the objective retained by United Nations experts for the 'first development decade' (the 1960s) was a total growth rate of 6%, which implied a per capita growth of over 4%.

This leads us to a further example of the implicit dangers of myths. If nineteenth-century economic growth had been indeed rapid, it implies the possibility of such a growth in the first stages of economic development. Had we fully understood the historical reality of the nineteenth century in relation to economic growth in the twentieth, the disappointment would have been less after the first development decade, during which the Third World economic per capita growth was of the order of 2%. More important is the fact that the realization that growth was slow at the beginning of the take-off would have perhaps led to earlier and stronger measures to slow down population growth.

## Was the traditional world little urbanized?

One of the major findings arising from research on urbanization undertaken over the last 20 years has been a radical change in our understanding of the importance of towns in traditional societies. This also provides an interesting example of the ways in which, in some cases, thinking about post-industrial society can influence negatively the study of pre-industrial societies and can create a myth. In fact, between the mid-1960s and the mid-1970s the only estimate of the scale of urbanization on the eve of the Industrial Revolution derived from the work of Kingsley Davis, a specialist in contemporary urbanization and Third World urban problems. Davis's study was written in the mid-1950s and, although never published, was frequently cited in subsequent research, not least in that of Hauser, the eminent Chicago geographer.[11] Davis's study was written in collaboration with H. Hertz and concluded that the urban population represented less than 3% of world population in 1800. This date provides a good base for measuring levels of urbanization prior to industrialization since, at that time, Great Britain was the only country undergoing the Industrial Revolution yet it represented less than 1% of world population. Davis used the same estimates in two essays that appeared in 1965, one of which was published in *Scientific American*.[12]

For historians of the contemporary period, reliable estimates on urbanization start with 1850–60 and indicate with reasonable accuracy that between 1850 and 1910 the level of urbanization in Europe rose from less than 15% to 32%. Backward interpolation suggests a level of urbanization of about 7–8% in 1800. Since the data were derived mainly from the larger cities, which grew fastest, it was suggested that this '1800 point of departure' of Europe should probably be reduced further. Furthermore, it was 'reasonable' (although in fact quite inaccurate) to expect that the rest of the world was much less urbanized than Europe, and therefore the proposed '3%' could be seen as a reasonable estimate of the percentage of the world's urban population in 1800.

After their appearance, Davis's figures were repeated by many other researchers who were looking for a point of reference and who, as a result, were led into drawing totally incorrect conclusions about the importance of urbanization in many traditional societies. It was not until 1974 that a more correct figure appeared in a book by Doxiadis, an expert on urban planning, which few historians or geographers read. Doxiadis suggested that for 1800 the world's level of urbanization was 6.2%, but this figure was not really documented or considered by any historian or geographer. Nor did two other estimates published in 1977 attract much attention. The first was Grauman's calculation that, on the basis of the data collected by Chandler and Fox, the level of urbanization (for the world in 1800) was between 5.0% and 5.5%; the second was my own estimate: 7.9% with a margin of error of minus or plus 12%.[13]

Let us now see what was probably the real level of world urbanization around 1800. The new estimates we now have at our disposal are based on extensive historical data banks of individual cities' populations, and on an increasing number of studies of specific countries. The data banks have benefited from the research into demographic history, which has expanded rapidly over the last 30 years. These new estimates suggest that the level of urbanization in the pre-industrial world was at least three and probably four times higher than the earlier '3%' estimates had indicated. Taking settlements with more than 5,000 inhabitants to define an urban population results in a rate of urbanization between 9% and 11%; for settlements with over 2,000 inhabitants, a rate of between 13% and 16%. This is valid not only for the world in 1800 but also much earlier than that. It appears, in fact, that one may, without too much trepidation, formulate the following rule: in any society with normal geographic characteristics, some 1,000 to 1,500 years after the appearance of the first city, urbanization reaches a level close to the maximum possible in the framework of traditional societies, a maximum somewhere around 10–15%.

The exceptions lie in regions subject to climatic extremes, especially of cold, and in very mountainous areas. Since such regions are, as a rule, thinly populated, the level of urbanization in the world as a whole approached the maximum possible in the framework of traditional societies very early in its history.[14]

Certainly, a 9–11% level of urbanization seems very low compared to that which will lead to industrialization. In Britain, as early as 1880, 56% of the population were city dwellers. The 1990 level of urbanization in developed countries was of the order of 68%; even for the Third World it was 36%. However, an average level of urbanization of traditional societies of 9–11% puts world history into a completely different perspective and allows us to correct important conclusions about the importance of urbanization in many traditional societies. Even a scholar as well informed and subtle as the late Moses Finley[15] could write in the framework of his explanation of the important role that cities had played in Graeco-Roman civilization that: 'The Graeco-Roman world was more urbanized than any other society before the modern era.' His error was not that he had overestimated the level of information available on the Graeco-Roman world but that he had used the low figures then accepted by all academics.

Change the millennium and the continent and much the same could be said of Rozman, of Hanley and Yamamura, and, above all, of Kornhauser, all of whom claimed that in the seventeenth and eighteenth centuries Japan was the most urbanized civilization in the world. While it is true that Japanese society was highly urbanized, with about 11–14% of the population living in towns with over 5,000 inhabitants, this was in fact much the same level as in pre-industrial Europe. In order to absolve (if this is needed) those good historians let us cite the geographer, Dwyer, who in the introduction to a collection of essays published in 1974 referred directly to Davis's figures of 3% urbanization in 1800 to argue that before the Industrial Revolution there were 'relatively few' towns.[16] Taking into account the accepted figure for 1800 could his conclusion be different?

## Was the West the only major colonizer?

Although this is seldom expressed in such straightforward terms, the extensive literature on underdevelopment unquestionably gives the impression that colonization was initiated by Europe. The reality is quite different. In fact, if one exaggerates a little, we can say that world history is almost synonymous with the history of colonialism. Also, even if colonialism is defined in terms of the main negative aspects of European colonization, the European case has numerous historical precedents. The following summarizes the major negative aspects of European (or other forms) of colonization:

1. An attempt to impose by persuasion or by force (or by a combination of the two) the civilization of the colonial power on the inhabitants of colonies; the term 'civilization' here means religion and language;
2. The introduction of a set of rules that subordinates the economic and political interests of the colonies to that of the colonial power;
3. Discrimination based on race, origin or religion against the inhabitants of the colonies and in favour of those of the colonial power.

Although the history of non-European colonization remains largely to be written, there is no doubt that it had the same negative elements as Europe from the sixteenth to the twentieth centuries. Furthermore, those colonizations in many cases lasted as long, or even longer, than that of Europe. Let us mention the duration of a few of those colonial empires: the Egyptian Empire, five centuries (from the sixteenth to the eleventh centuries BC); the Persian Empire, three centuries (from the seventh to the fourth centuries BC); the Roman Empire, four centuries (from the first century BC to the fourth century AD). Further away from Europe the Chinese and Mongolian Empires as well as those of pre-Columbian America must be mentioned. Coming closer to the contemporary period, one should not forget the Arab and Ottoman Empires, which colonized parts of Europe for much longer than Europe colonized the Middle East.

The fact that all these empires did not expand beyond a certain size is not attributable to a lack of colonial appetite but to the military and economic constraints of that period, which set limits on the extent of the largest empire (see Chapter 7). But this does not imply that the non-European colonial empires were small, especially in relative terms. We have seen in Chapter 7 (Table 7.2) that even at its peak (on the eve of World War I) Europe's colonial empire had a population 1.4 times that of Europe (excluding Russia). The Ottoman Empire in the eighteenth century had a population 2.5–3 times that of Turkey proper, and a much higher ratio was reached by the Roman Empire. An important reservation should, however, be made: the intensity of economic relations between the colonial powers and their colonies was much more limited than those of European colonization after the Industrial Revolution. However, these more limited economic relations did not prevent colonial domination from disrupting pre-existing local cultures and forms of social organization.

Seen from the cultural angle, the picture of a colonization process was, and still is, radically different, depending on how it is viewed. For example, the expansion of the Muslim or Christian cultures can be considered either as the progress of civilization or as colonization, depending on the observer's cultural background. Historically, many contributions to the wide spectrum of civilization are after-effects of colonizations; this, however, was not a one-way process, since in many cases the colonial power also profited from its colonies. There is, however, a probability that the negative aspects of European colonization on pre-Columbian America before the Industrial Revolution were more severe than those of most of the other traditional colonization processes; a probability, but not a certainty, since the compilation of balance sheets in this field is made difficult by the almost total lack of studies on the effects of non-European colonization as against a profusion of studies on European colonization. This profusion implies, *ipso facto*, a wide range of points of view, from underestimation to overestimation of the negative aspects.

## Was the West the major slave trader?

Finally, one of the most negative stigmas of European colonization, the African slave trade, was unfortunately also not unique in its large scale, even if this is often assumed to be the case. Before dealing with this myth, let us recall that the word 'slave' (used not only in English but in almost all European languages) comes from the word 'Slav' (reflecting the fact that the Slavonic races were frequently conquered and enslaved in the Middle Ages).

First, let us see how important was the European slave trade in Africans, a trade that lasted for more than three centuries. The first shipment of slaves to America started in the first decades of the sixteenth century, were greatly reduced after 1815 and became very small after 1870. According to the most recent data,[17] the number of African slaves that reached their destinations amounted to 9.5–10 million, with some 6 million during the eighteenth century alone. But if an estimate is made of the number of slaves that were taken out of Africa, the number is higher, since casualties during transportation were high. Incidentally, it should be noted that the casualty rates of European sailors were probably higher than those of slaves: the replacement cost of sailors being lower! Even the average life expectancy of Europeans living in many areas of Africa in the sixteenth and seventeenth centuries was very low due to health hazards: no more than 3–4 years! If the losses due to transportation are taken into account, the total number of slaves shipped from black Africa to European colonies or European settlements was of the order of 11–11.5

million during the entire European slave trade period.

The Islamic slave trade is certainly not unknown, but it has generally been grossly underestimated, even by Africans. As the French historian Marc Ferro notes in analysing history textbooks, from the moment the subject concerns the Islamic world 'the hand of the [African] historian begins to shake.'[18] Compared to the European slave trade, that conducted by the Islamic world started earlier, lasted longer and, crucially, involved a larger number of slaves. It began in the seventh century and lasted to the end of the nineteenth. For this whole period, the transport of people from sub-Saharan Africa to the Muslim world totalled 14–15 million, of which some 8–8.5 million were from 1500 to 1890. Thus the number of slaves shipped from sub-Saharan Africa to the Muslim world and to the European colonies may have been of the order of 25–6 million. Taking only the period during which the flows to the Muslim world and to the European colonies ran concurrently, that is, from 1500 to 1880–90, the total was 19–20 million. All this does not include casualties due to slave wars.

There are now fewer descendants of slaves in the Islamic world than in Christian America. This is due to the fact that a great number destined for the Islamic world were castrated. Furthermore, their mortality was high and their birth rate low. In fact, the 'visible' descendants of those slaves can be estimated at only a few million in the Middle East (including North Africa), whereas in America their number is approximately 70 million.

If the Western and Islamic slave trades were probably the two most important in world history, they were certainly not the only ones. I wrote at the beginning of the previous section that if one exaggerates a little, we can say that the word 'history' is almost synonymous with 'colonial history'. It is even less of an exaggeration to claim that all colonial histories (before the middle of the nineteenth century) were also histories of slavery. Colonizations and many wars had as a major motive the acquisition of slaves. The only fact that made the European slave trade so important is that it was the last in a very long series and it became the last because the West decided, and had the power, to stop large-scale international trade in slaves.

We have now concluded our survey of the seven less important myths which complement the thirteen previously described. All these myths are quite different, even if they can be assembled into three or four groups. This means that a concluding paragraph can only stress the large number of economic myths in world history; indeed, without being exhaustive we have presented, in all, twenty myths. It is, however, true that especially with the myth on slaves, I have perhaps stretched too much the domain of economics. But, all things considered, slavery had an economic motivation and also very important economic consequences. The generally unnoticed important historical turning points which we will now describe concern more strictly economic matters and I will then give more general conclusions.

## Notes

1 Denison, E. F., *Why Growth Rates Differ*, Washington, 1967.
2 Kendrick, J. W., 'Why productivity growth rates change and differ', in Giersch, H., (ed.), *Toward an Explanation of Economic Growth*, Tübingen, 1981, pp. 111–40.
3 Ohkawa, K. and Rosovsky, H., *Japanese Economic Growth. Trend Acceleration in the Twentieth Century*, Stanford, 1973, p. 17.
4 Maddison, A., *Les phases du développement capitaliste*, Paris, 1981.
5 Riedel, J., 'Trade as an engine of growth: theory and evidence', in Greenaway, D. (ed.), *Economic Development and International Trade*, London, 1988, pp. 25–54.
6 Bairoch, P., *Commerce extérieur et développement économique de l'Europe au XIXe siècle*, Paris, 1976, pp. 266–70. See also Nunes, A. B., Mata, E. and Valerio, N., 'Portugese economic growth 1833–1985', *The Journal of European Economic History*, **18**, No. 2, 1989, pp. 291–330.
7 The data presented here are based on the following sources. For individual countries: Deane, P., 'New estimates of Gross National Product for the United Kingdom 1830–1914', *Review of Income and Wealth*, No. 2, June 1968, pp. 95–112; Hoffmann, W. G. (with the collaboration of Grumbach, F. and de Hesse, H.), *Das Wachstum der Deutschen Wirtschaft seit der Mitte des 19. Jehrhunderts*, Berlin, 1965; Toutain, J.-C., 'Le produit intérieur brut de la France de 1789 à 1982 (Economies et sociétés)', *Cahiers de l'I.S.M.E.A.* Série AF, No. 15, 1987; US Bureau of Economic Analysis, *Long-Term Economic Growth, 1860–1970*, Washington, 1973. For European data: Bairoch, P., 'Europe's Gross National Product, 1800–1975', *The Journal of European Economic History*, **5**, No. 2, Rome, 1976, pp. 273–340; Bairoch, P., *Commerce extérieur et développement économique de l'Europe au XIXe siècle*, Paris, 1976.
8 Organsky, A. F. K. O. and Kugler, J., *The War Ledger*, Chicago, 1980.
9 Kuznets, S., *Modern Economic Growth*, New Haven, 1966.
10 The term 'Industrial Revolution' was apparently first used by Arnold Toynbee (the uncle of the author of *A Study of History*, Arnold J. Toynbee), in 1884, in a book titled *Lectures on the Industrial Revolution in England*. The term 'Take-Off' was coined by W. W. Rostow in 1960 in his book *The Stages of Economic Growth* and *The Unbound Prometheus* is the title of David Landes's book published in 1964.
11 Hauser, P. M. (ed.), *Urbanization in Asia and the Far East*, UNESCO, Calcutta, 1957, pp. 55–6.
12 Davis, K., 'Urbanization of human population', *Scientific American*, **213**, No. 3, 1965, pp. 41–53; Davis, K., 'The origins and growth of urbanization in the world', *American Journal of Sociology*, **LX**, No. 5, 1965, pp. 429–37.
13 Doxiadis, C. A. and Papaioannou, J. G., *Ecumenopolis, The Inevitable City of the Future*, Athens, 1974, p. 405; Grauman, J. V., 'Orders of magnitude of

the world's urban population in History', *Population Bulletin of the United Nations*, No. 8, 1976, New York, pp. 16–33; Chandler, T. and Fox, G., *3000 Years of Urban Growth*, New York, 1974; Bairoch, P., *Taille des villes, conditions de vie et développement économique*, Paris, 1977, p. 27.

14  For more details see Bairoch, P., *Cities and Economic Development from the Dawn of History to the Present*, Chicago, 1988. For Europe see Vries, J. de, *European Urbanization, 1500–1800*, London, 1984; and Bairoch, P., Batou, J. and Chèvre, P., *The Population of European Cities, 800–1850: Data Bank and Short Summary of Results*, Geneva, 1988.

15  Finley, M. I., 'The ancient city: from Fustel de Coulanges to Max Weber and beyond', *Comparatives Studies in Society and History*, **19**, 1977, pp. 305–27.

16  Rozman, G., *Urban Network in Ch'ing China and Tokugawa Japan*, Princeton, 1973; Hanley, S. B. and Yamamura, K., *Economic and Demographic Change in Preindustrial Japan, 1600–1868*, Princeton, 1977; Kornhauser, D., *Urban Japan: its Foundations and Growth*, London and New York, 1976; Dwyer, D. J. (ed.), *The City in the Third World*, London, 1974.

17  For a recent short summary of this problem see Etemad, B., 'L'ampleur de la traité négrière (VII–XIXe siècles: un état de la question', *Bulletin du Département d'Histoire Economique*, University of Geneva, No. 20, 1989–90, pp. 43–6.

18  Ferro, M., *Comment on enseigne l'histoire aux enfants*, Paris, 1981, p. 41.

$$\overline{14}$$

# Generally Unnoticed
# Historical Turning Points

In the introduction to this part of the book I noted that ignoring some unnoticed historical turning points can be as misleading as myths. Let us give one example. To ignore the fact that during the past half of a century the rate of increase in agricultural productivity in Western developed countries has been almost twice as rapid as in manufacturing can lead to a wrong interpretation of economic events, such as negative evolution in the terms of trade of Western agricultural products. In fact, the belief that gains in productivity in manufacturing were more rapid than in agriculture can be described as a myth. Since I gave the example of productivity, let us begin with this.

## *A reversal in the comparative rate of growth in productivity in industry and agriculture*

The physical and climatic constraints on human activity have from the dawn of history led to a slower growth in agricultural productivity compared to industry. The varying types of land, climatic differences, and the limited contact between agricultural workers and rural populations in general, all contrast strongly with urban-based industrial activities. With the Industrial Revolution the gap in productivity between agriculture and industry widened even further. Although agricultural productivity began to increase much more rapidly after the Industrial Revolution, it was, nevertheless, for more than two centuries, much slower than that of manufacturing.

Before proceeding further, it is worth considering the concept of

150

agricultural productivity. There is always a risk of confusion when one speaks of agricultural productivity, since, in some cases, this term is used in place of 'yields'. For this reason, it is common to add the term 'labour' (productivity) for what is, strictly, productivity and the term 'land' (productivity) for yields. The distinction is a very important one, since there is no necessary link between these two concepts. Both historically and geographically, there can even be a contradictory evolution of these two important aspects of agriculture. Let us give two examples. In nineteenth-century Europe there was an increase in both yields and productivity, while in the United States yields, especially of cereals, remained stable while productivity increased even more rapidly than in Europe. In the 1930s cereal yields in many Third World economies were higher than in most of the advanced industrial countries, while in the latter the level of productivity was some five to ten times higher.

Now let us return to the comparative rate of growth in productivity of the two sectors. If, for the sake of better comparisons, we limit ourselves to the Western developed countries, between 1850 and 1950 productivity increased annually by 1.8–2% in industry compared to 1.1–1.3% in agriculture. But between 1950 and 1990 this increase was 3.4–3.6% in industry and 5.4–5.6% in agriculture.[1] The turning point came earlier in the United States than in Europe: in the United States it had started at the end of the 1930s, whereas in Europe it began with the 1950s. As can be deduced from the above-quoted figures, this reversal was mainly due to the more rapid increase in the growth of agricultural productivity. The total increase in the Western world's agricultural productivity over the last 40 years has been greater than during the preceding 900 years.

This new trend in productivity has very far-reaching consequences and allows us to interpret some evolutions more correctly. Let us take the second point first. Farmers in Western countries often complain that their terms of trade are deteriorating; for example, they need to sell increasingly more wheat to buy the same type of tractor. This is, if not inevitable, at least a normal trend, since their productivity has increased more rapidly than that of machinery manufacturers. The very rapid decline in the agricultural workforce, which is a factor in productivity growth, is also a consequence, since food consumption cannot, for physiological reasons, increase as rapidly. The more rapid decrease in the share of food in consumers' expenditure is also explained by the turning points. Among the major consequences of the large increase in agricultural productivity is a rapid rise in production, leading in Western Europe to the disappearance of imports of cereals. This also meant a turning point, since from the 1860s to 1983 Western Europe was a large net importer of cereals. As late as 1961/5 Western Europe had an annual cereal deficit of 30 million tons, compared to an annual excess of 22 million tons for 1986/90. As other Western countries were net cereal exporters this created a production surplus throughout the Western world. It also had consequences for the rest of the world, both in the Third World and in developed countries in the East. These consequences are related to the other two turning points concerning the Third World which we will now consider, and to the turning point of the East, as we shall see later.

## *The Third World has become a net importer of food and almost a net importer of agricultural products*

In what can be called the traditional phase of colonialism, i.e. that preceding the Industrial Revolution, the trade of the future Third World was already characterized by a large surplus of exports in agricultural products. This was certainly the case in Latin America from the sixteenth century onwards, whose exports (if we exclude precious metals) were almost entirely tropical agricultural products and whose imports almost entirely manufactured goods. The same is true of the limited flow of trade that Europe had with Africa. As far as Asia is concerned, the situation was quite different since, in addition to tropical products, this region also exported large quantities of manufactured goods, especially textiles. But as most of the exports of the future Third World came from Latin America, in total terms, exports of agricultural products far exceeded their imports. Around 1800 Asian exports still had more or less the same product export structure as before, and we can conclude from the reliable figures that exist for total exports and from plausible estimates for product distribution that exports of agricultural products from the future Third World probably exceeded their imports by 120–180%.

For the nineteenth century we have reasonably good figures as far as exports are concerned.[2] Nevertheless, to determine the Third World's ratio of exported to imported agricultural goods we must engage in some statistical detective work, deducing the number from incomplete data. From these, it appears that agricultural products represented, for the 1830–1913 period, the very stable and high share of total exports of 82–3%. In imports, for which figures are much less reliable, it can be estimated that less than 10% were of agricultural origin from developed countries and 80–85% for those originating from other Third World regions. Since during this period the Third World's total exports were 5–10% higher than its total imports, this means that exports of agricultural products exceeded agricultural imports by 175–200%.

We have relatively good figures for the inter-war period and very good ones for after World War II. For obvious reasons, I will restrict my analysis to the Third World market economies, excluding Argentina. During the inter-war period and probably until the end of the 1940s, the Third World's agricultural trade surplus was in the order of 190% (see Table 14.1) or, in other words, almost three times more exports than imports, as in the nineteenth century.

Despite the fact that some exports of cereals from Western developed countries to the Third World were food aid (less than a fifth of cereal imports), the value of Third World imports of agricultural products increased very rapidly from the mid-1950s onwards. On the other hand, the growth of agricultural exports from the Third World slowed down. The rapid increase in oil prices in the 1970s reinforced both the growing trend of imports of cereals and the slowing down of exports of agricultural products. Indeed, as a result of the very large increase in oil revenues, almost all oil-exporting countries experienced a rapid acceleration of a pre-existing trend: the substitution of local food production by imports. All this led to a gradual disappearance of the favourable trade balance. By 1969–71, agricultural exports were only 67% ahead of similar imports. The 1970s saw a further rapid deterioration: the trade surplus fell to only 7% for 1979/81, and this trade surplus disappeared almost totally at the beginning of the 1980s. For the 1981/4 period there was even a deficit of the order of 7%, and after four years of more balanced trade the deficit appeared again from 1989 onwards. But even a balanced trade represents an important turning point compared to the huge export excess that was the rule for centuries.

As is almost always the case, there are wide regional (and country) differences in this evolution and Table 14.1 provides a very good illustration of this. The evolution was very negative in Africa and West Asia (i.e. the Middle East). In the latter region, at least there were oil resources to compensate for declining agricultural exports, while in Africa this evolution is a good illustration of this continent's difficult situation.

Since food represented a very large share of agricultural exports (for example, 48% for 1911–13) and a marginal share of imports, the Third World also traditionally had a very large trade surplus of food products. In 1955, for the Third World countries (excluding Argentina), this trade surplus was 115% (or more than twice as many exports as imports). But this represented a deteriorating situation since, in the inter-war period, the excess was of the order of 150%. In 1970 this surplus fell to 12%. It is in 1973 that, for the first time in over two hundred years, there was a deficit. If we take into account the fact that import values include transport and other related costs, which is not the case for

**Table 14.1** Trade in total agricultural products of Third World market economies, excluding Argentina, 1928–1988/90 (year or annual average; billions of current dollars)

| | | | Trade balance in: | |
|---|---|---|---|---|
| | Imports | Exports | $ billion | Imports (%) |
| **Total** | | | | |
| 1928 | 2.10 | 5.90 | 3.80 | 180 |
| 1937 | 1.60 | 4.80 | 3.20 | 200 |
| 1955 | 5.04 | 12.71 | 7.67 | 152 |
| 1965 | 8.00 | 15.02 | 7.02 | 89 |
| 1969/71 | 9.40 | 15.87 | 6.47 | 69 |
| 1974/6 | 27.01 | 35.65 | 8.64 | 32 |
| 1979/81 | 56.85 | 59.66 | 2.81 | 7 |
| 1984/6 | 56.36 | 58.02 | 1.66 | 3 |
| 1988/90 | 77.48 | 74.48 | −3.00 | −4 |
| **Of which:** | | | | |
| Africa | | | | |
| 1955 | 1.02 | 3.21 | 2.19 | 115 |
| 1969/71 | 1.96 | 4.49 | 2.54 | 130 |
| 1979/81 | 13.84 | 11.14 | −2.70 | −20 |
| 1988/90 | 14.60 | 10.27 | −4.33 | −30 |
| Latin America[a] | | | | |
| 1955 | 1.37 | 4.39 | 3.03 | 221 |
| 1969/71 | 2.30 | 5.86 | 3.56 | 155 |
| 1979/81 | 12.59 | 25.24 | 12.65 | 100 |
| 1988/90 | 12.75 | 27.33 | 14.58 | 114 |
| West Asia | | | | |
| 1955 | 0.51 | 0.39 | −0.12 | 24 |
| 1969/71 | 1.23 | 1.05 | −0.19 | −15 |
| 1979/81 | 13.88 | 3.95 | −9.94 | −71 |
| 1988/90 | 16.40 | 5.67 | −10.73 | −65 |
| Rest of Asia | | | | |
| 1955 | 2.15 | 4.67 | 2.53 | 118 |
| 1969/71 | 3.86 | 4.30 | 0.44 | 11 |
| 1979/81 | 15.82 | 18.62 | 2.87 | 18 |
| 1988/90 | 32.84 | 30.00 | −2.84 | −9 |

[a] Argentina excluded.

*Sources:* Author's calculations derived from:
For 1928 and 1937: League of Nations, *The Network of World Trade*, Geneva, 1942; and Bairoch, P. and Etemad, B., *Commodity Structure of Third World Exports, 1830–1937*, Geneva, 1985.
For 1955 and 1965: United Nations, *Unctad Handbook of International Trade and Development Statistics*, New York, various issues; and FAO, *Trade Yearbook*, Rome, various issues.
For 1969/71 and after: FAO, *Trade Yearbook*, Rome, various issues.
The data for the different periods are not strictly comparable, but the differences are small.

exports, we must subtract 9–11% of the value of imports to make the figures more comparable. On this basis, the first deficit year was 1975. By 1981–3 the (uncorrected) deficit reached 35%, and after 1984 the situation improved a little, but there was still a 23% deficit for 1988–90.

It is worth noting that in physical terms or, if one prefers, in terms of calorific value, the deficit is much larger than the above-quoted figures. This results from the fact that, among imports into the Third World, cereals predominate, whose price per calorie is low, whereas in exports products predominate whose prices per calorie are high (fruit, cocoa, etc.).

### The case of oils and fats and of sugar

The turning point in agricultural trade was accompanied by more minor ones for some tropical agricultural products. Among those the most significant is the reversal of the trade balance in oils and fats for Africa, one of the main export regions, and the near-disappearance of the net oils and fats export surplus, as well as that for sugar, for the Third World market economies taken as a whole. Let us consider these two cases.

The important role of the Third World as a producer of edible oil seeds began in the middle of the nineteenth century, when demand in the developed countries began to increase sharply as a result of higher standards of living and new techniques, leading to an increase in the use of tropical oilseeds. From the beginning of the twentieth century Africa took an increasing share in the export of these products. Around 1937, this continent, which then represented 12% of the Third World's population, provided 32% of oil seeds. This increased further in the post-war period. In terms of oil equivalent, the net export of African vegetable oil products was still 1,390,000 tons for 1966. This diminished to 210,000 tons in 1975. Apparently, the first deficit year was 1979. For 1979–81 the annual trade deficit was 800,000 tons and reached 1,300,000 tons annually for 1984/8 and more than 1,400,000 tons for 1989/90. Even if we limit discussion to black Africa there was a deficit for 1989/90 of the order of 75,000 tons.

Let us now see the evolution for the whole of the Third World market economies. In 1934/8 this region's annual net exports of those oil products amounted to 3.4 million tons (of oil equivalent) or 46–50% of Third World production. By 1984/8, as we saw in Chapter 11 (Table 11.1), this trade surplus was reduced to 8% of production. The situation would have been much worse if Malaysia had not become a major exporter within a very short period. Malaysia's net output of those products rose from less than 0.5 million tons in 1970 to over 6 million tons in 1990. Therefore without Malaysia the Third World would have a global deficit.

From the beginning of the seventeenth century to the end of the nineteenth, sugar was by far the most important Third World agricultural export. As mentioned in Chapter 10, beet sugar, whose production began at the start of the nineteenth century, was the first important agricultural product from developed countries to challenge the Third World's dominant position for a primary good. But since the demand for sugar rose so quickly, the volume of net exports of this product from the Third World continued to increase until 1967–8, when it reached 12.5 million tons compared to 0.2 million tons for 1790 and 7.5 million tons for 1909–13. But recently the volume of net exports has fallen rapidly from 12.4 million tons in 1968–72 to 4 million tons for 1986–90.

Therefore globally the Third World's international trade in agricultural products has suffered a considerable reversal in recent years. This implies that the Third World's large cereal dependency is no longer counter-balanced by the developed countries' reliance on some of the most important traditional export crops originating from the Third World. This in turn implies an additional risk of an indiscriminate use of what some have called the 'food weapon'.

## The production costs of food become cheaper in the developed Western world than in the Third World

I noted above that the rapid increase in food imports in the Third World is related to the significant rise in agricultural productivity that has characterized Western agriculture since the early 1950s. This had, among other things, two important consequences, the first being the large availability of food products, the other the total reversal of relative production costs.

In the early 1950s, as was probably also the case during most of the preceding century, despite the fact that agricultural productivity was higher in the Western world, its agricultural production costs were greater due to higher labour costs. Around 1950 agricultural wages in the Western developed countries were fifteen to twenty times higher than those in the Third World economies. Since productivity was some seven times higher, this means very roughly, that production costs in the developed countries were two or three times higher than in the Third World. Around 1985 salaries in the Western developed countries were some twenty-two to twenty-eight times higher, but since the level of productivity was then thirty-six times higher, production costs in the Third World were 1.2–1.6 times higher than in the developed countries. The turning point must have taken place between 1972 and 1978.[3]

Such a situation explains the success of the drive for external markets for Western agricultural products and will certainly lead in the future to an emphasis on this drive. The real price of food, especially cereals, in international markets has declined since the mid-1950s. For example, the price of wheat in real terms declined by at least 57% between 1955/9 and 1985/9.[4] The Third World was and will continue to be the major outlet for cheaper Western agricultural products, probably leading to further disruptive effects on their local economies. Also, since the early 1970s the developed countries in the East have rapidly become large net importers of agricultural products from the West, as far as food is concerned.

Here, in fact, we are confronted with another turning point. The former USSR, which had been a major cereal exporter for centuries, has become since 1972 a chronic and important net cereal importer. The annual deficit for 1986/90 was 31 million tons or 15% of its production (for 1984/5 it reached 24%). This led to a rapid increase in the region's trade deficit in food products, which rose from less than $0.3 billion per year in 1970 to $13.1 billion for 1979/81 and has remained at a high level since then. The other Eastern countries have also become net importers of agricultural products. For all the Eastern countries combined (including the former USSR) the annual trade deficit in agricultural products rose from $1.6 billion for 1969/71 to a peak of $19.7 billion for 1980/82 due to a peak in cereal imports in the former USSR. It is not assumed that the changes now taking place in the East will lead to a decline in food imports: in the short term the opposite is even probable.

Therefore, globally, low Western production costs will probably lead to further increases in Western agricultural exports. However, since the West is also very competitive in manufacturing exports, and can no longer increase substantially its per capita consumption of tropical products, what will the West import from tropical regions?

Before considering the last of the important turning points in history, which is related to the crucial problem of energy supplies, let us deal with a minor but interesting one.

## Bringing coal to Newcastle or cotton to the Third World

For centuries, raw cotton, like sugar, was one of the principal primary goods exported by the future Third World to Europe. This trade probably began in the thirteenth century and for a long time the main source of cotton was the Middle East (hence the Arabic origin of its name), and its importance in Europe was limited. However, at the end of the seventeenth century and much more so in the first decades of the eighteenth, cotton manufactures developed all over Europe, imitating Indian textiles which had become fashionable. At the beginning of the eighteenth century, Europe consumed 3,000–4,000 tons of raw cotton and this increased to 9,000–12,000 around 1750. In terms of volume, raw cotton was probably the second largest export product of the Third World after sugar.

As cotton lent itself much more easily to the process of spinning mechanization than wool or linen, this fibre played a crucial role in the first stages of the Industrial Revolution, the cotton spinning mill being almost the symbol of the new era. Between 1750 and 1810 European cotton consumption multiplied six to eight times, reaching 70,000–80,000 tons. At the same time that cotton became an important textile fibre for Western industries a new and important supplier appeared: the United States. This country became the main cotton supplier but demand rose so quickly that the Third World increased its cotton exports. The peak was reached somewhere around 1969/70, when the net exports of cotton from the Third World (to the developed one) reached 1,760,000 tons.

Since then exports have decreased gradually, due to a decline in consumption by the developed countries and an increase in the Third World industries resulting from a shift in the geographical location of the cotton textile industries. In 1972, for the first time since the middle of the nineteenth century, the textile industries of the Third World consumed more cotton than those of the developed countries. In 1980, for the first time in history, the Third World imported more cotton than it exported. According to data for 1988/90, in that period the Third World production of cotton was 11,700 tons and its consumption was 12,000 tons.

## *Petroleum becomes cheaper than coal: sweet and sour effects*

As for every group of products, price comparisons are not simple. In general, three major points must be considered: differences in quality, differences in the stages at which prices are measured (retail, wholesale, import, etc.) and international price differences. In the case of the two products described here, it is obvious that differences in calorific value must also be taken into account.[5] But this does not imply that other matters can be settled so easily. For example, coal does not need any processing for most of its uses whereas petroleum needs to be refined even before being used as fuel oil. On the other hand, oil leaves no ash after burning and can be transported more easily.

In the early 1880s, when petroleum began to be produced in large quantities in the United States – then and for a long time the main oil

**Table 14.2** Pre-World War II selected prices of coal and crude petroleum (in current dollars per ton of coal equivalent

|  | 1880/84 | 1909/13 | 1925/9 | 1934/8 | 1952/4 |
|---|---|---|---|---|---|
| **UNITED STATES[a]** |  |  |  |  |  |
| Coal (bituminous) | 1.21 | 1.24 | 2.15 | 2.02 | 5.28 |
| Coal (anthracite) | 2.04 | 2.19 | 5.86 | 4.45 | 10.12 |
| Petroleum (crude) | 4.56 | 3.58 | 7.25 | 5.22 | 13.21 |
| **FRANCE[b]** |  |  |  |  |  |
| Coal | 3.26 | 4.50 | 5.33 | 6.01 | 19.67 |
| Petroleum (crude) | 23.64 | 17.33 | 23.96 | 8.92 | 27.83 |
| **ITALY[c]** |  |  |  |  |  |
| Coal | 4.44 | 4.63 | 7.03 | 9.21 | 20.58 |
| petroleum (crude) | 9.31 | 8.14 | 8.56 | 16.73 | 14.52 |

[a] Production prices.
[b] Wholesale prices.
[c] Import prices refer to ten-year averages until 1934/42 (1881/90; 1901/10).

*Notes:* Crude petroleum has been converted into coal equivalent using the standard 1.47 ratio.
In order to obtain the price of petroleum per barrel the figures quoted in this table should be divided by 4.966. (The standard weight ratio used for petroleum is 7.3 barrels per ton.)

*Sources:* Calculated by the author on the basis of the following sources:
US Bureau of Census, *Historical Statistics of the United States. Colonial Times to 1970*, Washington, 1975. *Annuaire statistique de la France*, Paris, various issues. Istituto Centrale di Statistica, *Sommario di statistiche Storiche, 1926–1985*, Rome, 1968.

producer – the average cost of a barrel of petroleum at the well head was $0.92 (for 1880/84). For the same period, a short ton of bituminous coal at the mine was $1.10, but that of Pennsylvania anthracite, also at the mine, was $1.86. When expressed in comparable weight and calorific value (see Table 14.2), the comparison shows that petroleum was then (if we take the average of the two coal series) some 1.7 times more expensive than coal. On the eve of World War II (1934/8) petroleum (in the United States) was still 1.6 times more expensive than coal. In Europe, although extraction costs for coal were higher than in the United States, the price differential was, in general, much larger, because most of the petroleum was imported. In Europe, petroleum was three to four times more expensive than coal (always, as above, in calorific value). As an approximate world estimate it can be claimed that, on the eve of World War I, petroleum was three times more expensive than coal. Between the two world wars, especially in the 1930s, the price of petroleum came closer to that of coal, but a price differential of 50% still remained.

After World War II the discoveries of low extraction-cost oil reserves, especially in the Middle East, led to a rapid increase in production and a

**Table 14.3** Post-World War II selected prices of coal and crude petroleum (in current dollars per ton of coal equivalent)

|  | 1952/4 | 1955/7 | 1958/60 | 1970/72 | 1980/82 |
|---|---|---|---|---|---|
| **PRODUCT PRICES** | | | | | |
| **Coal** | | | | | |
| Germany[a] | 11.69 | 13.11 | 14.75 | 19.90 | 52.94 |
| United States (bituminous)[b] | 9.31 | 10.33 | 10.36 | 17.09 | 61.85 |
| France[c] | 19.67 | 19.80 | 18.20 | 25.00 | 108.30 |
| **Petroleum** | | | | | |
| Saudi Arabia[b] | 8.59 | 9.13 | 9.24 | 10.18 | 152.49 |
| OPEC weighted average[b] | 8.93 | 8.94 | 8.11 | 8.11 | 159.08 |
| **COUNTRY PRICES** | | | | | |
| **United States** | | | | | |
| Coal (anthracite)[a] | 10.12 | 9.20 | 9.20 | 12.74 | 50.21 |
| Petroleum[a] | 13.21 | 14.32 | 14.55 | 16.37 | 142.19 |
| **United Kingdom** | | | | | |
| Coal[b] | 15.00 | 15.54 | 18.37 | – | – |
| Petroleum[d] | 16.24 | 15.29 | 14.04 | 10.82 | 169.00 |

[a] Production prices.
[b] Export prices.
[c] Wholesale prices.
[d] Import prices.

*Sources:* See Table 14.2 to which the following sources should be added: United Nations, *Monthly Bulletin of Statistics*, New York, various issues. IBRD, *Commodity Trade and Price Trends*, Washington, various issues. US Bureau of Mines, *Mineral Yearbook*, Washington, various issues. Statistical abstracts of individual countries, various issues.

reduction in real prices. In Western Europe petroleum became cheaper than coal in the mid-1950s. Complementing the price figures given in Table 14.3, a further indicator of this turning point is provided by the changes in the consumption of fuels to produce electricity. In Western Europe in the early 1950s, coal provided almost 100% of the energy used for this process. The reduction in this share began in the mid-1950s, and in 1960 coal provided 84% of the energy used, and petroleum 13%. In 1970 the share of coal was 57%, and the low point was reached in 1975, with 47% for coal and 36% for petroleum. The two-year time lag between the oil price increase and the increased use of coal can be explained by the need for modifications to some of the electricity-generating equipment.

    In the United States this turning point came later, since coal was more abundant and more easy to extract and therefore cheaper. From 1963 onwards the share of petroleum for generating thermal electricity increased rapidly. Between 1960 and 1975 that of coal declined from 66% to 59% and that of petroleum rose from 10% to 20%, with gas accounting for most of the remaining share.

The reversal in the relation between coal and petroleum prices led to very important worldwide indirect consequences: the rapid change in the relative and absolute roles of petroleum in Western energy consumption. This caused a reduction in local production of energy (mainly coal) and led to an external energy dependency where, until the mid-1940s the West was still producing more energy than it consumed. In Chapter 5 (especially Table 5.2) I have provided the main data for this point. For Western Europe, which, in a sense, represents the median situation (between the almost total dependence of Japan and the rather limited one of North America) this energy dependency reached, in 1973, 58% of its consumption, compared to 12% in 1950, and to an excess of production over consumption of 1% in 1937.

Among the more minor, but not marginal, indirect effects, we must mention the economic decline of almost all Western coal-producing regions. One of the first economic assignments at the end of the 1950s for the author of this book was to study the socio-economic impact of the closure of some Belgian coal mines and the possibility of 're-adaptation' in those regions. Some of our bleak conclusions were, unfortunately, confirmed by subsequent events, but that is another story.

Cheap oil also meant more cars, and this accelerated the break-up of cities. The discomfort of traffic congestion in large cities has led a growing number of inhabitants to move out to the suburbs, to which the car provided easier access. This displacement, in turn, results in the relocation of some of the commercial facilities that were formerly in the cities. The inner city thereby loses an important part of the amenities it once offered, and, as a result, becomes less appealing, thus accelerating the exodus of inhabitants.

However, the two major consequences of this external energy dependency are, from 1973 onwards, world economic instability and an unprecedented rise in international prices and interest rates resulting from the two large successive increases in oil prices that took place in 1973 and in 1980. In 1973 the price of petroleum quadrupled and tripled by 1980. Expressed in current dollars, the price rose from less than $2 a barrel from 1960 to 1970 to $33 in 1981.

These price increases led to the first two serious recessions in the post-war history of the West. In the 26-year period between 1946 and 1972 there has not been one year in which the GNP of the Western developed countries, as a whole, declined, and only one in which the rate of growth has been below 1%: in 1958 (0.9%). In the 19-year period between 1973 and 1991 there has been two declines (1975: −0.5%; and 1982: −0.3%)

and two years of a growth below 1% (1974: 0.9%; and 1991: 0.6%).

Even if prices began to increase in the 1964–71 period, it was a very moderate rise compared to the effects of the two oil shocks. The world's wholesale prices, which increased on average by 3.6% per year during the 1964–71 period (2.6% for 1956–63), rose 13.7% in 1973, 22.9% in 1974, 17.6% in 1984 and 12.8%, on average, for the 1973–83 period.

Even if other factors had intervened, there is no doubt that economic instability and inflation caused by the oil price increases were the major elements in the rapid rise in international interest rates, an increase that adversely affected the Third World, which had, and still has, a high external debt. If we take the US Central Bank discount rate as an indicator of international level of interest, we see that between 1948 and 1962 this fluctuated around 2%, and between 1963 and 1972 around 5%. The highest rate observed between 1948 and 1972 was 6%. In 1973, it rose to 7.5%, and then fluctuated around 6% between 1975 and 1977. It reached a peak of 13% in 1980, which is the highest level achieved in US history. From 1985 to 1990 the discount rate fluctuated around 7%. This rate is modest compared to the peak of the 1979–85 period, but is still about 50% higher than that prevailing between 1963 and 1972, and 250% above that between 1948 and 1962.

Before moving to the next phase of developments in petroleum prices it is worth noting that the petroleum price increases would probably have been more gradual, and certainly more realistic in economic terms, if political factors had not intervened. Obviously, we are referring here to the dominant role of the Arab countries in OPEC (Organization of Petroleum Exporting Countries), and this was more influential in the 1973 increase than in that of 1980. The rapid 1980 price increase, on top of the already high prices resulting from the 1973 rise, meant that petroleum became, despite an increase in coal prices, three times more expensive than coal (see Table 14.3). Therefore it was 'normal' to expect a decline in oil prices, which began in 1983 and accelerated in 1986.

But here we are digressing from history to current events, which led to the 'Gulf crisis' the world was experiencing when I was writing the final chapters of this book. I do not want to end on a sour note, so I will mention another turning point, a sweet one, which nevertheless has some connection with petroleum. Let us see the connection first.

One of the commodities whose price increased very rapidly following the 1971 and 1973 oil price increases was sugar. The reference price of sugar, which was $55 a ton in 1966/70, reached $655 in 1974, and has remained at a relatively high level since then. The large increase in incomes for the population of many Middle East countries, very fond of sweet products, explains the soaring price of sugar. Middle East net imports of sugar, which amounted to 0.86 million tons for 1968/70, increased to 1.63 million tons for 1973/4 and reached 3.32 million tons for 1988/90 (this last amount represents 12% of the world's sugar imports, while the Middle East contains only 5% of the world's population).

The historical turning point relating to sugar was in the early 1960s, when it became cheaper than wheat. For centuries, as we saw earlier (Chapter 8), sugar was a very expensive product. Even in 1913, it was still three to four times more expensive than wheat, and in the early 1950s there was still a 20–30% difference. For the 1965–9 period the reference price of a ton of wheat (No. 2, hard red winter, f.o.b. Gulf) was $61.9 and that of sugar (f.o.b. Caribbean ports, bulk basis) $48.1. This, incidentally, explains why, at the beginning of this century and indeed well before it, good biscuits were sweet biscuits and after the 1960s, as a rule, cheap biscuits were very sweet. Since then, due to oil's large price variations, sometimes sugar was much cheaper than wheat and vice versa. In 1974, the year of the steepest oil price increase, sugar was almost three times more expensive than wheat, whose price fluctuations were more moderate. Since then, the price of sugar is influenced almost as much by oil prices as by fluctuations in the volume of its production. So the non-petroleum producer countries, i.e. most of the world, must hope for sweet years, years when there are no sharp increases in oil prices.

## Notes

1 Bairoch, P., 'Les trois révolutions agricoles du monde développé: rendements et productivité de 1800 à 1985', *Annales, E.S.C.*, No. 2, March–April 1989, pp. 317–53; with updated figures.
2 Bairoch, P. and Etemad, B., *Commodity Structure of Third World Exports (1830–1937)*, Geneva, 1985. See also Hanson, J. R., *Trade in Transition. Exports from the Third World, 1840–1900*, New York, 1980.
3 Bairoch, P., 'Les trois révolutions agricoles du monde développé: rendements et productivité de 1800 à 1985', *Annales, E.S.C.*, No. 2, March–April 1989, pp. 317–53.
4 The magnitude of the decline in prices can vary significantly according which price deflator is used. In this case, we used world wholesale prices; if retail prices are used, the decline is 63%, and if the world GNP price deflator is used the decline is 78%, or an international price of wheat divided by five.
5 The standard conversion coefficient used is that a ton of crude petroleum is equivalent to 1.47 tons of coal. The other conversion is 7.3 barrels of crude petroleum equals one ton.

# Conclusions: The Paradox of Economic History or the Absence of Absolute Economic Laws

If I had to summarize the essence of what economic history can bring to economic science it would be that there is no 'law' or rule in economics that is valid for every period of history or for every economic structure. Let me choose one example that will return us to the problem of commercial policies. After all, foreign trade is, *par excellence*, a field in which, to quote Haberler, 'economic history can offer more than economic analysis'.[1]

## The varying effects of the same commercial policy

As we have seen (Chapter 3), it is almost certain that during the nineteenth century, contrary to the classical model, free trade coincided and was probably the main cause of depression and protectionism and was probably the main cause of growth and development for most of today's developed countries. In fact, the only real exception was the United Kingdom. However, this was a country which by 1846 (when it adopted free trade) had a very large lead over the rest of the future developed world as a result of being the 'cradle country' of the Industrial Revolution. On the other hand, and here we can be even more affirmative for the future less developed countries, free trade meant, as we have seen, the acceleration of economic underdevelopment.

Does this mean that protectionism can always be equated with economic growth and liberalism with stagnation? Certainly not, and I am sure that in this respect I am in full agreement with most economists. History can also corroborate the benefits of liberalism in some cases.

The UK's decision to introduce free trade in 1846 was certainly a good move for what was then the most advanced country in the world. Its per capita level of industrialization was more than three times higher than that of the rest of the future developed countries and more than twice the level of its closest competitors such as France, Belgium, Germany, Switzerland and the United States. In the field of iron industries and also especially in cotton textiles, which was then by far the largest item in exports of manufactures, Britain had a very dominant position. It had more than the half of the world's iron production capacity and two-thirds of the cotton spindles, and Britain's liberal commercial policy was certainly one of the factors that contributed to two decades of very rapid economic growth. Per capita GNP, which increased from 1831/5 to 1841/5 at an annual rate of 0.6%, rose by 2.3% between 1841/5 to 1851/5 and by 1.8% between 1851/5 and 1861/5. This was the best achieved in the United Kingdom's history over a 20-year period until after World War II, when we find a similar but not markedly higher growth rate (in terms of per capita growth).

Let us leave, for the moment, the nineteenth century and move to the post-World War II period to see another example of the positive impact of liberal trade policy. Even if most econometric analyses show that foreign trade is not such a powerful booster as is generally believed (see Chapter 13), it is certain that the rapid economic growth of the Western world in the 1950s and 1960s was due in part to trade liberalization and is generally seen as a confirmation of free trade theories. Even leaving aside the period of very rapid reconstruction after World War II, between 1950 and 1973 the per capita GNP annual growth rate of Western Europe reached 4%. This can be compared to 1.3% for the preceding best 23 years, i.e. the 1890–1913 period (which was also, as mentioned earlier, the most protectionist period and to which I shall return later). The best shorter-term period before the 1950s in terms of economic growth was 1920–9, when per capita GNP increased at an annual rate of 3.2%.

However, the classical model does not call for historical support. Its argument against protectionism and in favour of free trade is ahistorical and theoretical. It also assumes a perfectly competitive world, when the real world in which we live, or the past world in which our parents and grandparents lived, was one of imperfect markets and discontinuities. Let us recall the main aspects of the classical and neoclassical theories of international trade.

The basic building block of this theoretical approach is the law of comparative advantage or comparative costs. Let us cite here the very good book by Charles Kindleberger, who is one of the rare specialists in international trade theory who has a good knowledge of history:

One country may be more efficient than another, as measured by factor inputs per unit of output, in the production of every possible commodity; but so long as it is not equally more efficient in every commodity, a basis for trade exists. It will pay the country to produce more of those goods in which it is relatively more efficient and to export these in return for goods in which its absolute advantage is least.[2]

The most important parts of any trade theory are the discussions of the effects of trade on economic development; the expansion of international trade not being a goal in itself, especially if it is unfavourable to the rest of economy. If the classical model is not very explicit on the economic gains of international trade, especially in trade between countries at different levels of development, the neoclassical theory is very explicit. According to neoclassical theory, trade liberalization is *the* way to an equalization of the levels of development, and an equalization that pulls up the low levels and not vice versa.

So, so far the theory . . . But what does history show about what happened in the real world? We have given above cases which supports the arguments that both unilateral and bilateral liberalization had positive repercussions. The case of Britain in the mid-nineteenth century is of paramount importance for at least three reasons. It was the first major case of liberalization following the Industrial Revolution; it was experienced by the dominant economy, and Britain was the Mecca of economic theory.

However, if Britain chose the right trade policy in 1846, 60 years later its voters, in 1906, in following Alfred Marshall's advice, were wrong to reject Chamberlain's 'fair trade policy'. It is obvious that factors other than trade policy contributed to accelerate the relative decline in the British economy. But the persistence of free trade in an international context of increasing protectionism at a moment when the British industrial lead over its closest competitors had been reduced to a mere 30–40% certainly appears to have been a mistake. In his advice, Marshall noted (as we saw in Chapter 2) that

> it is absolutely essential for England's hopes to retain a high place in the world, that is should neglect no opportunity to increase the alertness of its industrial population in general, and its manufacturers in particular; and for this purpose there is no device to be compared in efficiency with the plan of keeping its markets open to the new products of other nations, and especially to those of American inventor genius and of German systematic thought and scientific training.

This proved to be wrong or at least insufficient, since by 1913 the most industrialized country was no longer the United Kingdom but the United

States, who (in per capita terms) exceeded it by some 10%. In 1932, when Britain abandoned its liberal trade policy, the US level of industrialization was 50% higher than that of the United Kingdom. Furthermore, Belgium and Germany were also then very close. Again, this trade policy does not explain all the negative evolution; as mentioned earlier, among other things, the ability to sell easily non-sophisticated manufactured goods to its colonies forestalled the need for modernization. However, I cannot refrain from recalling another 'odd' evolution that we saw in Chapter 1. In the United Kingdom the 1930s were a much better decade than the 1920s. However, I must hasten to add that the main cause of the poor performance of the 1920s was to be found in fixing the exchange rate at too high a level, which handicapped exports. On the other hand, recent research on the 1930s shows that the historic decision of Britain to return to protectionism in 1932, after almost a century of free trade, is an important element in explaining the prosperous 1930s.[3]

## The limits of export-led development in the Third World: the 'Four Dragons'

However, to repeat myself, things are different for different periods and different regions. What is true for the other success story of liberalization, i.e. that of the Western developed countries in the 1950–73 period, certainly does not apply to the less developed countries during the same period. In all of those countries who had more liberal tariff policies than nineteenth-century Europe, the process of industrialization was hampered by the influx of manufactured products. Even if this more liberal policy was not always the sole factor, it is significant to note that despite the fact that all countries from the mid-1950s onwards made efforts to industrialize themselves, there remains a very large number that can be considered as quasi-industrial deserts. According to a UNIDO handbook on industrial statistics[4] in 1985, the per capita value added in manufacturing was $2,554 for the developed market economies and only $144 for the developing ones. Despite this low average, among the 121 developing countries for which data are reported we can find 15 countries with a level below $50 and 30 additional countries below $20.

In almost all countries where local industrial production increased substantially, this was essentially through import substitution (mainly tariff) measures. However, even this policy reached its limit after about 20 years, when the majority of products that could be easily manufactured were locally produced, i.e. essentially consumer goods and textiles. Therefore we see a slowdown in industrial growth. The volume of manufacturing production of the Third World market economies (excluding the 'Four Dragons', Hong Kong, South Korea, Singapore and Taiwan), which had risen at an annual per capita rate of 4.2–4.6% between 1953 and 1970, increased by only 2.5% per annum between 1970 and 1990.

Another factor that contributed to the expansion of the Third World's manufacturing production was through exports to developed countries that gave them relatively easy access to their markets partly for political reasons. But it is very important not to overlook the fact that the export-led industrialization strategy was possible only for a limited share of the Third World. The 'Four Dragons', manufactured exports (excluding re-exports) represented in 1990 almost 53% of those of the entire Third World, while their manufacturing capacities were some 14% of that region while their population represented less than 2% of that of the Third World. A very simple but illustrative calculation shows that if the entire Third World now had to export per capita the same amount of manufactures as the 'Four Dragons', this would be the equivalent of almost all of the consumption of manufactures of all the Western developed countries. In other words, that those Western countries would see the almost complete disappearance of their manufacturing industries. As we shall see later, the part of the West that had a liberal policy regarding manufactured imports lost a very large share of its workforce in this sector between the early 1960s and the early 1990s. This leads us to another point.

## Those who don't obey the rules win

But there is another limitation to the success story of post-World War II Western liberalization: one can ask to what extent the trade policies followed by the West in that period were beneficial to them (as far as manufacturing was concerned). The move to liberalism in the Western developed countries began in the early 1960s. But it is well known that liberalism in imports of manufactured goods was not at the same level in all countries and that, due largely to non-tariff barriers, Japan adopted one of the more restrictive policies compared to the other great industrial powers during the same period.

One should, however, bear in mind that at the beginning of the 1960s, although Japan had doubled its pre-war per capita level of industrialization, it was still less industrialized than the advanced Western countries. In 1963, its per capita level of industrialization was a third lower than that of Western Europe and half of that of Germany. However, it was about the same as Italy and much higher than Spain. But even compared to the less industrialized countries of the West, Japan's level of protection was much higher.

Thus, and without necessarily connecting these two phenomena, one is tempted to recall the fact that Japan's industrial growth has been much more rapid than that of its partners in the developed world. Furthermore, and this is more important, between 1964/6 and 1972/4 (we shall discuss the more recent period later) while the six earliest industrialized countries of Western Europe lost 0.9 million jobs in their manufacturing industries, Japan gained some 3 million.[5] From 1965 to 1973 the total Japanese trade surplus in manufactured goods rose from $5.9 billion to $23.4 billion; as far as trade with Western Europe was concerned, this surplus rose from $0.2 billion to $2.5 billion.

Obviously, the loss of industrial employment cannot be explained only, and at times not even mainly, by an imbalance in trade policies. Research in this field is rare, but I shall refer to one of the most recent studies concerning the cotton industry in Great Britain.[6] From 1950 to 1970 this sector lost 168,400 jobs; increase in productivity accounted for the loss of 33,100 jobs (or 20%), but the changes that took place in external trade were responsible for 87,000 job losses or 52% (62,000 of which were the result of a loss in exports and 25,000 due to an increase in imports). All the remaining losses were due to a drop in domestic demand and to the use of other fibres, mainly synthetic.

In 1973 the Japanese per capita level of industrialization was almost the same as that of the average in other Western countries. Although the West's economic evolution became, after 1973, more unstable as a result of the successive oil crises, it is equally necessary to emphasize the fact that the negative trends became worse. Following more or less the same restrictive policy with regard to imports of manufactured goods, Japan, between 1972/4 and 1988/90, increased its workforce in the manufacturing industry by another few hundred thousand while the earliest industrialized European countries, with much more *laissez-faire* policies, lost 6.1 million jobs, that is, more than a fifth of the workforce of 1972/4 in this sector! In the field of external trade it should be noted that, between 1973 and 1990, the Japanese surplus in manufactures in relation to the rest of the world rose from $23.4 billion to $176.2 billion, and with regard to Western Europe from $2.5 billion to $31.6 billion.[7] So globally, between 1965 and 1990, Japan's trade surplus in manufactures with the rest of the world was multiplied by 30 in nominal terms and 12 in real ones. Japan's awareness that it had gone too far in its unbalanced commercial policy is not only very limited but also recent. So much so that, referring to the statement made on television in April 1985 by Prime Minister Nakasone, in which he encouraged his fellow citizens to buy more foreign products,[8] Minister Watanabe, of the influential

MITI,[9] commented, 'Only half joking' and that 'if he [the Prime Minister] had done that 10 years ago, he would have been hauled off to a lunatic asylum'.[10]

As noted earlier, it is obvious that the Japanese success cannot be explained completely, or maybe not even as largely, just by differences in import policy. As Eva Ehrlich[11] pointed out, one of the most important factors that explains the rapid growth of Japanese productivity is the ethics of the workforce. In spite of this, it is obvious that protectionism has, in many sectors, played an important role. Moreover, the openness of other countries' markets is probably also a major cause of the disappearance of so many jobs in manufacturing.

## *Six hard facts of nineteenth-century history*

However, much more than contemporary history, nineteenth-century history reveals that liberalism in international trade had more negative than positive consequences and that, conversely, protectionist measures had predominantly positive outcomes. We shall now briefly present six hard facts that illustrate this.

The first hard fact is that what economic historians call the great European depression began during the period 1869–73, when trade policies in Europe had reached an unprecedented degree of liberalism (and which was to be equalled only after 1962). This depression was very serious, more severe and much longer than that of the 1930s. It can be estimated that from 1867/9 to 1889/91 the volume of per capita gross national product increased by only 0.2% annually, against the 1.1% of the preceding 25 years and the 1.5% of the following 25. Let us recall that between 1929 and 1939 the per capita GNP increased at an annual rate of 1.2% (for Europe excluding the USSR).

The second hard fact is that not only was there a severe slowing down of economic growth but also, and all the more paradoxical in the period of greatest liberalism, a decrease in international trade. Indeed, from 1870 to 1890 expansion in the volume of European exports was very modest: slightly less than 3% per annum, as against the 4.5% between 1830 and 1860.

The third hard fact is that the United States, which did not take part in the free trade movement (on the contrary, it increased its already strong protectionism), during the period of the great European depression went through a phase of rapid growth. Indeed, this period can be regarded among the most prosperous in the economic history of the United States.

The fourth hard fact is that economic growth started to rise again when

Continental Europe resumed and intensified its protectionist policies. At the individual country level and independently from the period in which policies were revised, a return to protectionism was quickly followed by an increase in economic growth. On the other hand, it is significant that, during this phase of economic expansion (1889–92 to 1913), economic growth in the United Kingdom, which had remained faithful to free trade, was slower than on the Continent, which had turned protectionist, i.e. 0.9% and 1.5%, respectively (in terms of per capita GNP). It should, however, be noted that the reintroduction of protection was for some years (from five to eight, according to country) followed by a slowdown in external trade. But once this period had ended, external trade expanded more rapidly than during the free trade era. Between 1891/3 and 1913 the volume of European exports increased by 3.9% per year, compared to less than 3% for the free trade period.

The fifth hard fact is that, even if some uncertainties remain on the causes of such an evolution, it is very interesting to note that in the case of the great European depression, both the liberal and the protectionist theories were incorrect. The major cause of the slowdown in the economy was the decline in rural income due to a fall in agricultural prices caused by the influx of imported cereals and not by imports of manufactured goods to Continental Europe. One of the reasons for this evolution is that European tariff barriers for manufactured goods did not disappear as in the United Kingdom, whereas, for agricultural products they disappeared completely in all countries.

Last but not least of the six hard facts is that, in the nineteenth century, the liberal trade experience in the Third World was a complete failure. It is no exaggeration to say that the opening up of those economies was one of the major reasons for their lack of development during the nineteenth century. In fact, the term non-development is an understatement since it led to a process of de-industrialization and to structural changes that made later development more difficult.

## The balance sheet of colonies is not a simple one

Beyond the major myths surrounding the major problems of trade policies addressed above there are numerous other important or less important myths. Among the important ones is that of the crucial role played in the development of the Western world by colonization, or, more generally, the Third World. If there is no doubt that the Third World, especially through the availability of cheap raw materials and energy products, was one of the contributing factors to the rapid growth of Western economies in the 1955–73 period, but the situation was quite different in the nineteenth century and during the first half of the twentieth. During this period the developed world even exported energy to the Third World and was almost totally self-sufficient in raw materials. So, other times, other situations.

The two other important myths in this area concern the scope of Third World outlets for developed countries' industries and the role of colonialism in the triggering of the Industrial Revolution. Let us begin with the second point. As we saw in Chapter 7, it appears that there is little relation between these two major events. Not only was Britain before and during the first stages of the Industrial Revolution a minor colonial power but markets outside Europe played a minor role in the first decades of the Industrial Revolution. If, indeed, as the history of modern development unfolded, the Third World markets became more important than previously, this does not imply that those markets were important in relative terms. Let us recall here three impressive percentages. For the whole of the developed countries during the period 1800–1938, only 17% of total exports went to the Third World and those exports represented less than 2% of the total volume of the production of the developed countries. The share of manufacturing production exported to the Third World was larger but was below 10%. Obviously, this does not imply that for some periods and for some countries those outlets were not important. However, a greater share of Third World markets was apparently not by itself a recipe for rapid economic development, since if one compares the rates of growth during the nineteenth century, it appears that non-colonial countries generally had a more rapid economic development than colonial ones.

The fact that the West did not need the Third World is good news for the Third World. Such a statement may sound paradoxical or provocative, but the fact that the development of the West was not due to exploitation of the Third World is positive. If such exploitation had been the main cause of the Industrial Revolution and/or of the first century of the West's development, this would have a very significant consequence. Indeed, if such had been the case, it would imply that development needs the exploitation of large outside regions and, since the Third World cannot fulfil today this essential condition, it would imply the impossibility of its economic development. So it is very fortunate that the experience of the West shows that a process of development is possible without exploitation of other parts of the world.

Does this mean that colonization had no negative consequences on the future Third World? This was not the case: economy is not a 'zero sum game'. For example, if exports were not important for Western industries, their low cost led to an almost complete de-industrialization of the future Third World. I will not mention the other negative consequences of colonization, but even here there are numerous and important myths. Part III of this book presented four of the major myths concerning the historical roots of underdevelopment and the actual situation in the Third World, and three of the more minor ones, described in Chapter 13, relate to the same problem. Therefore, as with the six hard facts of nineteenth century history, I will summarize briefly these seven myths:

1. The poor countries are not poor because they were already so before the Industrial Revolution. It is very likely that the level of Western income around 1700 was no higher than that of the future Third World.
2. There was no deterioration in the Third World's terms of trade between the 1870s and the 1930s. On the contrary, since productivity increased much more rapidly in the developed countries' manufacturing industry the terms of trade in primary goods, which formed the bulk of the Third World's exports, improved. However, they did deteriorate in the 1950s and 1980s.
3. Rapid growth in population is not a minor factor in the economic problems facing the Third World. If the slowing down of population growth is not a major factor in economic development, failure to do so is certainly a major handicap to this development.
4. Exports of tropical agricultural products are not the cause of the increasing food imports that affect large areas of the Third World. There is no connection between these two aspects: the reasons for the Third World's increasing food imports are more deeply rooted. They are linked to a rapid urbanization process combined with a very slow growth in agricultural production and productivity, as well as to the availability of cheap cereals.
5. Exporting primary products is not a road to underdevelopment. Most of the richest developed countries have been exporters of primary goods.
6. Returning to more important events in world history, the West was far from being the only major colonial power, numerous other civilizations were more important in this respect and lasted longer.
7. The Western slave trade was important but not the largest in world history; the Islamic slave flow began earlier, lasted longer and was more important.

## The 1929 and 1987 crashes and the structural changes

In conclusion, let me return to the 1987 crash with which I began. The June 1988 *OECD Economic Outlook,* which was the first published after the crash, elicited similar comments. Let us first recall the main factors. The 1987 annual growth rate for all the OECD countries was estimated at 3.1% (or 2.5 per capita), the highest since 1980 (if one excludes 1984), and a similar rate was expected for 1988.

In *The Economist* of 11 June 1988 the leading article, whose title was '1988's economic miracle', began as follows: 'Last October's equity crash could have dragged economies down with it. So far, miraculously, it hasn't. At the time, even the breeziest forecasters thought that growth would slow down; the gloomiest looked to a slump.' *The Economist* gave full credit to our profession by declaring that 'The Fed staved off deflation last October, by avoiding the mistakes of the 1930s'.

However, as Joseph Schumpeter wrote: 'Cycles are not, like tonsils, separate things that might be treated by themselves, but are, like the beat of the heart, of the essence of the organism that displays them.'[12] Indeed, what the columnist of *The Economist* failed to take into consideration is that the 1980s were not the 1930s. Let us see two structural differences that may have played an important role. In the beginning of the 1930s the workforce in the tertiary sector represented 33% of the total workforce in the Western developed countries, and in 1987 the share was more than 60%. Since, as a rule, employment in this sector is generally more stable than in manufacturing, it probably means that, to a certain extent, this alone helped largely to make the advanced economies more stable. The other structural difference is the relative importance of transfer incomes through various channels, mainly social security benefits. In the late 1920s these incomes represented probably less than 4% of GNP but in the late 1980s close to 30%. However, all this does not rule out the possibility of a 1930s style depression. Incidentally, more stable employment also means a slower increase in the workforce, a factor that can, to a certain extent, explain the slower than expected decline of unemployment in good years in most Western countries, even if other factors are also intervening. This factor may also explain in part the length of the 1991/2 depression.

Therefore, once again, different structures mean different evolutions and different laws. History does not necessarily repeat itself, and never exactly. The changes in employment are only one of the many profound structural modifications to the developed countries' economies. It is not often realized that the increase in the volume of per capita GNP during the last 40 years has been larger than that of the preceding two centuries, thus contradicting the ideas developed between 1938 and 1950 by the 'Stagnation' or 'Maturity' schools (notably A. Hansen, B. Higgins, P. Sweezy and to a certain extent by the famous J. M. Keynes). To take the example of Western Europe, we can see that between 1949 and 1990 the volume of per capita GNP has been multiplied by some 3.6 compared with 3.2 between 1750 and 1949. This also means that during the last 40 years the structural changes in almost all aspects of economic and social life have been greater than during the preceding 200 years. It does not, however, imply that the previous changes were minor. The Industrial Revolution was one of the two most fundamental turning points in history (the other being the Neolithic Age, which led to the birth of civilization), and in almost every aspect the nineteenth century marks the real transition between traditional societies and the modern world.

During the last 40 years there has also been generally unnoticed reversals or turning points of some of the major economic trends, leading very often to paradoxical situations. The most important of these concerns the growth of productivity in the Western developed countries. As we have seen, whereas during the nineteenth century and until the end of the 1930s in North America and until the beginning of the 1950s in Western Europe the manufacturing productivity increased at a rate almost twice as fast as that of agriculture, since the 1950s the converse is true. Among other unnoticed turning points, two are largely related to the one we have just considered. They concern the fact that production costs of food have become lower in the developed Western world than in the Third World; and that the Third World has become a net importer of food and almost a net importer of agricultural products. Less important but more paradoxical is what happened recently to one major raw material imported for centuries to the West and originating from the Third World. Since the early 1980s Third World textile mills are using more raw cotton than the region produces. Also, in the mid-1950s petroleum became cheaper than coal, leading to many problems resulting from the two successive very rapid increases in oil prices.

This brings us again to contemporary events, so let us also recall here another recent turning point. The former USSR, which has been a cereal exporter for at least a century and a half, has become an important net cereal importer since 1972. This is one of the symptoms of the economic failure that central planning encountered in that region after the initial, successful and rapid, but costly, creation of an industrial base. But even in the advice that some Western economists give today to the former USSR, in disarray and 'rushing to capitalism', there is much ignorance of history. As John Kenneth Galbraith writes:

In my view, some, and perhaps much, of the advice now being offered the Central and Eastern European states proceeds from a view of the so-called capitalist or free-enterprise economies that bears no relation to their reality. Nor would these economies have survived if it had. What is offered is an ideological construct that exists all but entirely in the minds and notably in the hopes of the donor. It bears no relation to reality.'[13]

Thus world history is full of myths, of important turning points and of paradoxes. To a very large extent, modern history is characterized more by economic discontinuities than continuities. This brings us back to the first statement of those conclusions concerning the absence of economic laws valid over history even if we limit the discussion to modern history.

So does it mean that there are no absolute laws in economics? I am increasingly inclined to answer that, indeed, there is no absolute law in general economics, or if one uses a more technical term, in macro-economics. I am also inclined to think that this also holds true for microeconomics, unless we postulate stable human behaviour: in other words, a stable and real *homo economicus*. I doubt that such a *homo economicus* ever existed and I hope that he or she never will. Human attitudes and behaviour can change and have changed more in the past 40 to 50 years than ever before. Those changes are also in part related to the modifications to economic and social structures and, in turn, can influence those structures. For example, attitudes to work can modify the levels of unemployment and social benefits which, in turn, can lead to modifications in personal behaviour and in public policy.

So does it mean that economists are right not to ask too many questions of economic historians? Yes . . . if we take the paradox at its face value. No . . . if we take into account that, to a very large extent, the experience of more developed countries can be beneficial for today's less developed ones. Certainly no, since experiments that go wrong are very costly in economics, and certainly no, to make economists aware that their task is a very difficult one, since they have to find solutions for many rapidly changing problems.

Being by training more an economist than an historian, I cannot end this book, which has described a number of important myths that are more common to economists than to historians, without repeating the comment I made in the Introduction. A book could certainly be written presenting the myths historians believe to be true of economics, and the list of myths would probably be at least as long. But this is a task more fitting for an historian than for an economist, and the title of such a book, instead of *Economics and World History*, could be *World History and Economics*.

# Notes

1 Haberler, G., *A Survey of International Trade Theory*, Princeton, 1961, p. 58.
2 Kindleberger, C. P., *International Economics*, 4th edn, Homewood (Ill), 1968, pp. 36–7.
3 See especially Kitson, M. and Solomou, S., *Protectionism and Economic Revival: The British Inter-War Economy*, Cambridge, 1990.
4 United Nations Industrial Development Organization, *Handbook of Industrial Statistics, 1988*, Vienna, 1988.
5 'Earliest industrialized countries' includes the following: Belgium, France, Germany, Sweden, Switzerland, United Kingdom. The data concerning employment are taken from Bairoch, P., 'A major shift in Western European labour force: the decline of manufacturing industries' (presented to the ESRC Symposium on Socio-Economic Change in the West, Cambridge, 11–12 April 1986). Figures have been updated for the present book.
6 Singleton, J., 'Lancashire's last stand: declining employment in the British cotton industry, 1950–70', *Economic History Review*, 2nd series, **XXXIX**, February 1986, pp. 92–107.
7 According to OECD, *Economic Outlook. Historical Statistics 1960–1986*, Paris, 1986; and data provided by the GATT Secretariat, Geneva.
8 A speech made on television on 9 April 1985, in which Nakasone, admitting that certain measures had restricted access of foreign goods to the Japanese market, insisted that the trade surplus was due to the quality and low prices of Japanese goods. With reference to this statement, it should be noted that the list of the foreign products the Prime Minister suggested his fellow-citizens should buy (to reach $100 per capita) included mainly those that were not really important for technological development.
9 As its name suggests, this ministry (Ministry of International Trade and Industry) has played a leading role in the past, and still does, in supporting policies for Japanese industries, especially exports.
10 'Will Japan really change?' *Business Week (International)*, 12 May 1986, pp. 29–34 (especially p. 34).
11 Ehrlich, E., *Japan. A Case of Catching-Up*, Budapest, 1984, p. 122.
12 Schumpeter, J., *Business Cycles. A Theoretical, Historical and Statistical Analysis of the Capitalist Process*, 2 volumes, New York, 1939 (**I**, p. V).
13 Galbraith, J. K., 'The rush to capitalism', *The New York Review*, 25 October 1990, p. 51.

# Index